P9-DFN-679

GERMAINE BRÉE

CAMUS

REVISED EDITION

RUTGERS UNIVERSITY PRESS

New Brunswick   *New Jersey*

TO FRANCINE, CATHERINE, AND JEAN

Preface to the Third Printing

Just over a decade after Camus' death, his first novel, *La Mort heureuse* (A Happy Death) has come out (1971) and, deservedly, shot to the top of the best-seller lists. Camus was twenty-three when he started on this first novel, which vibrates with the warmth and lyrical intensity of a directly personal experience. Although Camus had not entirely integrated all its episodes to his satisfaction, it tells a complete story; clearly its hero Patrice Mersault— not Meursault—is young Camus' mythical double, like Camus shocked into a passionate awareness of what it is to live by "the encounter with death of a life rich in blood and vigor."

Camus' experience of illness is the ground of what he had to say. His Mersault, in an initial symbolic act, leaps beyond the constraint of mediocre routine and relationship into the freedom of existence, from where he slowly touches the limits of the happiness it holds in the communion of friendship, love, solitude and the beauty of the world itself until, at the highest point of his *ascesis* and ecstasy, he encounters death—in the physical assault of illness upon his body. Mersault has acceded at that instant to a point of awareness in which he can see himself in double perspective—as a totally expendable particle of an immense whole and as a being endowed with a passionate awareness and love of the life that inhabits him. The single life, the single moment not to be wasted; to be enhanced, enlarged and lived in the full awareness of its vastness.

Young Camus' revolt was not against death, but against the docility with which human beings accept the mediocrity of their lives; not against the simple joys of daily living, but against men's indifference to them. At twenty-three, it was his own limitations and potentialities he was objectifying in Mersault, too uncertain as yet to give writing a place on Mersault's path to happiness and death—although he had, seemingly, been tempted to do so. But the pattern of the story is clear. "A man's will," wrote Saint Bonaventura, "is as simple or as composite as his love. By the will being simple we mean that its affective energies are without division or dissipation, because they are concentrated on one or a few objects."

The tenderness and quiet humor in the book are closely tied to that love. The years that Camus lived, out of which he wrote, were terribly demanding of men's energies. But Camus' will was indeed concentrated on the few objects of his love: the simple bonds that bring happiness to human beings, the freedom that men may achieve in this world, the love of beauty and of justice that animates their lives, the moments of awareness when, as for Mersault, there wells up from within them the pain and glory of knowing—often beyond words—that they partake in something far greater than themselves. These are the moments when human beings concentrate their will and discover the nature of their love—the moment in *The Plague* when two men can withdraw from the desperate turmoil of an unflagging struggle to see the whole of life again—and these are the moments which the greater stories in *Exile and the Kingdom* describe.

Since my book was written, before Camus' death, his work has not ceased to be discussed with varying degrees of understanding and sensibility. Much has been added to our understanding of his work since then, and this study can be seen only as a kind of schematic preface to that work. Although I see the limitations of this study in the light of the many other studies that have appeared, I should not wish to change it, nor for that matter, could I. Some critics have attempted, not always impartially, to destroy what they considered a "cult," which Camus himself would surely not have rejoiced in, and some have read into his work their own political views and prejudices. In this regard *La Mort heureuse* brings a corrective. The interest in Camus has not waned, all prophecies to the contrary notwithstanding. Statistics in 1970 showed *The Stranger* and *The Plague* topping the list in the number of copies sold in the pocket book series alone, with *The Myth of Sisyphus* and *The Rebel* still making a good showing in the essay series. Camus wanted to speak to the "common reader" and yet had the artisan's respect for his craft. So his work, esthetically speaking, is outside the main literary trends of our time. Camus is now living simultaneously the posthumous life of the writer in academic debate and yet as an active presence in the imagination and midst of some millions of readers. *La Mort heureuse* will renew that interest.

I had seen the work in manuscript and briefly mentioned it in this volume. But the draft available to me was not complete or was in an intermediate stage in its development. The end I describe is different, and the difference is significant. Mersault, I noted, goes down to his death, voluntarily in the "sea and the sun." In the published work, illness strikes him: he does not participate in his own death directly. This would, of course, be a necessary change in pattern—in terms of Camus' own sensitivity—his rejection of the "romantic" evasion of reality, his refusal to betray the life that seems to betray us. It was that betrayal which most deeply revolted him in our recent history, a history that spoke more loudly of man's hatred of and contempt for life than of his love and in which so large a role was played by the irresponsible and monstrous bureaucratic machinery that had made that war possible and threatened the future. We are perhaps more aware of the thrust of Camus' thought than before; but we have possibly stressed its anxieties more than its affectivity—Camus' will to concentrate on those "few objects" that enhance life and the human beings that partake of it.

GERMAINE BRÉE

University of Wisconsin
July, 1971

Foreword (1960)

On January 4, 1960, just two years after he had been awarded the Nobel Prize for literature, Albert Camus died, at the age of forty-six. The car in which he was traveling to Paris, driven at a high speed by his friend Michel Gallimard, crashed into a plane tree, instantly killing the writer. As the news spread over France, then beyond France, to Camus' readers all over the world, grief and consternation were widespread. Moving tributes in press articles and radio broadcasts appeared in great number. Meanwhile, in a bare room of the small town hall of the village of Villeblevin stood his coffin, covered with a sheet on which was placed a single wreath. With only a very small group of his family and friends in attendance, it was transported to the village of Lourmarin in the South of France, where Camus had spent much of his time since the award of the Nobel Prize. It was, on the whole, the brutal "absurdity" of Camus' death, the stupid trick of chance, that struck most imaginations: the railroad ticket in his pocket, evidence of a last-minute decision to take the journey by car. But for many of Camus' friends it was the quiet dignified burial in the Lourmarin cemetery, not the lurid accident, that most exactly evoked the quality of the man.

This book, begun before Camus had won the Nobel Prize, finished a year before his death, spoke of a writer still in mid-career. Since it was written only one major work by Camus has appeared, his stage adaptation of Dostoevsky's *The Possessed*. Many other works were in the making: a novel, *The First Man*, to which in Lourmarin Camus was giving much of his time, a play, another essay perhaps. In the summer of 1959, when I last saw Camus in Lourmarin, he was full of energy and projects, dreaming of the theater which he was soon officially to direct. To a journalist who, that same year, asked what wish he would formulate, he answered: " 'In a superabundance of vivifying and healing forces, misfortunes themselves have a solar brilliancy and engender their own consolation,' says Nietzsche. It's true. I know it. And I ask only that this strength and superabundance be given me again, from time to time at least." [1]

Many friends helped me in the preparation of the book. The American Philosophical Society gave me a grant from the Penrose Fund and New York University from the Research Fund of the Graduate School of Arts and Sciences, which enabled me to work in Paris on the unpublished notebooks and the manuscripts of Albert Camus. Marguerite Dobrenn of Paris was of great help to me in the preparation of the manuscript of this book. I wish most warmly to thank Ruth Field, who brought me her invaluable, patient, and constructive assistance.

To Albert Camus, himself, I owe much: free access to a great deal of unpublished material; a direct and friendly welcome; the patient reading of the manuscript; a careful checking of facts which scrupulously avoided any attempt to influence critical evaluations or interpretations.

[1] Jean-Claude Brisville, *Camus* (Paris: Gallimard, 1959).

Contents

CAMUS

1

Camus and His Time

"La peine des hommes est un sujet si grand
qu'il semble que personne ne saurait y tou-
cher . . ."

"Do you know that over a period of twenty-five years,
between 1922 and 1947, 70 million Europeans—men, women,
and children—have been uprooted, deported, and killed?" [1]
Probably most of us today would answer a somewhat reluctant or an impatient Yes to this question, but few would want
to consider it with the dramatic urgency implicit in the works
of Albert Camus.

The recent history of Europe was the constant object of
Camus's preoccupation, a preoccupation which he shared with
many contemporary writers and thinkers. We can reach no
really penetrating understanding of the significance and value
of his work if we take it out of the historical context of our
time. Two major wars within a quarter of a century, revolutions, mass deportations, concentration camps, have accustomed us to think in terms of the widespread possibilities of
imprisonment, torture, and violent death for persons like ourselves. We are no longer astonished by systematic brainwashing and mass propaganda; the atom bomb is now a part of
our everyday life. That we live in a disconcerting epoch we
are willing to agree, but if our century is, as Albert Camus
called it, "a century of fear," [2] for many of us the fear is a

[1] *Actuelles II,* p. 33.
[2] *Actuelles I,* p. 141.

3

diluted one and, most of the time, dormant. But to Albert
Camus these characteristics of our time were subjects of scandal, a scandal that he himself found it impossible to evade.
It was his strength as an artist to refuse to write any work that
did not take into account and express directly or indirectly
the latent anxieties of his generation.

The name of Albert Camus became familiar to many people in the years immediately following World War II. To
some, not particularly interested in literary achievements, he
was then essentially the young and vigorous combatant in the
clandestine Resistance movement, the director of the newspaper *Combat,* who after the 1944 liberation expressed in his
editorials opinions, anxieties, and hopes which they shared.
To others he was, rather, the author of *L'Etranger,* a short
novel published in 1942 whose meteoric success rapidly spread
far beyond France. It soon reached textbook status and is cur-
rently used as such in the French literature courses of many
colleges and universities. Camus's second novel, *La Peste,*
was widely and in general quite favorably reviewed in literary magazines, European and American. But it was with
L'Homme révolté, a volume of essays, which raised widespread commentary and controversy, and a third novel, *La
Chute,* that he really reached his public. "The Fall [*La Chute*]
is an hors d'oeuvre for cocktail parties," reported Leslie Hans-
com in the New York *World Telegram and Sun* (Feb. 15,
1957), and indeed it was.

But even if we disregard the mundane notoriety shared
with other, lesser works, Camus's success as a writer was immediate and, within the limits of the somewhat restricted
circles of the reading public, world-wide. A book by Camus
was a literary event. Eagerly anticipated and greeted in Paris
itself, discussed, attacked, defended, it was promptly translated into many languages, and as it crossed national frontiers
it was once again attacked, praised, or refuted.

Some critics, like Henri Peyre,[3] took exception to a certain hagiography that seemed to be developing around the work of Camus, objecting to statements such as the one which appeared on the dust jacket of the American translation of *La Chute* claiming that Camus was "Europe's greatest living writer." But in the fifties it was undeniable that, at least to many of his contemporaries, Camus appeared to be the most significant European writer of his generation. The 1957 Nobel Prize for "his important literary production, which with clear-sighted earnestness illuminates the problems of the human conscience of our time"[4] was an important recognition of the quality of Camus's work. Although it was the logical climax of his growing international prestige, the greatness of the honor awarded to so young a writer—Camus at the time was just forty-four—added fuel to the controversy that *L'Homme révolté* had inspired. The controversy was political at its source rather than literary. To the questions raised by the cold war was now added the burning question of Algeria. For twenty years Camus had been deeply concerned with the economic and political problems of his native land, warning, protesting, suggesting. As the struggle became more bitter and the factions on both sides more fanatical, he was called upon to pronounce, to take sides. His answer was to publish *Actuelles III*, an "Algerian Chronicle" containing, besides a selection from the articles he had written since 1939, a clear statement of his position, a position which seems now to have prevailed among Algerians whether of European or of Arabic extraction.

It was Camus's death, however, when all surface controversy and dissension was silenced, that revealed the extent of

[3] Henri Peyre, "Man's Hopelessness," *Saturday Review*, Feb. 16, 1957.
[4] From the citation read by Dr. Anders Osterling, permanent secretary of the Swedish Academy.

the writer's influence and prestige. The work of the still "young" writer, only in mid-career, was now terminated. Future works projected—an unfinished novel, Notebooks as yet unpublished—might throw much light on the work already completed, but further speculation as to the evolution of the writer had now come to an end. "A man dies," wrote his friend, the Italian critic Chiaromonte, "and we pursue through a living face, gestures, actions, memories, an image forever effaced. A writer dies: we examine his work, each one of his books, we reflect on the thread which ties each to the others . . . and we attempt, in our appraisal, to evaluate the inner impetus so unexpectedly interrupted." [5] The perspective changes for the critic, and the work begins to live a life of its own.

The scope of Camus's work is greater than might generally be understood: articles, prefaces, lectures, adaptations of foreign plays, and essays of considerable length, such as "Réflexions sur la guillotine," add to the bulk and significance of the more widely known novels, plays, and essays. At least four of his books, *L'Etranger*, *La Peste*, *L'Homme révolté*, and *La Chute*, have been labeled, each in its time, as "the most important writing" of a generation, and no one of his works could be said to be without some measure of importance.

It is curious that the adjective "European" should be applied to a writer who, though European in descent and education, was a native of Africa, an Algerian for whom Europe, in one aspect at least, never ceased to be the "sad," "dark," "dreary," and all too often "ignoble" Europe of war and mass murder: "From the shores of Africa where I was born, helped by distance, we have a clearer view of the face of Europe

[5] Nicola Chiaromonte, *"La Résistance à l'histoire,"* Preuves, April, 1960, p. 17.

and we know it is not beautiful." [6] Yet Camus sometimes
thought of himself as a European. In the preface to his
Lettres à un ami allemand he wrote: "When the author of
these letters says 'we,' this does not mean 'we the French'
but 'we Europeans.'"

Camus was deeply attached to France, his country,[7] as both
his actions and his political writings testify, but the uni-
versality of his appeal was perhaps due to the fact that he did
not approach the questions that preoccupied his countrymen
from an entirely French point of view. Born and educated in
Algeria, he was twenty-three when he first visited France, but
apparently it was not France in Europe that attracted him
most strongly. His first trip abroad in 1935 had taken him to
the Balearic Islands; though his second trip took him to Paris,
it was via Central Europe, more specially Italy, and it was in
Italy that he felt most at home.

Camus was thus astonishingly free of the intellectual attitudes which most Frenchmen inherit from their long historical past and the milieu into which they are born. For Albert
Camus this very "innocence" was, in a sense, both a problem
and a strength. It explains in part his tendency to consider
each question from scratch, and it also explains, perhaps,
why the intricacy and greatness of the problems of our historical experience weighed heavily on the work of a man
who, by the time he was in his late twenties, unexpectedly
found himself cast in the role of moral mentor to his generation.

Although Camus's claim to our attention does not lie primarily in his political writing, several of his volumes, and
particularly the three-volume *Actuelles* and *L'Homme révolté*, deal directly with political problems; in a sense, his

[6] *Actuelles II*, p. 63.
[7] Camus answers questions put to him by Jean Bloch-Michel, *The
Reporter*, Nov. 28, 1957, p. 37.

political thought reached its fullest expression in *L'Homme révolté*. He had long experience as a journalist and, like most men of letters today, gave opinions—spontaneous or solicited—on all contemporary events of general or local interest that seemed to him worthy of comment. Of these there were many. He did not, however, at any time set himself the task of formulating a political theory. A writer, in his eyes, should be "a man who observes the world without ceasing to play his part in it." It so happens that the "part" of the writer in contemporary France, perhaps more than in any other country, is not a small one, and in the years of war and occupation it became very exacting. But most exacting of all is the writer's own conscience. In order to "play his part" as an artist in the world of the past quarter of a century, Camus could not avoid becoming deeply involved in political controversy and political action. How greatly this, too, weighed on his work, we shall consider later.

For Camus, however, political problems were of interest only in so far as they touched one of his major preoccupations, that is, the daily life of human beings, their freedom and the human justice meted out to them on this earth. He consistently refused to refer to the abstract universe of systematic ideologies and always stubbornly based his arguments on the individual universe of everyday living in relation to the general principles of freedom and justice. Here again he was beset by the essential limitation of the man of letters. Except in the years of the German occupation, when thought and action coincided, Camus keenly felt the gap that separated formulation from action.

In the world of politics it is well to remember that Camus did not speak as a technician; in one sense this could doubtless be a limitation, for while it is, for example, relatively easy to evaluate the impact of the atom bomb on international policy, it is far more difficult to formulate the articles of an agreement that might preclude its use. But Camus did not, after all, make any claim to being a technician. In answer, perhaps, to Sartre's contention that an artist must be "engaged" in the political issues of his time, Camus wrote: "It is not the struggle that makes artists of us, but art that obliges us to be combatants. By his very function the artist is the witness of freedom, and this is a justification for which he sometimes must pay heavily." [8] And Camus assumed this function with all the hazards it involved: "My role . . . is not to transform the world nor mankind. I have not enough virtue nor sufficient wisdom for that. But it is perhaps to serve, in my place, those few values without which a world, even transformed, isn't worth living in, without which a man, even new, is not worthy of respect." [9]

To a lesser degree this is true also of his attitude toward the moral and metaphysical problems his work poses. Philosophical and ethical systems, as such, did not interest him, and he himself stated on several occasions that he was not a philosopher. His first long essay, *Le Mythe de Sisyphe,* is the cause of some misunderstanding in this respect. Because Camus studied philosophy at Algiers, because *Le Mythe de Sisyphe* stated and discussed a problem which belonged to the realm of philosophy, Camus and his works have frequently been discussed in reference to a somewhat simplified and vague system of thought centering around the notion of "the absurd." If we think of a writer whose essential effort is directed toward elucidating his own experience through an effort of his intelligence as a "philosopher," then Camus most certainly is a philosopher, but nothing could be more erroneous than to consider him an "existentialist" writer. Camus, himself, was most explicit on this point; his work supports his opinion; and his controversy with Sartre when *L'Homme*

[8] *Actuelles I,* p. 264.
[9] *Ibid.*

révolté was published emphasized the difference in the orientation of their thought. "I have little liking for the too famous existential philosophy, and, to speak frankly, I think its conclusions are false," [10] he wrote in 1945, a point of view he never altered.

In contrast to Sartre, Camus was first and foremost an artist, an artist who had an exacting idea of what both art and the artist should be. His artistic conscience explained and supported all his other activities. According to him, the artist's task is essentially to "transfigure" his experience and not to "revel" [11] in it. But no experience can be transfigured unless it is first understood. It is not easy at any time, and more specifically in our time, for a man to elucidate and simultaneously attempt to transfigure all the problems raised by his experience. This is particularly true in the case of a man like Camus, who had no preconceived system of belief. Yet this is what Camus set out to do, not in order to give definite answers but in order to bring out of the chaos and often the violence around him the material that, in his own eyes, could be "transfigured" and made into a valid work of art. Camus had to start by "creating" his own values, a perilous task, no doubt, and one in which an individual must reveal his limitations. But Camus's persistent effort explains in great part the unusual force of the work that resulted and its power of attraction for many readers today.

As a writer, Camus, at the time of his death, was just reaching the years of maturity. It was characteristic of him that he had planned many future works, made notations about them in his Notebooks, and even spoken freely about them. These will remain unwritten, but all that went before them develops as an organic whole, revealing the complex progress of a strong personality. Both the work and the man deserve our

[10] *Actuelles I*, p. 111.
[11] *Actuelles II*, p. 48.

attention, and one of the first tasks of the critic—avoiding the extraneous biographical material that through imagination and even error can obscure the personality of a contemporary writer—should be to start with as accurate a description as possible of those aspects of a writer's life that appear to be directly relevant to the understanding of his work.

2

Algerian Summer, 1913-1932

"J'ai grandi dans la mer et la pauvreté m'a
été fastueuse, puis j'ai perdu la mer, tous les
luxes m'ont alors paru gris, la misère intol-
érable."

"The love one shares with a city is often a secret love." [1]
Algiers, where Camus spent the first twenty-seven years of his
life, was always for him more than just a city. It was a
source of passion, the inner kingdom to which his writing
constantly referred. Beyond Algiers stretches all Algeria: to
the east, the inland city of Constantine, near which Camus
was born in the small village of Mondovi on November 7,
1913; to the west, the port of Oran, which he visited in 1939
and where he lived for a few months in 1941 and 1942; to the
south, beyond the mountain ranges, lie the high deserted
plateaus of alfa grass and the interminable Sahara desert; and
to the north, for miles on end the high rocky cliffs, deep bays,
and beaches of the Algerian coast border the glittering expanse of the Mediterranean. Around the ports, from early
spring until well into the fall, the beaches teem with the
brown bodies of the youth of Algeria, men and women leading
the lives of young gods in the clear, warm water and the sun.

For Camus, Algeria was essentially the land of an "invincible summer." The sun, the sea, the flowers, the desert, and,
in contrast, the teeming cities composed his inner, passionately cherished landscape. The carefully cultivated plain, pride

---

[1] *Noces* (Algiers: Charlot, 1938), p. 53.

12

of the Algerian "colon," and the mountain ranges of the Atlas have little place in this inner Africa, which was typified in the landscape of Tipasa, the old Roman city lying to the west of Algiers. There the pure lines of the Chenoua hills link sea and sky. Silent ruins remind one of Africa's age-old indifference to the fragile empires built upon her soil. The atmosphere is fragrant with the aroma of a thousand Mediterranean plants and, in the long days of summer, time stands still. "In the spring, Tipasa is inhabited by the gods and the gods speak in the sun and the fragrance of the absinthe plants, the sea in silver armor, the stark blue sky, the flower-covered ruins and the great swirls of light amid the masses of stone." [2]

There seems to have been no winter in Camus's childhood world. It was only much later in his life, when he returned in 1952 to his native city after an almost unbroken absence of thirteen years, that he found the dark, shivering Algiers of certain winter days. Though he must have known many such days in the poverty-stricken section of Belcourt where he had lived, they apparently left no trace in his memory. At the heart of Camus's sensitivity, imagination, and thought, and at the heart of his work, are the beauty of the African coast and the glory of an "inexhaustible sun." These he described as none before him, and also the peculiar temperament, ethics, attitudes, and language of the native Algerians with whom he felt more at home than with anyone else.

Of French, Spanish, Italian, Maltese, and Jewish extraction —European, Berber, and Arabic—the working-class population of Belcourt is impervious to the racial barriers that exist in more prosperous, middle-class milieus. The Berber and the Arab never seemed "strangers" to Camus. The primitive mores, elementary moral code, freedom and limitations, idiom, humor, and idiosyncrasies of the Algerian working class gave him his basic understanding of a humanity un-

[2] *Ibid.*, p. 11.

touched by middle-class inhibitions and codes of conduct. "It is in this life of poverty," he wrote later in his Notebooks, "among these humble or vain people that I most surely touched what seems to me to be the real meaning of life."

L'Envers et l'endroit (1937), Camus's first published work, and *Noces* (1938) owe their marked originality to his passionate desire to convey the unique quality of his native country, its men and its landscapes. France gave him her language but Algeria unmistakably gave this language new inflections, a new brilliance, intensity, and starkness which, in themselves, set Camus apart among French writers. Until September 2, 1939, when with the outbreak of World War II Camus found he must "come to terms with darkness" and become familiar with the European cities of "blood and iron," his thought and its expression were rooted totally in his Algerian experience.

What Algeria gave him he generously returned. Besides *L'Envers et l'endroit* and *Noces, L'Etranger,* a first draft of his play *Caligula,* and *Le Mythe de Sisyphe* were all conceived and in part written in the years before 1939. To Algeria, too, are dedicated many of Camus's most admirable pages, those written over a long period of years and published in a single volume, *L'Eté* (1954). North Africa not only furnishes the *décor* of *L'Etranger* and *La Peste,* it also plays a role in all Camus's work, bearing those essential images and symbols that give a writer his individuality, his own clearly differentiated style. This is so true of Camus that the absence of North Africa in, for example, *La Chute,* is equivalent to the presence of a sort of hell. The sun, the sea, the vast expanse of the sky, the dry wind, the clear contours and large dimensions of North Africa, these become a spiritual landscape. When Camus spoke of "Greek" or "Mediterranean" values, it was to this inner landscape that he referred, to the values it embodied for him, to the "strange joy" it meted out to him in his adolescence and young manhood. In its totality it remained for him the symbol of pure life.

In many ways Camus's childhood was typically Algerian. His father, a day laborer, was French, of Alsatian descent. He had had little schooling but had taught himself to read and write when he was past twenty. Mobilized in 1914, he was killed at the age of thirty-four at the battle of the Marne, leaving a widow and two young sons. The younger of the two, Albert, was one year old at the time. The tall man with the pale eyes, who so painstakingly wrote postcards to his wife anxiously inquiring about the health of his two boys, was soon little more to them than a photograph and a name. His wife, of Spanish origin, could not read those short messages from distant France, for she had never learned to read or write. A childhood illness neglected in the isolated village where she lived and where doctors were scarce had left her deaf and with a speech impediment. The silent presence, the patient brown eyes, the life of labor, the brief discontinuous sentences of this woman who "thought with difficulty" haunt the pages of her son's books.

Camus's widowed mother and her two children moved to a two-room apartment in the crowded Rue de Lyon in Algiers, where she earned a living for her family as a cleaning woman. The children grew up under the supervision of a domineering, unloved grandmother, who educated them with a whip and who was slowly dying of that terrible sickness, cancer of the liver. An uncle, partially paralyzed, shared the apartment. It was not a happy environment for the child who seems to have centered all his need for love upon the silent figure of his mother. At night she sat by the one small window of the apartment and when her son came in she did not hear him, but "he could distinguish the thin silhouette and the bony shoulders and he stopped: he was frightened. He was begin-

ning to feel many things. He was hardly aware of his own
existence. But he suffered to the point of tears from that animal silence. He felt pity for his mother, was that love? . . .
He stayed for long moments watching her. Feeling himself
a stranger he became conscious of his sadness." [3]

He was a stranger, too, in the unlovely *décor* of poverty.
"I remember a child who lived in a poor section. . . . There
were only two floors and the staircase was not lighted. Even
now, many years later, he could find his way to the house in
the dark. . . . His very body is impregnated by that house.
His legs remember the exact height of the steps. His hand, its
instinctive, never-dominated horror of the banisters . . . because of the roaches." [4] Camus was never to forget the closed,
silent "world of poverty" of his childhood. Asking nothing,
expecting nothing, it had its own dignity. Its inhabitants, stoic
rather than resigned, silently and perhaps unconsciously de-
spised the glib rationalizations and easy consolations in which
the more fortunate middle class sometimes indulges.

The mother, the grandmother, the stark poverty around
him would have constituted the child's entire world had it not
been for that "other side of the coin," the luxurious beauty of
the land of Africa:

> There is a solitude in poverty, but a solitude that gives
> each thing its real price. At a certain degree of wealth, the
> sky itself and a night filled with stars seem natural riches.
> But, at the bottom of the ladder, the sky regains all its
> meaning: a grace without price. Summer nights, mysteries
> amid the crackling of the stars. Behind the child stretched
> a stinking corridor and his broken little chair gave slightly
> under him. But his eyes raised, he drank from the purity
> of night. [5]

[3] *L'Envers et l'endroit* (Algiers: Charlot, 1937), p. 27.
[4] *Ibid.*, p. 25.
[5] *Idem.*

Thus, in his early childhood began Camus's "long love affair with Africa," an affair that, he wrote, "no doubt will never end."

Some twenty years later in the preface to a re-edition of *L'Envers et l'endroit*, Camus evaluated what he owed to his childhood:

> Born poor in a working-class section of the town, I never knew what destitution was before I saw our cold suburbs [of Paris]. . . . The warmth that reigned over my childhood freed me from any resentment. I lived amid privation but also in a sort of delectation and felt infinite forces within me. The only problem was to discover where I should apply them.[6]

For a time Camus seems to have applied them in much the same way as did most of the young boys of Algiers. Free of intellectual complexities and moral restraints, they concentrated on the development of the healthy young animal in them.

But in the meantime, and unknown to himself, Camus was starting out on a path which was to lead him rapidly away from Belcourt and eventually from the glorious beaches of Algiers. In the grade school of Belcourt, which he entered in 1918, Louis Germain, one of his teachers—to whom Camus was to dedicate his Nobel Prize acceptance speech—took interest in the boy, supervising his work outside class hours and preparing him for a scholarship which would allow him to continue his schooling in the *lycée* of Algiers. Camus won the scholarship and in 1923, at the age of ten, entered the *lycée* and followed the regular course of studies that took him step by step to the University of Algiers, where he studied philosophy from 1932 to 1936.

In his early adolescence Camus seems to have taken little

[6] *L'Envers et l'endroit* (Gallimard, preface to 1958 printing), p. 17.

interest in his work at the *lycée*. He was passionately addicted to the physical world, to the development of a perfect body. At fifteen and for the next two or three years football was the center of his life. He told of his impatience as he waited "from Sunday to Thursday, the day he practiced, and from Thursday to Sunday, the day he played." [7] His friends still remember the serious goalkeeper with the impeccably rolled white socks; all his life Camus took a passionate interest in football.

Swimming, too, was, and remained, one of his great joys: "Once in the water, it's a seizure, the surging of an opaque and cold glue, then a dive, the humming in one's ears, a running nose and a bitter taste in the mouth—swimming, arms polished by the water, lifted out of the sea to become golden in the sun then plunging back with a torsion of all the muscles; the flow of the water over my body, the turbulent possession of the sea by my legs—and the absence of horizon." [8] At Algiers "one swims in the harbor and rests on the buoys. When one passes a buoy already occupied by a pretty girl, one shouts to one's friends 'I tell you it's a sea gull. . . .' All the morning passes in diving, in the flowering of laughter amid the spray, in long strokes of the paddle around the red and black merchant ships. At the hour when the sun overflows from all the corners of the sky, the orange canoe loaded with tanned bodies brings us back in a wild dash. And with the last long glide into the calm water of the harbor, how can I be sure that I am not guiding through the smooth water a tawny cargo of gods in whom I recognize my brothers?" [9] For Camus the act of swimming always held a particular significance and was often a symbol of a kind of purification, a ritual that freed the swimmer from the burdens and the evils of his daily life.

[7] R.U.A. (*Racing universitaire d'Alger*), April 15, 1953.
[8] *Noces*, p. 19.
[9] *Ibid.*, p. 62.

During these years the only ethics he knew were the ethics of his football team, but "when one lives this way, close to bodies and through the body, one finds out that it has its delicacies and, if I may risk an absurd statement, a psychology of its own." [10] The robust sensuality of these Algerian youths was in itself a form of equilibrium and sanity. When a few years later, in 1939, Camus described the young people of Oran, he described them with an indulgent humor as very similar to what he himself must have been at that age: "Between the years of sixteen and twenty," the young Oranese boys and girls walk up and down the boulevard every evening, "the boys with waved and carefully brilliantined hair," the girls made up as meticulously as an American actress. And in fact, as Camus pointed out, the American movie actor Clark Gable was the model for the boys and Marlene Dietrich for the girls, and that was why "the critical minds of the town commonly call the young men, thanks to a carefree pronunciation, the 'Clarques,' while the girls go by the name of 'Marlenes.' " [11] Movies, dancing in one of the popular cafés built into the sea on wooden piles, these are the recreations of adolescents astonishingly free of the often austere restrictions imposed on them in the French provinces. ". . . on the boulevards of Oran one does not raise the problem of being and one is not concerned with the road to perfection." [12] And these problems were apparently of no great concern to young Camus, the goalkeeper of the football team.

It was a great shock to the lad of seventeen when in 1930 he suffered his first and virulent attack of tuberculosis. The year 1930 marks a turning point in his life. His first lonely encounter with death, a public ward at the clinic, the other patients around him, seem to have awakened him to a full

[10] *Ibid.*, p. 59.
[11] *L'Eté*, pp. 24, 25.
[12] *Ibid.*, p. 26.

consciousness of what it really meant to be a living human being. His initial reaction appears to have been one of fear, shame, and revolt. He felt no romantic delectation in his state and no resignation. The next ten years were to be perhaps the most active years in an unusually active life. Camus broke with his past life. He left home, where he could not take adequate care of himself, and after a short stay with an uncle started to live independently, supporting himself as best he could. His intellectual life seems to have begun then to develop at an unusual tempo. At the University of Algiers he found a master, the philosopher and writer Jean Grenier, formerly his professor of philosophy at the *lycée* of Algiers, for whom his affection and gratitude never wavered. Though not yet at its end, the Algerian Summer had acquired new overtones.

3

Passion for Life, 1932-1939

"... cette matière magnifique et futile qui
s'appelle le présent."

The 1930's in Algiers were propitious years for a young man
with latent possibilities as a writer. Because of its distance
from France and the very character of the land and population, Algiers, a prosperous, picturesque city of 265,000 inhabitants, was developing as an independent cultural center for
the entire province. A group of young intellectuals, many of
them students, were taking stock of what they liked to think
of as their own rich heritage. This heritage went back beyond
France to Rome and, through the early medieval Arabic
civilization and Byzantium, to Greece. For these young men
and women, Algeria was not the exotic land to which Europeans traveled when they wanted to shake off the dreary
shackles of civilized living. Their North Africa was not that
of Flaubert, Fromentin, Loti, or Pierre Benoît, nor even that
of Oscar Wilde, André Gide, or Henri de Montherlant. Nor
was it the Africa of the mystics, those seekers after the stern
spiritual discipline that the desert has ever meted out to its
devotees, such as, in the generation that preceded theirs,
Ernest Psichari, Renan's grandson converted to Catholicism,
or Charles de Foucauld, the Trappist monk. In their eyes
Algeria was neither a refuge nor an adventure. It was their
land and they felt its newness and originality, an originality
they wanted to express in a literature that was their own.

Besides Albert Camus, a whole crop of writers was developing on African soil: Jules Roy and Emmanuel Roblès, both well-known novelists; Raoul Celly and Max-Pol Fouchet, later to be known as essayists and critics; the future painter and novelist René-Jean Clot. The political ferments of the time were, to be sure, at work, but they scarcely penetrated beyond the calm surface of a peaceful land where many Mohammedans, too, were preparing to write in French: Mohammed Dib, Mouloud Feraoun, Mouloud Mammeri, and, a little older than these, Jean Amrouch, whose career had already begun. Edmond Charlot, a publisher in Algiers, was willing to print the works of his compatriots and the ephemeral reviews they launched. Camus was soon actively involved in this milieu and perhaps it was a great advantage that his first intellectual contacts were made in Algiers and not in Paris, where so many talents are weakened or lost. Algiers was small enough to bring him the friendships which were to last through many years and it furnished him with a small appreciative audience that played a role in the rapid maturing of his personality.

In the years immediately following his first attack of tuberculosis young Camus's activity reveals something of his desperate reaction to the threat that hung over him. Much of the time he was a sick man, though no one would have guessed it, and his career was directly affected. Since his professors had warned him that he could not hope to pass the medical examination required of candidates to the Agrégation—the final step before the Doctorat d'Etat which opens up a university career—he had to abandon any thought of teaching as a profession and with it the security it would bring. The year 1937 when he refused a minor teaching job at Sidi-bel-Abbès, in the south of Oran, seems to have been a crucial one for him: "a burning and disordered year," he recorded in his Notebooks, "uncertainty as to the future, but absolute freedom with regard to my past and to myself." In the light of a problematical future, the present seems then to have become for Camus "that magnificent and futile" substance of life which must be savored to the full.

The explosion of energy that characterizes these years is not merely the manifestation of a disorderly appetite for living. It originates in an inner life unusual in its intensity. The first manuscripts he wrote (or, at least, preserved) date from 1932; in 1935 he started to keep Notebooks, jotting down his plans, his observations, his thoughts, and by 1937 his first book was being published. His personal life, to be sure, had its vicissitudes: a brief unhappy marriage at the age of twenty to Simone Hie, daughter of an Algiers doctor; an impressive array of occupations to keep himself alive—clerk in an import-export firm (a job he remembered when writing *L'Etranger*), salesman for automobile accessories, meteorologist, private tutor. It was not until 1938 that he finally decided in favor of journalism.

Some of these years were happy ones. For a time after his divorce young Camus and three other students shared a house overlooking the magnificent bay of Algiers. They called it "the house facing the world." The beauty, the freedom, the gaiety, the affection, and understanding he then experienced came as an unexpected and delightful interlude in a difficult life. But through it all what essentially mattered was his discovery of his need to write and his decision to become a writer.

Camus had his literary preferences which he shared with most of his contemporaries: Proust, whom he always greatly admired, then Gide. At first André Gide's aestheticism and self-conscious sensuality annoyed the lad from Belcourt, but he soon felt the deeper value of Gide's writing: ". . . the sensual message of *Les Nourritures terrestres* taught me nothing. On the contrary, something in that admirable exaltation smacked of conversion and disconcerted me. . . . It is the asceticism of the work that struck me; and since then I have never ceased to learn with Gide that there is neither art nor greatness without a freely accepted discipline." [1] Montherlant's nihilistic moral code was a temptation, Montherlant, whose nonchalant elegance, felt hat, and meticulously gloved hands Camus also liked to imitate. André Malraux was more directly an admired master about whom Camus planned to write an essay. But these writers were in many ways far removed from his own sphere. At the time of his first journey to Europe, Camus, who traveled third class, stayed in poor hotels and sometimes went without food, commented somewhat ironically on the "virtues" which the relatively wealthy Gide and Montherlant found in travel as they moved in luxury through Europe or North Africa.

It was probably his master, Jean Grenier, to whom Camus dedicated his first work, *L'Envers et l'endroit,* and later *L'Homme révolté,* who most deeply influenced him: "Grenier gave me a taste for philosophical meditation." [2] And it was Grenier who introduced him to the first two books that strengthened his conviction that he too had something to say: a little-known novel, *La Douleur,*[3] and Grenier's own book of essays, *Les Iles. La Douleur* described lives such as those Camus had known in Belcourt, whereas *Les Iles* spoke of the Mediterranean and its significance, of the values of life, and contained a personal approach to the problem of happiness by a man who, though a believer, was never inclined to be dogmatic. The two books directly touched the core of Camus's sensitivity, hence their impact.

Of Breton origin, a Christian, and something of a mystic, Jean Grenier was a passionate devotee of Greece. To Camus he transmitted his love of Greek literature, of the great tragic

[1] *Le Figaro littéraire,* Saturday, Feb. 24, 1951.
[2] Quoted in an interview in *Les Nouvelles littéraires,* Thursday, May 10, 1951.
[3] By André de Richaud.

poets as well as the philosophers. It was thus through Plato and Plotinus that Camus first considered those problems of essence and existence which, with the German philosophies of Hegel, Heidegger, Husserl, and Jaspers, were later to cause so much ink to flow in the Occidental world. Camus's line of thought, unlike Sartre's, can be traced through St. Augustine, Pascal, Kierkegaard, and Chestov, with Plato and the Neoplatonists as a constant check and reference.

For Jean Grenier philosophy does not consist merely in the analysis and criticism of the main systematic philosophies. The very titles of his books show a mind itself involved in scrupulous philosophical meditation. The topics upon which he likes to ponder are pertinent to our time: *Essai sur l'esprit d'orthodoxie; Entretien sur le bon usage de la liberté; De l'Indifférence.* The essay is Grenier's chosen medium. His meditations, based on personal observations of both inner and outer experience, on historical facts and anecdotes, draw on a vast store of knowledge. His method, somewhat akin to that of Montaigne, is the very opposite of the rigorous logical demonstration. He has no great respect for abstractions and seems concerned mainly with a scrupulous examination of the concrete data of experience.

The impact on the young student of a mind of this quality was incalculable. It was under Grenier's influence that Camus worked on a philosophical thesis which he completed successfully [4] in 1936, the subject of which was the influence of Plotinus on St. Augustine. To the layman this may seem a purely academic subject, but for the North African, who could think of both Plotinus and St. Augustine as his countrymen, it was an unusually apt choice. The impact of Neoplatonism on the formation of the Christian dogma was of no mean interest to a young man who, though devoid of

[4] His director was Professor René Poirier, later professor of philosophy at the University of Paris.

faith, sought to understand the meaning of his own life. Camus would not soon forget the teaching of Plotinus nor Augustine's deep involvement in the problem of evil.

The average reader today, protected by standards of morality still uncritically accepted in our everyday world, often finds it difficult to understand a whole trend of twentieth-century European thought which grew out of a painful awareness of the impossibility of finding a rational justification for any system of moral values. With the turn of the century, and in France most particularly, an intellectual crisis developed, the depth, intensity, and complexity of which seem to have been equaled only at times of such great historical transition as, for example, the breakdown of the Roman Empire. Often alluded to by philosophers and critics, this crisis still awaits its historian. It was heralded by a wave of nihilism: the Christian beliefs seemed to many to belong to the past, and the rationalist philosophies of the past three centuries had lost their power of conviction, unsuited as they seemed to a rapidly changing world. The age-old questions of the significance of man's odyssey on this earth were being posed anew and no new satisfactory answers were being offered. But for many young Europeans it seemed essential to find an answer to the question Why live? More or less directly they were all the sons of Nietzsche, of Dostoevsky, familiar with the ideas—if not always the text—of Spengler's *Decline of the West*. To some the only possible justification for life was participation in some form of social and political action, while others were drawn to various forms of individualistic ethics—hedonistic or heroic, as the case might be.

If we can distinguish Albert Camus from among his contemporaries it is perhaps because, in this realm, he started from nothing and had nothing to question or reject except precisely that very nihilism that might have led him passively to accept illness and death. His Notebooks in these early years reveal his intense concern with ethical values, his need to establish a passionately loved life on intellectual foundations that seemed valid to him. Camus was never to abandon this search. It was the strongest driving force behind his work, and it made a writer of him.

By now "the tall young man, slim and pale, indefatigable though sick, passionate . . ." [5] had moved far away from his childhood world—but not without scruples. "What I should like to say," he wrote at the very beginning of his Notebooks, is "that one can feel—without any romanticism—the nostalgia for a lost poverty." Not that he was rich, far from it, but he felt organically linked to a working class to which he no longer belonged. For this reason, perhaps, he had a strong sense of responsibility in the face of social injustice.

In 1934 Camus joined the Communist party, and yet politics, except in a very general way, seem at the time to have interested him very little. His attitudes were fairly typical of the student "left" in the 1930's. Opposed to fascism and yet pacifistic, keenly conscious of the dangers of the Hitlerian adventure across the border and yet suspicious of any show of nationalistic reaction at home, the liberal "leftist" student opinion was anti-Mussolini, anti-Hitler, anti-Franco, rather vague on facts and enthusiastically in favor of social reform in France. The myth of a peaceful, benevolent Russia slowly realizing a paradise on this earth was one of the generous illusions that it quite uncritically accepted. Among Camus's friends it was no uncommon thing to hold membership in the party. These, after all, were the years when Gide, traveling to Russia at the invitation of the Kremlin, addressed enthusiastic audiences in Moscow's Red Square, when Malraux more or less equated his own vision of man's grandeur with the communist fight for liberation, when Aragon abandoned sur-

[5] Blanche Balain. Quoted by Roger Quilliot in *La Mer et les prisons,* p. 12.

realism in favor of the "real" world of Marxism. What was more surprising was how brief for Camus the experiment proved to be—for him it lasted less than a couple of years.

Camus's particular task as a party member was to serve as a propaganda agent among the Arabs to whose cause he was dedicated. When a few months later, for tactical reasons, the party line with regard to the Arab population changed, he was deeply shocked. The Kremlin in its concern over Hitler's Germany had signed an agreement with Pierre Laval, an action with which Camus disagreed violently, naïvely distressed by so blatant an example of opportunism. He and a group of his friends left the party and the party, in turn, excluded them. In a sardonic little paragraph of his Notebooks, dated March, 1936, Camus laconically disposed of a question that was later to prove a good deal tougher than he then thought:

> Grenier, on the subject of communism: "The whole question is the following one: for an ideal of justice, should we subscribe to absurdities?" One can answer Yes: beautiful! No: honest!

For the moment the young man was thinking only of his private commitment and not of his time as a whole. Although his courageous public stand against communism was to come several years later, at a particularly crucial time in the history of French politics, this first political adventure was characteristic. In general, his political positions eventually proved to be sound, both practically and ethically, but they were often assumed a little in advance of his contemporaries and were a good deal more decisive.

Though the party line had changed, Camus's interest in the lot of the underprivileged Algerian Arabs, whom he considered as his fellow countrymen, did not waver. In June, 1939, as a journalist on the staff of the leftist paper *Alger-Républicain*, he was sent to investigate the conditions of the Kabyle tribes in the mountains to the south of Algiers. Berbers, still marked by the vague memory of Rome and a Christianization that had not survived the Arab conquest, the hardy and independent Kabyles were undergoing a severe economic crisis which was particularly intolerable in a region where geographic conditions limited their resources to the necessities of bare survival. The report Camus brought back revealed the qualities which later marked his work as director and editor of the postliberation daily *Combat*. Up to that time Camus's contributions to *Alger-Républicain* had not been very important. Only a few short topical articles—one very moving description of a convict ship en route to French Guiana—gave some inkling of his unusual sensitivity to all forms of human suffering. The Kabyle report showed how powerful this sensitivity could become when allied with two other basic qualities: a scrupulous attention to the accuracy of his facts and a deadly irony relying for its effect on a cold form of studied understatement. From June 5 to June 15, 1939, *Alger-Républicain* ran a daily installment of the report, which is even today illuminating.[6] It contains a lot of hard common sense and precise, very clearly limited proposals of reform, among them a form of self-administration for the Kabyles. Justice was no abstract concept for Camus even at that time; it was a necessity born of his intense power of understanding the misery of others. It was later to become a passion.

But at this stage the problems of social injustice were not of paramount concern in his life. Because of his past youth he was fully aware of them, but from afar and somewhat theoretically. The immediate and unexpected consequence of the brief interlude with communism was the discovery of what was to be another of the passions of Camus's life, one almost as strong as his passion for Algeria, and quite as lasting. In the

[6] Certain sections of the report are reproduced in *Actuelles III*, pp. 33-90.

1930's the Communist party stressed cultural activity, favoring a close collaboration between intelligentsia and working class. Cultural centers, theater workshops, *avant-garde* movie societies or clubs, more or less ephemeral in nature, appeared in many places and almost overnight. In 1935 *Le Théâtre du travail* (Workers' Theater) was founded in Algiers and on Camus's initiative. Algiers was far from the metropolis and the half-dozen performances given each year by Parisian troupes did not constitute any serious competition. *Le Théâtre du travail* outlasted its commitment to the party and managed to continue until 1939. Because of the spirit it reveals and because Camus was at the heart of the affair, this venture is well worth relating.

Le Théâtre du travail opened its doors in May, 1936, with a dramatic adaptation of Malraux's *Le Temps du mépris* (*Days of Wrath*). The actors were all amateurs, students and workmen. The stage was set up in one of the characteristic wooden cafés built out into the sea on piles in the popular section of the port, the Salle Padovani, normally used as a popular "dancing," as the French call it, and the beating of the waves punctuated the performances. A great effort had been made to draw the working-class public, with which students and a handful of the *avant-garde* bourgeoisie mingled. In line with the century-old traditions of such initiatives in France a manifesto had been prepared. Self-consciously didactic in tone, serious and studiedly modest, it had all the overtones of a certain style Camus was often to use in his editorials:

A Workers' Theater is being organized in Algiers thanks to a collective and disinterested initiative. This Theater is conscious of the artistic value inherent in mass literature, wishes to prove that art can sometimes profit by moving out of its ivory tower, and believes that a sense of beauty is inseparable from a certain sense of humanity. These are not very new ideas. And the Workers' Theater is well aware of

it. But it is not concerned with originality. Its aim is to reinstate certain human values, it is not to bring new themes
of thought. The means of production had to be adapted to
the theoretical aims. Hence certain innovations in the application of ideas that are still new in Algiers. Desirous
above all to avoid all the "commonplaces" of propaganda,
the organizers, for their first experiment, have adapted
André Malraux's novel *Le Temps du mépris*. Their future
effort will consist in creating, producing, and interpreting
by their own means. . . .

Though the "collective" and "social" overtones are recogniz-
ably communistic in inspiration, there is an obvious element
of technical and artistic excitement: the pleasure with which
the "organizers" announce their "innovations" and their desire to avoid obvious political themes are intellectual and not
political in nature.

Le Temps du mépris, which was well received, was followed
by an attempt to fulfill the second objective of the announced
program, that is, to "create" a play "collectively." The concept of "collective creation," like that of a "literature of the
masses," would probably have made Camus smile in later
years. And yet a curious work exists, the four-act *Révolte dans
les Asturies*, published in Algiers in 1936, for the friends of
Le Théâtre du travail, surely a rare and not too bad example
of that paradoxical idea. This "attempt at collective creation"
was never produced, however, having been judged too dangerous by a rather timid municipality. The young authors took as
their theme the revolt of the miners in Oviedo, a revolt that
had been savagely repressed two years earlier. There was no
question at all as to where their sympathies lay. Unabashed by
censorship, the group published the play, dedicating it "to
Sancho, Santiago, Antonio, Ruiz, and León," who are in the
play itself among the miners. The introduction bears the mark
of Camus's personality and, with some youthful paradoxes,

develops a theme which he was to make his own, the theme of the futility and yet the grandeur that accompany certain human actions, placing upon them the seal of "the absurd":

> Theater is not written, or only as a last resort. This is true of the work we are offering the public today. Since it could not be produced, at least it will be read.
> But the reader should not judge. He should apply himself to translating into forms, movements, and light what is merely suggested here. At that price only can he see this tentative in its true light.
> We claim that this is an attempt at collective creation. True. This is its only value. And also that, as a tentative, it introduces action into a frame that is not suited to it: the theater. For this action to reach absurdity, that form of grandeur particular to men, it is enough that it should lead to death.
> And that is why if we chose another title we should choose *Snow*. The reader will understand why later. It is in November that it covers the mountain ranges of the Asturias. Two years ago it covered those of our comrades who were killed by the bullets of the Legion. History did not record their names.[7]

Révolte dans les Asturies is a curious play with a naïveté and a sincerity that may still please and amuse the disinterested reader. The *décor* in itself is worth considering; it was no doubt inspired partly by the authors' didactic intentions and partly by intellectual—one dares not say philosophical—considerations. "The spectator," the text explains, "is to be the center of the spectacle. The play takes place in a square in Oviedo. The spectator must feel he is *in* Oviedo, not *in front* of it; everything goes on around him and he must be the center of the tragedy." The poor spectator thus has no alternative but to "participate" in the action and "the set is so con-

[7] Introduction to *Révolte dans les Asturies*.

ceived as to prevent him from defending himself." What is more, though the participation will be collective, each spectator will participate "according to his personal geometry. Ideally, seat 156 will see things differently from seat 157." This is itself only a transposition of what takes place in the play, where various voices arise diversely describing the event taking place: the capture of Oviedo by the miners and the defeat of the miners at the hands of the Legion. The whole play is a vast dialogue between the struggling voices of the miners and the voice of an immense loud-speaker placed on the stage. It is the loud-speaker that eventually prevails, a symbol of that essential evil or plague, abstraction, which Camus never ceased to fight. At the end of the play the voices of the dead rise in a kind of chorus somewhat reminiscent of the voices of the dead in *Our Town*. Their words come directly from the pen of Camus and acquire a certain moving grandeur. The snow then covers the bodies, symbolizing the indifference of nature toward men's hopes and the tragic absurdity of man's fate.

This "collective creation" was not again attempted. The troupe presented several other plays, among them an adaptation by Jacques Copeau of *The Brothers Karamazov* and Gorki's *The Lower Depths*. It was then that the controversy latent in the manifesto of *Le Théâtre du travail* reached its height. Was the Workers' Theater to be essentially a theater with a social message or was it to present good theater the quality of which guaranteed its human value? Firm on the second point, Camus forestalled any possible accusation that he was catering to a "bourgeois public" by rather unexpectedly pointing out that he could make no distinction among the spectators, the "colon" in his eyes being just as illiterate as the worker. He won his point. *Le Théâtre du travail*, thus transformed into *Le Théâtre de l'équipe*, pursued its career, presenting as its next play Camus's own adaptation of Aeschylus's *Prometheus Bound*. *Prometheus* was followed by plays as varied as Rojas's *Celestina*, directed by Camus amid vociferous disputes, Pushkin's *Don Juan*, Gide's *Le Retour de l'enfant prodigue*, Vildrac's *Le Paquebot Ténacité*, Synge's *Playboy of the Western World*.

At the heart of all this effort was Camus, actor, adaptor, director, "possessed by the love of the theater," involved in all phases of the enterprise. The experience he had gained served him well when for about a year he acted in the troupe of Radio Algiers (formerly the troupe of Alec Barthus), which played in the small towns and villages around Algiers. An important phase of his career had thus begun, for his interest in the theater never lessened. Both as writer and as director he was to continue to give a great deal of thought to the problems of the contemporary theater, and in particular to the questions raised by *Le Théâtre de l'équipe*: how, for example, to bring back to the theater the popular appeal it had enjoyed in England or Spain at the time of the Renaissance.

But 1939 was moving toward the fateful month of September. In spite of the Spanish war, of the annexation of Austria and then of Czechoslovakia, Camus's world was still essentially the world of his Algerian Summer, of "the house facing the world," of *Le Théâtre de l'équipe*. He was preparing to satisfy a long-time wish to go to Greece, he was not preparing for war. His state of mind at the time is clearly described in the letters he wrote a couple of years later and in a very different atmosphere to a "German friend." He had given little real thought either to war or to the affairs of his country. He did not think of himself as a patriot. At twenty-six his life was full to overflowing. He had had two short works published and several others were taking shape in various notebooks and files. He had left far behind him his adolescent friends of the football team.

"In 1933," he wrote later, alluding to Hitler's rise to power, "began a period that one of the greatest among us rightly called the days of wrath.[8] And for ten years every time we were informed that naked and unarmed human beings had been patiently mutilated by men whose faces resembled our own, our heads swam and we wondered how such a thing was possible." [9] For Camus the days of wrath, with all their implications, began only late in 1939, and it was not until 1941 that he was to know the full extent of their power.

"As a writer . . . I started to live in admiration. This, in a sense, is paradise on this earth. As a man, my passions have never been 'against.' They have always addressed themselves to what is better and greater than I." [10] The values coined in Africa, under the Mediterranean sun, were now in the fall of 1939 to be put to a severe test. The outbreak of war coincided almost exactly with Camus's first successful creative efforts. It need not have touched him directly. He had more reasons than most to wait on the sidelines: his physical condition, his home in North Africa, his commitment to his career as a writer. His inner, personal enemy was tuberculosis, death installed in his flesh, a "fall" concerning him alone and which he had had the strength to dominate. But events of a different nature now overtook a life that, up to that time, had been so decisively conducted. The trials they brought were not of his own choosing; the choice of how he should meet them was in his hands. The Algerian Summer was at an end.

[8] Allusion to André Malraux: *Le Temps du mépris*. The title is a quotation from Nietzsche's *Thus Spake Zarathustra*.

[9] *Actuelles I*, p. 25.

[10] Preface to the 1957 edition of *L'Envers et l'endroit*. Reproduced in the 1958 edition (p. 20) with a slight variation: "As a man, my passions have never been 'against.' The people I have loved have always been better and greater than I."

4

Days of Wrath, 1939-1944

"Il avait fallu se mettre en règle avec la nuit,
la beauté du jour n'étant qu'un souvenir."

War has broken out. Where is the war? Outside of the
news we must believe and the posters we must read, where
can we find the signs of this absurd event? Not in the blue
sky over the blue sea, the whirring of the cicadas, nor in the
cypress trees on the hill. Nor in the youthful surge of the
light in the streets of Algiers.

One wants to believe in it. One looks for its visage and
it evades us. The world alone, with its magnificent visages,
is king.

To have lived in the detestation of the beast, to be confronted with it and not be able to recognize it. So little has
changed. Later, no doubt, will come the mud, the blood and
an immense nausea. . . . But today one realizes that the
beginning of a war is comparable to the beginning of a
peace: the world and one's own heart are unaware of them.[1]

Camus noted scrupulously yet with surprise that, in spite
of his concern, the first days of the war were for him "days of
prodigious happiness": like many others, he was astonished to
find his life unchanged. Later, during the somber years of the
Resistance, he was to equate the cause of justice with that of
France,[2] but in these early days of the war he firmly believed

[1] Notebooks.
[2] In 1952, at the time of the controversy raised by *L'Homme révolté*,
Francis Jeanson reproached Camus for having equated the cause of
justice and that of France, but he failed to recall the particular circumstances that explain Camus's attitude at that precise time.

that war was the result of a stupid human error. In 1939 there is not a trace in his writing of what might be termed "patriotism," the word "France" is never even mentioned. In this respect Camus's reaction was quite typical of the young French intellectual. In reaction against the militant nationalism of fascist Italy and nazi Germany—not to mention the rightist groups in France—many young intellectuals were self-consciously internationalist and antimilitaristic, studiously avoiding any attitude that might smack of chauvinism.

War, Camus noted, brought out in human beings a capacity for hatred and violence, favored "a universal flood of cowardice, the mockery of courage, the tawdry imitation of greatness, the degradation of honor." [3] He was not a conscientious objector. In fact, he volunteered for service in the armed forces, explaining this gesture to himself both by arguments apparently borrowed from the Montherlant of *Service inutile* and by other, more sincere arguments born of his own reflection. From Montherlant no doubt came the idea that, in the universal imbecility of the times, it was up to the individual to choose the attitudes most suited to his inner code of personal nobility; more personal was Camus's feeling that there was really no choice:

> It is always futile to want to dissociate oneself even from the stupidity and cruelty of others. One cannot say: "I know nothing about this." One collaborates or one fights. Nothing is less excusable than a war and its appeal to national hatreds. But once war is there it is futile and cowardly to draw aside under the pretext that one is not responsible. Ivory towers have crumbled. Indulgence is precluded for both oneself and others. [4]

His gesture in volunteering proved useless:

[3] Notebooks.
[4] *Ibid.*

"But the boy is very sick," said the lieutenant, "we can't take him." [5]

The refusal touched Camus deeply:

I'm twenty-six, I have my life, and I know what I want. To accept. And, for example, to see what is good in what is bad. If I'm not wanted as a combatant, it shows that my lot is always to remain apart. And it is from my struggle to remain a normal man in exceptional circumstances that I have always drawn my greatest strength and usefulness. [6]

There is pride and courage in this observation and a clear indication that he accepted no decision but his own. Nonetheless as far as he was concerned the whole problem remained a strictly personal and not a national one.

The dreary routine of the "phony war" that followed seems almost completely to have driven the fact of war from Camus's horizon. Finding himself *persona non grata* in Algiers after his articles on the Kabyles, he moved first to Oran and then to Paris, where he worked as a journalist on the staff of *Paris-Soir*. Though not an enthusiast for Paris, in a certain Parisian solitude he was able to concentrate on his writing, finishing *L'Etranger* in May, 1940, just before the German invasion. In the subsequent mass exodus from Paris he followed the staff of *Paris-Soir* to Clermont-Ferrand in the center of France, and then, abandoning the paper, moved to Lyons. In Lyons, in 1940, he married his second wife, Francine Faure, a young woman who, though born and brought up in Oran, was of French origin. [7] Camus hated the darkness of Lyons, a manufacturing city, and the

[5] *Ibid.*
[6] *Ibid.*
[7] Their twin children, Catherine and Jean, were born in Paris in 1945.

coldness of its climate, and in January, 1941, having finished *Le Mythe de Sisyphe*, he returned to Oran and Algiers. In the spring of 1942, a virulent attack of tuberculosis brought Camus to the mountains of central France. The allied landing cut him off from his wife, who had left for Oran earlier.

In the three dramatic years that followed, Camus's only concern apparently was with his own private life and the development of his work. His Notebooks show him voraciously reading, meditating on the theater, particularly on the Greeks and Shakespeare, planning future works; there is no direct echo of the exodus in either his work or in his Notebooks. But the surface is deceptive; *La Peste* and *Le Malentendu*, works which were at that time in the process of development, show how intense was Camus's awareness of the catastrophe into which the world had plunged.

Only two short essays, *"Oran, ou la halte du Minotaure"* (1939) and *"Les Amandiers"* (1940), different in context though not in atmosphere, belong exclusively to this period. The first is one of Camus's most delightful essays, a text for anthologies; with grace and humor he describes the particular physiognomy of the town of Oran, and over these pages war casts not the slightest shadow. Although the second essay does concern war, the first of hundreds of such articles that he was to write in the years that followed, in spirit it is serene, rather far removed from the burning anxiety and despair of the French defeat in 1940:

> The first thing is not to despair. Let us not listen too attentively to those who shout that this is the end of the world. Civilizations do not die so easily and even if this world were to succumb, there would be others after it. . . . When I lived in Algiers I always patiently waited through the winter because I knew that in one night, in one single, cold and pure night in February, the almond trees of the

Valley of Consuls would be covered with white flowers.[8]

The flowering almond trees of Algiers were a long distance from Paris. As early as 1942 Camus seems already to have become involved in some clandestine activity. At this time he lived on a farm, Le Panelier, in the small village of Mazet-Saint-Voy in the province of Auvergne, not far from the mining town of Saint-Etienne. He found satisfaction in his work among the miners, for he felt closer to them than to any but his own native Algerian countrymen. His activities took him back and forth between Saint-Etienne and Lyons, two cities he thoroughly hated: "This town of boredom and ugliness," he wrote of Saint-Etienne, "plunging me into the most unpleasant horrors." And again, "In my opinion, if hell existed it would resemble those endless streets where everyone was dressed in black." [9]

It was not until Gabriel Péri, a workman and an active force in the rising communist opposition to the Nazis, was executed in France by the Nazis that Camus's inner preoccupations came sharply to the fore. By 1943 he was a member of the underground network Combat. To the question Why? he never gave a direct answer beyond recalling Péri's execution and saying he could not imagine himself elsewhere.[10] His underlying reasons, sharpened by a year of experience in this particularly cruel form of warfare, were stated a little later in his *Lettres à un ami allemand*. He had little to say about his activity in the underground.[11] The network he entered had come into existence in December, 1941, as the result of the fusion of two smaller groups. Its headquarters at the time was

[8] *L'Eté*, p. 73.

[9] René Leynaud: *Poésies posthumes* (Paris: Gallimard, 1947). Preface (1945) by Camus.

[10] *Actuelles I*, p. 185.

[11] For a history of the network, see *Combat* by Marie Granet and Henri Michel (Presses Universitaires de France, 1957).

in Lyons and it was destined to become one of the most active and powerful of the groups that, in February, 1944, joined forces in the Movement of National Liberation.

The clandestine printing and diffusion of *Combat*, the news sheet with the same name as the network, was of primary importance to the network, though by no means its only form of activity. The news sheet served as a link between the various branches; it was an organ of recruitment and, not the least among its functions, a source of information. It refuted false news and disseminated accurate facts about the war, seeking to counteract in every way the efforts of German propaganda. It gathered and published exact data concerning German reprisals, executions, deportations, and other acts, in an appeal to the pride and indignation of the French. It spoke constantly of hope, of the great future of a victorious and free France, for these "days of wrath" were paradoxically days of hope. Its voice was eloquent, for the men who risked their lives in this work believed what they said.[12]

There is no "passive resistance," nor a resistance for V-day, nor a "political resistance." It is now, immediately, that we must harm the foe. For the honor of France. For its participation in the war. For Victory [February, 1944].

All the French today are united by the enemy, by such ties that the gesture of one creates the impetus of the others and the absent-mindedness or indifference of one causes the death of ten others [March, 1944].

We must state things as they are: we are vaccinated against horror. All the faces disfigured by bullets or men's heels, the men shattered, the innocent assassinated, at first gave us the revolt and disgust we needed to start fighting

[12] Camus wrote the last two of the three quotations that follow.

deliberately. Now the daily fight has submerged everything else [May, 1944].

The paper also had a generous program for the future, for a "new society, a vigorous and just regime." Social justice, the end of colonialism, and internationalism were more than slogans, they were in all reality articles of faith.

Combat appeared first as a typed and then as a mimeographed sheet, not even as large as a page from a notebook of standard size, then as an equally small printed page, until that triumphant August 21, 1944, the first day of the battle of Paris, when it appeared at last in the full light of day with the name of Albert Camus as its director. Camus, who in the clandestine sheet had been one of the three men who wrote the anonymous editorials, now took charge of the editorial column. During the occupation he had worked first in the Lyons sector of Combat, then was assigned to the editorial staff of the paper. In the spring of 1943 he had moved to Paris ostensibly as a reader for the publishing firm of Gallimard, a position he continued to hold after the war. In the fall of that year, he assumed responsibility for the publication and diffusion of the news sheet *Combat*, organ of the underground network, where he was known under various names, "Bauchart" and Albert Malté among others.[18] He narrowly escaped from the Gestapo when he was arrested in a round-up while carrying a lay-out for an issue of *Combat*. He was awarded the Medal of the Liberation for his activities, a rare honor.

It was through the former director of *Alger-Républicain*, Pascal Pia, who had been one of the initiators of *Combat* in its first stages, that Camus first made contact with the group. There he found, among others, a man he greatly admired, André Malraux, and formed a friendship with an exceptionally

[18] I am indebted for the information concerning Camus's names in the underground to Madame Albert Camus. Professor Jacques Hardré (University of North Carolina) also furnished corroborating facts.

courageous man, René Leynaud, who was the chief of the Lyons sector of the Combat network. His friendship for Leynaud was unusual in its depth and intensity even in a life which invited friendship. On May 16, 1944, Leynaud was arrested and a month later executed. "In thirty years of life no death reverberated within me like this one," wrote Camus in his preface to the posthumous volume of Leynaud's poems,[14] the only pages in which he ever spoke directly, in his own name, of those momentous years. He recalled the warmth of the evenings spent with Leynaud and his wife, their discussions and the nobility of the faith that sustained this dedicated man. He recalled, too, the meeting with Leynaud which was destined to be their last. It was one of those furtive meetings characteristic of the Resistance. They separated on a bridge in Paris: "sunk in my stupid human confidence, sure of him and of his future, I merely nodded to him from across the bridge." The execution of Péri had provoked a first indignation in Camus; the execution of Leynaud nourished a cold and desperate fury: "His death . . . made my revolt blinder. One does men no good by killing their friends, I know it only too well. And some of the moments of anger of which I am not proud today came from there."[15]

These two executions were not the only ones which might have provoked Camus's anger. By the very nature of his work he was close to the inferno of murder and torture that was the lot of those who chose to fight with the underground. His revulsion was so deep that it left indelible marks. In these years he seems to have lost his spontaneous confidence in an essential goodness of life, despite the suffering, death, and injustice it encompasses; and, more particularly, he lost that easy abandon and optimistic view of human relations which

[14] Leynaud, *op. cit.*
[15] *Ibid.* This is an allusion to certain very rare editorials on the treatment meted out to collaborationists at the time of the liberation.

give his first works their distinctive grace. The man who, in 1944, emerged so honorably from this period of trial was in many ways very different from the man who had accepted its challenge.

These are the years when, at the very outset of his career as a writer, Camus knew success, a rapid, unexpected success that placed him in the first rank of contemporary French writers. *L'Etranger* in 1942 and *Le Mythe de Sisyphe* in 1943 made him famous. But the reality in which he was plunged at the time overshadowed these triumphs. In contrast to the years that preceded, his private life almost disappeared. Though working steadily at *La Peste* and his future essay *L'Homme révolté*, he found it hard, if not impossible, not to yield to a kind of despair. The *Lettres à un ami allemand* and his Notebooks contain the immediate expression of his inner tension and suffering.

Published in 1945, the four letters "to a German friend" were written between July, 1943, and July, 1944. Two had already appeared in the clandestine press, the other two were previously unpublished. All four were written in the turmoil of the Resistance. In the preface to these letters Camus goes to some pains to emphasize the significance of the context: "I cannot allow these letters to be reprinted without saying what they are. They were written and published in the clandestine press. They had a purpose, which was to throw some light on our blind struggle and to make our fight more effective. They are topical and therefore may appear unjust." That is, however, precisely why they are so revealing. It is not surprising, under the circumstances, that the letters constitute an indictment of nazi Germany and a passionate defense of France, that "admirable and preserving" nation of which Camus speaks with a depth of love and compassion quite new to him. The "hundreds of thousands of men assassinated at dawn, the terrible walls of prisons, a Europe whose soil steams with the millions of corpses that were her children"—that is the part of Germany. In contrast, France is the suffering and heroic France of the present, the France of the past, defeated because of her very ideal of justice, the France of the future which will incarnate humanity and justice: "I belong to a nation that in the last four years has begun over again the entire course of its history and which, calmly and with assurance, is preparing amid ruins to make another history for itself and to take its chance in a game in which it holds no trumps."

To reproach Camus for this clear and simple view of the right and the wrong in the situation is to forget under what pressure these lines were written and the burning faith that alone made it possible for men to act as they did—heroically. The tone of moral superiority which sometimes—a little too often perhaps—colored Camus's political reactions is not infrequently the object of criticism, but to search for its origin in self-complacency is to ignore what the letters reveal. Camus's indignation was born not of the intellect but of an unusually acute, exacerbated sensitivity to human suffering and indignity. Right and wrong in this realm are things of the flesh. However greatly in the years that were to follow Camus may have yearned to free himself from the memory of those "millions of corpses," it was to remain with him and, at the slightest provocation, induce reactions so violent that they disconcerted and disturbed the interlocutors who were more detached or more forgetful or sometimes not too charitable by any standards.

The *Lettres à un ami allemand* are also a confession, the expression of a personal credo. The letters recall the discussions of two young men—a German and a Frenchman—before the war and evoke the fundamental skepticism they shared: "We both believed, for a length of time, that there was no superior meaning to this world." To the German's decision in 1939 to give a meaning to his life through the cult of his country, and his justification of the role it must play in history,[10] Camus opposed his own uncertainties, his unwillingness to separate the idea of France from the idea of Justice. Camus then considers and broadens the problem of the respective choices made by the two men, the separate roads which led them eventually to stand against one another as irreconcilable enemies. "I tell myself now that if I had really been with you in what you thought, I ought to say that you are right to do what you are doing. And this is so serious that I must stop to consider it . . ." What takes shape in these letters is a personal ethic based not on logic but on experience and passionate inner conviction. So strong is the conviction, however, that, like most convictions, it mistakes itself for logic:

> You see, from the same principle we drew different ethics . . . you chose injustice, you aligned yourself with the gods. Your logic was only apparent. I chose justice, on the contrary, to remain faithful to this earth. I continue to believe that this earth has no superior meaning. But I know that something in it makes sense and that is man, because he is the only being who insists upon it. This world has at least the truth of man, and our task is to give man his justification against fate itself. And he has no justification other than man, and it is man we must save if we want to save the idea we have of life. You smile and you disdainfully answer: "To save man, means what?" But I shout it at you from the depths of my being, it means that one should not mutilate him and that one should give a chance to justice which he alone conceives.

The dramatic repetition of the word "man" shows how desperately Camus was fighting to preserve the values of his Algerian Summer, his very *raison d'être*. His logic is the logic of life and death, not the logic of philosophers. This dialogue with the former friend who is now implacably to be destroyed

[10] An attitude perhaps derived from meditation on the last pages of the *Decline of the West*.

is an attack upon the intellectual nihilism Camus knew only too well. It is easy to refute the logic of Camus's arguments, the fallacy in his explanation both of his own situation and that of France, but it is impossible to question the inner truth of the experience nor its corroboration by facts. The *Lettres à un ami allemand* demonstrate that Camus's truths were personal and passionate in nature, that they were arrived at intuitively, that they were reasoned only *a posteriori* and in the light of their evidence in his eyes. They are the record of an experience, they are not a mental exercise.

That these certainties were hard come by, the Notebooks are there to attest. "All that does not kill me strengthens me," young Camus had noted, culling from Nietzsche in happier days. And in 1942 he again reflected: " 'All that does not kill me strengthens me.' Yes, but . . . and how hard it is to think of happiness. The crushing weight of it all; it is best to be silent forever and to turn toward the rest.'"[17] What threatened Camus's idea of life was thereby threatening his very power of creation, besides constantly sapping his physical strength. "In the act of writing there is proof of a personal certainty which I am beginning to lose. The certainty that what one feels and is, is a valid example—I am losing all this." [18] And most revealing of all since it is the lament of the artist: "I cannot live away from beauty." [19] Those years were, indeed, years of exile.

Of the three main works that preoccupied Camus in this period—*La Peste, L'Homme révolté,* and *Le Malentendu*—it was his play, *Le Malentendu,* that most nearly embodied the deep underlying anxieties of the man and a despair which stands in almost direct contradiction to the defiant assertions of confidence which fill the *Lettres à un ami allemand.*

[17] Notebooks.
[18] *Ibid.*
[19] *Ibid.*

5

Trial by Solitude, 1944-1955

"J'ai refait toutes les étapes de l'époque."

"Paris is firing all its bullets on this August night." [1] Liberation had come at last, bringing with it a great surge of relief and hope. Those who had been secretly engaged in the fight could now come out of hiding and be recognized. Few were the people who knew that the successful young author of *L'Etranger* was also an active participant in the Resistance. As *Combat* came off the press on August 24, 1944, Camus found himself becoming doubly famous. In the months that followed, and in spite of himself perhaps, he rose to the status of leader in both politics and ethics. Sartre, whom he had met earlier in 1944 and whose prestige reached its zenith in the postliberation years, later recalled, in an open letter to Camus, the aura with which Camus was surrounded at this time:

It was in 1945: we were discovering Camus, the Resistant, as we had discovered Camus, the author of *L'Etranger*. And when we compared the editor of the clandestine *Combat* with Meursault [the main character in *L'Etranger*] . . . when we realized especially that you had never ceased being both one and the other, this apparent contradiction made us advance in our knowledge of ourselves and of the world. You were almost exemplary. For you bore within yourself all the conflicts of our time and went beyond them because of the ardor with which you lived them. You were

[1] From the first openly distributed issue of *Combat* (*Actuelles I*, p. 19).

a real *person*, the most complex and the richest, the last and the most gifted of the heirs of Chateaubriand and the scrupulous defender of a social cause. You had all the luck and all the merits, bringing to a sense of greatness a passionate love of beauty, to the joy of living, the sense of death. . . . How we loved you then.[2]

Camus became a familiar figure in the Paris scene: the tall, dark, well-set-up young man with steady gray eyes, in the inevitable raincoat, a cigarette between his lips, charming all who met him and, it was said, something of a Don Juan. "Camus's physical appearance is not of those one easily deciphers at first sight," wrote Mme. Théo van Rysselberghe, Gide's octogenarian friend, a woman of unusual insight. "He must come and inhabit it consciously before one can discover its spirit." She notes "the high forehead" and "the well-shaped hands" that "have surprisingly exact, expressive gestures" emphasizing "the words spoken in a quiet voice." But most of all she stresses the "weight" of his presence. "The most effective arm of any man, according to Malraux," she concludes, "is to have reduced to a minimum his share of histrionics. Are there any histrionics left in Camus? Where can they take refuge?"[3]

In 1944 Camus was thirty-one and the role he was being called upon to play lay heavy upon him, taxing to the utmost his determination to have no part in any public spectacle. He was not then nor was he at any later time attached to a political party, though the general aims of the Socialist party corresponded most nearly with his ideas of social justice. He was a journalist and a writer and it was in these capacities that he set out to serve the new France that was to emerge with the Liberation. Among the men who had worked together in the

[2] J.-P. Sartre: *Les Temps modernes*, August, 1952, pp. 345, 346.
[3] M. Saint-Clair: *Galerie privée* (Paris: Gallimard, 1947). M Saint-Clair is the pen name of Mme. Théo van Rysselberghe.

years of underground warfare some were committed to a political party (a number to the Communist party); others, like
Camus, were committed only to France. But for each of them
the commitment was a serious one. A cause for which so many
men had faced torture and death was a sacred cause. Small
wonder that the tone was solemn and forbade any form of
cynicism. The moment, too, was critical. In the *Lettres à un
ami allemand* Camus had written: "I think that France has
lost her power and glory for a long time to come." [4] It had
become a question of what could be saved, what future prepared. The men in the underground thought in terms of revolution, a "New Deal" through which the institutions and
political practices of the Third Republic would be definitively
amended. The dawn of a new era in French history was what
they expected from so great a catastrophe as the defeat of
1940. In those first days of liberation the words "hope," "justice," "wrath," and "greatness" came easily from Camus's pen
and they all heralded a new human "happiness."

In a very general way Camus and his group dreamed of
"reintroducing the language of ethics into the language of
politics," that is to say, of cultivating in every realm that sense
of civic duty which under the Third Republic had not been
particularly characteristic of France. The press was to play a
paramount role in the transformation. The Liberation had
swept away large sections of the press marked by the stigma
of collaboration. The clandestine press was to introduce
France to a nonvenal, independent, high-caliber journalism,
scrupulously documented, impervious to any but the highest
motives, a real guide to public opinion—a "critical" press, as
Camus called it. At the helm of *Combat* Camus, with a
staff formed in the underground, was ready to play his part
in this reform. The experiment lasted, with one interlude

[4] *Lettres à un ami allemand*, p. 31.

in 1945, until 1947. For three years the paper kept afloat, reached a respectable number of readers, and "never dishonored any cause it mentioned." But the odds were against Camus. After a short period of uncertainty the prewar habits of the French press reasserted themselves; the "collaborationist" or "purged" papers soon reappeared under slightly different headings. The aftermath of war revealed deep rifts between the men on the staff of *Combat*. The paper, in need of funds, lost its independence; Camus resigned as its director and *Combat* turned its back on its heroic past to become a leftist-center sheet hardly distinguishable from a dozen others.

During his three years as editor of *Combat* Camus wrote hundreds of editorials. After he withdrew from the paper he did not contribute regularly to any one paper until, in 1955, the Algerian issue provoked a series of articles in Mendès-France's *Express*. But throughout the years, in many papers and on varied occasions, Camus expressed his opinion on political events both internal and foreign. It would be idle here to summarize those articles, a small number of which Camus published in the three volumes of *Actuelles*. But they make interesting reading. They constitute a chronicle of our times, a record kept by a man with the principles of the honest, informed citizen who follows no "party line." Camus made no claim to infallibility. Some of the opinions expressed in his daily comments proved to be quite transitory, as Camus admitted in the preface to *Actuelles I*. This is particularly true of some of the articles that immediately followed the Liberation, perspectives at that time being obviously narrowed by the isolation and inner passion of the Resistance groups. The emphasis, naturally, is on France, but the events considered are often of world-wide significance: the atom bomb; the cold war; Korea; the colonial problem in Madagascar or in

Algeria; the forced labor camps in Russia; the uprising of the workers in East Germany and much later in Hungary; the events in Algeria.

But these articles are documents too of another sort. Moving from hope and certainty to a kind of inner weariness and distress, they are the record of an evolution which was characteristic of many of Camus's compatriots, men of the "liberal left," baffled by the morass of French politics. Politics for Camus were inseparable from ethics.[5] This does not necessarily mean that his ideas were impractical. He was determinedly opposed to violence, to repression, to any action that would lead to the condemnation of men to death. Thus he was opposed to Franco's Spain, and all the more bitterly since he considered Spain "his second country." He was opposed to anti-Semitism; to Stalinism; to imperialism, whether it be economic or political; to the blind repression of national agitation in Cyprus, Poland, Hungary, or Algeria; and to the terrorism of the Fellagha. He was opposed to policies that compromised with what he considered injustice, for example the admission of Franco's Spain to UNESCO, and remained impervious to the argument that therein lay a means of influence and reform. He was in favor of international democratic institutions and early in the postliberation period stated openly that a strictly national policy was no longer possible for France in the present world. He was also in favor—already at the time of Hiroshima—of an international control of atomic energy.

As time passed, a certain evolution in Camus's point of view could be traced, one that had some bearing on one trend at least in the French ideological climate. It concerns the nature of political action itself. In 1944 Camus spoke the

[5] "Ni victimes ni bourreaux (Neither Victims nor Hangmen)," Actuelles I, pp. 142-179, are essential pages in this context.

language of absolutes: for example, absolute justice,[6] immediate and total revolution. It is the language of the French
intellectual, inherited from the French Revolution, and one
which explains, in part, the deadlocks in the French Parlia-
ment: each basic issue raises a question of principle on which
individuals and parties are intransigent and which successfully blocks measures that, in fact, concern the interests of
only individuals or groups. Camus was soon to prefer another
approach closer in spirit to the method favored by the
Anglo-Saxon countries, that is, the delimitation of a problem, the choice of a policy in line with the principles of
democratic action, its application within the concrete framework of the given situation—a policy of immediate, relative
solutions oriented in the direction of progressive liberalization.

This point of view is particularly evident and revealing in
the series of articles that Camus in 1945 devoted to the situation in his native Algeria.[7] They are well-informed, pertinent
articles written by a man most deeply concerned over the
future of a country he considers his own. They propose immediate, practical, moderate solutions—administrative, economic and political, liberal and undramatic—that, had they
been immediately applied, might have gone a long way toward
solving the question of Algeria. Again, in January, 1956, in
Algiers itself, to a joint group of French and Mohammedans
he proposed measures designed to limit the dangers to a
civilian population caught between the violent forces of po-

---

[6] The question of justice as applied to the "purge" of the collaborationists opposed him to François Mauriac, who was the spokesman of
"charity." Camus, fresh from the violence of the Resistance, defended
his point of view against Mauriac but later was to admit that he had
changed his opinion and felt that Mauriac was right.

[7] *Combat*, May 13-16, 18, 20-21 and June 15, 1945. Reproduced in
Actuelles III, pp. 93-122.

litical terrorism and the violent reactions they created.[8] It seemed to many moderates, both Mohammedan and French, a reasonable solution, but it appealed to a moderation and an objectivity that no longer existed. Camus, to his surprise and grief, was shouted down by an irate mob of excited extremists, by those very Algerians he had at one time felt he understood so well.

A second trend that can be traced in Camus's thought concerns his attitude toward Marxism. His first rejection of Marxism had been personal. Then in the Resistance years he had observed the Communists at work more closely and had come out of the Resistance with a strong conviction that their political aims and ambitions spelled death for the Occidental world. He felt that it was a crucial moment in the destiny of the West, acutely critical in the history of France.

Immediately after the Liberation, the French political parties in power—mainly the Christian democrats of the M.R.P. (Mouvement Républicain Populaire), the Socialists, and the Communists—observed an uneasy truce. The Communists were exploiting to the hilt their part in the Resistance movement. Unity was the key word. It was not long before *Combat*, attacked in the communist press, firmly though courteously marked its independence in respect to party line. Camus proceeded cautiously lest he in any way serve the dubious anticommunist reaction, a reaction which all too often led to regrettable confusions and practices.

What is interesting in his position is its underlying motivation, already visible in his *Lettres à un ami allemand*. Camus rejected the Marxist version of history and with it the so-called "realist" approach to political action. He was openly challenging as questionable myths ideas that had long appeared irrefutable to a certain large sector of the "liberal"

[8] *Pour une trève civile en Algérie: Appel d'Albert Camus* (Algiers, 1956). Reproduced in *Actuelles III*, pp. 169-184.

left. As a logical consequence, he also rejected the idea that in politics the end justifies the means. Since in his eyes there was no inevitable orientation in historical events, no predetermined March of History, as the Marxists believe, there existed no predetermined end to justify the means. In no sense did this bring Camus into the camp of the conservative right, for he believed firmly that the best form of government for France and for any other country was a people's democracy. What he objected to was the justification of violent political methods of repression in the name of "historical necessity."

His attitude made him an easy target for the communist press and at the same time held him at arm's length from such essentially rightist movements as General de Gaulle's Rassemblement du Peuple Français (R.P.F.). In 1947 his point of view was akin to Sartre's and he was on the whole in sympathy with Sartre's unsuccessful attempt to create a noncommunist left, that attempt of which Simone de Beauvoir was to give a highly fictionalized account in *Les Mandarins*. Sartre, who saw France as caught between the powerful "blocks" of two hostile powers, Russia and the United States, was persuaded that France needed a socialized economy, yet he was opposed to the methods of the Communist party now seceding from active participation in the government. He attempted, by creating the Rassemblement Démocratique Révolutionnaire (R.D.R.), to rally the working class around a noncommunistic program of social reform and to reintegrate it as an active force into the framework of national politics. Camus never joined the R.D.R., and the R.D.R. completely failed to achieve its aims.

Persuaded by this failure that effective social action could be taken only through the Communist party, Sartre then attempted a tactical "rapprochement" with the communist group, hoping thus to influence their party policies without weakening the chances of the social reform he thought essential for France. In Sartre's eyes open hostility to the Communist party, the only party which represented the French working class and therefore the vital future of France, was futile, in that it merely reinforced the negative elements in French politics. Camus, on the other hand, saw a mortal danger in any form of compromise with communism.

A bitter controversy soon separated the two friends. Camus accused Sartre, and with some justification, of using two weights and two measures, one for the capitalist countries—and in particular the United States—the other for Russia. Sartre accused Camus of being a reactionary bourgeois. In 1950 the controversy flared over the problem of Russian labor camps, a fact which explains in part the subsequent reaction of *Les Temps modernes,* Sartre's review, to *L'Homme révolté* and the bitter personal tone of the argument. Both men were sincere. Neither harbored personal ambitions; both were acutely concerned with the same problems. But between them there was a fundamental intellectual disagreement. Though Sartre rejected the philosophical foundations of Marxism, he accepted the Marxist version of historical determinism which Camus rejected.

By 1952, therefore, Camus had achieved a splendid political isolation. The violent attacks launched against *L'Homme révolté* from all political directions affected him, in spite of many favorable reactions, quite deeply. A whole section of *Actuelles II* (about seventy-five pages in all) contains articles in defense of his book. Yet the preface of *Actuelles II* struck a new note. Nihilism now seemed to Camus to be a thing of the past; peace, he felt, might finally bring the world, and France, the chance of a sane recovery; political events no longer blocked the horizon. For the word "revolution" he substituted the word "renaissance." He no longer thought that it would be brought about by a dedicated group; he saw it as merely an almost inevitable development. "We can no longer live without positive values. Bourgeois morality repels us by its hypocrisy and cruelties. We find equally repugnant the political cynicism that reigns in the revolutionary movement. As for the independent left, it is, in fact, fascinated by communist power and entangled in a Marxism of which it is ashamed." [9]

The aftermath of war had proved bitter to a man whose convictions and temperament had led him to stress the values of "dialogue" as opposed to the values of dogmatic totalitarian statement. And he sometimes laid himself open to charges that he was intransigent, too sure of himself, hasty in his judgments, dictatorial and pompous in his tone. In truth, he was all too often a much-harassed man. One of his short stories [10] tells the gruesome and humorous little tale of the fate of one Jonas, a Parisian painter who becomes a celebrity. Little by little, family, friends, disciples, and critics crowd Jonas out of his own life and apartment, interrupting his work, occupying his time, calling upon him to pronounce upon one issue after another, until finally out of sheer necessity he is driven to build a small hide-out for himself, one that hangs suspended between floor and ceiling. There one day he collapses out of sheer exhaustion as he traces on a blackboard the letters "soli—." His disciples wonder: solidarity? solitude?

Besides the everyday political battle, Camus was occupied with other duties: reading for Gallimard; directing a collection of essays under the over-all title *L'Espoir*; lecturing on official tours in the winter of 1946-47 to the United States and in 1949 to South America. Still more important was the development of his own writing: in quick succession four plays, *Le Malentendu* (1944), *Caligula* (1945), *L'Etat de*

[9] *Le Libertaire*, May, 1952.
[10] "Jonas," in *L'Exil et le royaume*.

siège (1948), and *Les Justes* (1949); and publication in 1947 of a novel, *La Peste*, and, in 1951, *L'Homme révolté*.

In Camus's personal life this period revealed a growing inner desire for a respite from external pressures. In his Notebooks and in many pages of his work [11] he appraised and reappraised the situation of the artist in his time and the value and significance of creative work. For Camus the writer these were not easy years: "I cannot withdraw from the times without cowardice. . . . Have I the right to be only a witness? In other words, have I the right to be nothing but an artist?" [12] "If everything really can be reduced to man and history, where is the place, I ask, of nature, of love, of music, of art?" [13] "One must love life before loving its meaning, says Dostoevsky . . . yes and when the love of life disappears, no meaning can console us." [14]

Fatigue from the strain of underground warfare, a temporary but distressing loss of memory, an almost desperate need for personal happiness and abandon, brought a crying need for solitude and privacy: "At the bottom of my heart, a Spanish solitude. The man only comes out for certain 'instants,' then he retreats to his island. Later from 1949 on I tried to join up, I went through all the stages of the times. But in an onslaught, on the wings of clamor, under the whip of wars and revolutions. Now I am through, and my solitude is rich in shadow and in works that belong only to me." [15]

A new and long attack of tuberculosis in 1949, lasting almost two years, and a crisis in his personal life deepened and accentuated his feeling of solitude and his need for privacy. After the publication of *L'Homme révolté* in 1951, Camus

[11] *"Création et liberté,"* *Actuelles II*, pp. 127-153; also the last section of *L'Homme révolté*, among others.
[12] Notebooks (1945-1948).
[13] *Ibid.*
[14] *Ibid.* (1949).
[15] *Ibid.* (1951).

turned away from politics and, though it was not apparent on the surface, turned inward and toward the planning of his future work. Between 1951 and 1956 he published no major work.

It was perhaps a sign of this inner evolution that, in 1953, he returned to one of his first loves: the theater. Since the end of World War II the summer festivals in the French provinces had become one of the features of the theatrical world. For a few days, sometimes for a couple of weeks, outdoor performances were given in such spectacular settings as the Avignon Palace of the Popes. One of these festivals was held at Angers, using for its stage the magnificent terraces of the château. In 1953 the director of this festival, Marcel Herrand, presented two adaptations by Camus: Calderón's *La devoción de la cruz* and a sixteenth-century comedy, *Les Esprits*. In the course of the rehearsals Herrand became ill and Camus took his place as director. Not only did he remain partly in charge of the annual festival but, in 1956, he directed the Paris production of his adaptation of Faulkner's *Requiem for a Nun*. It was then that Paris discovered in Camus the first-rate theatrical director to whom Algiers had been introduced twenty years before, and for Camus the theater was once again to move into the center of his life.

6

"My Work Is Not Begun"

> "Dans le songe de la vie, voici l'homme qui
> trouve ses vérités et qui les perd, sur la terre
> de la mort, pour revenir à travers les guerres,
> les cris, la folie de justice et d'amour, la dou-
> leur enfin, vers cette patrie tranquille où la
> mort même est un silence heureux."

In the 1950's Camus produced one volume after another
at an accelerated tempo. For the theater he produced a series
of brilliant and successful adaptations: *Un Cas intéressant*,
an adaptation of the Italian play *Un Caso clinico* by Dino
Buzzati; *Requiem pour une nonne*, the adaptation of Faulkner's *Requiem for a Nun*, which was one of the outstanding
successes of the 1956-57 theatrical season; *Le Chevalier
d'Olmédo*, an adaptation of a drama by Lope de Vega; and,
in 1959, his stage adaptation of Dostoevsky's novel *The
Possessed*. In 1956 came the much-discussed novel *La Chute*,
and in 1957 *L'Exil et le royaume*, a book of short stories. And
he freely admitted that there was more to come: a novel,
entitled *Le Premier Homme*; a play, *Don Juan*.

The years 1954-1955 seemed to mark a new stage in his
career. In 1954, having just reached his fortieth year, he wrote
a preface to a new and at first strictly limited edition (1957)
of his first book, *L'Envers et l'endroit*. This preface includes
a self-evaluation and a self-portrait. For any artist, he claimed,
there is a single source of inspiration. In his own case this
source can be found in *L'Envers et l'endroit*, his first pub-

lished work, which describes the world of his childhood. Though Camus questioned the literary value of the work, he did not question its fundamental significance. At the source of his artistic vocation he saw "the world of poverty and light in which I lived for a long time, which offered me emotion without measure, and the memory of which still preserves me from the two dangers that threaten the artist, complacency and resentment." The preface is a self-evaluation by a man who, as he looks back over his past, feels he has reached a certain measure of self-possession, a certain state of detachment:

. . . poverty was never a misfortune for me: it was always counterbalanced by the richness of light. And, because it was free from bitterness, I found mainly reasons for love and compassion in it. Even my rebellions at the time were illuminated by this light. They were essentially—and I think I can say it without misrepresentation—rebellions in favor of others. It is not certain that my heart was naturally inclined to this kind of love. But circumstances helped me and, to correct my natural indifference, I was placed halfway between poverty and the sun. Poverty prevented me from judging that all was well in the world and in history, the sun taught me that history was not all. I wanted to transform life, yes, but not the world, which was my god. And that is no doubt how I began this uncomfortable career in which I find myself, starting out with innocence on a fine line of equilibrium along which today I advance with difficulty, without being sure I shall reach my goal. In other words, I became an artist. . . . Later, even when a serious illness temporarily took this vital force away from me, in spite of invisible infirmities and the weaknesses they brought me, I may have known fear or discouragement but never bitterness. This illness doubtless added other very serious impediments to those I already had. But in the long run it fostered a freedom of heart, the slight distance with re-

A manuscript draft of the 1957 preface of *L'Envers et l'endroit*
(*Reproduced with the Permission of Albert Camus*)

gard to human interests which saved me from resentment. This privilege, since I have been living in Paris, I know to be royal. But it is a fact that I have savored it to the full and that, at least up to the present, it has illuminated my life.

Camus went on to explain how ill at ease he felt in the atmosphere of literary Paris, how demanding he found his profession as writer and how painful the "trial by vanity" to which Paris subjects its authors and to which he, like others, found it easy to succumb. He freely admitted that, in his need to escape from its insidious charm and the "discomfort" it caused him, he developed a cold and brusque appearance, refusing compliments with that "stupid and surly air" he knew only too well. Though this surliness was due in part to "the deep indifference" he felt within him "like a natural infirmity," he explained its more fundamental cause, that is, the feeling that such compliments did not refer to his universe, which was still essentially as it had been in *L'Envers et l'endroit*: "that old woman, a silent mother, poverty, the light on the olive trees in Italy, solitude and love, all those things which, in my eyes, are witnesses of truth."

He analyzed his hatred of comfort, of family or bourgeois life, and, as an artist, the violent anarchy he felt within himself, obliging him to a strict—almost too strict—discipline in form. This form, in his eyes, was what *L'Envers et l'endroit* lacked, but he knew he eventually would find the form he sought: "For at least I know, with certainty, that a man's work is nothing but the long journeying to recover, through the detours of art, the two or three simple and great images which first gained access to his heart. And that is perhaps why, at forty, after twenty years of work and publication, I continue to live with the notion that my work is not begun."

As to the rest, "in the secret of my heart I only recognize simple lives and the great adventures of the mind. . . . I have tried as best I could to be a man with an ethic, and that is what cost me most. . . . Man sometimes seems to me an injustice on the march, I refer to myself." Camus had attained the detachment that sometimes accompanies achievement and maturity.

When the Nobel Prize award was made in 1957, though deeply moved by the honor, Camus was troubled by the notoriety it brought him. He felt the weight of his responsibility and questioned his own future potentialities. He realized, however, as he himself said, that he must accept his fate in its entirety. For the first time in his life he found himself free from financial burdens. Turning his back, at least partially, on Paris, he could now return to the Mediterranean world in which he felt at home.

During the years of clandestine warfare he had formed a solid friendship with the poet René Char, who lived away from Paris, in the old and charming village of L'Isle sur la Sorgue, not far from the Fountain of Vaucluse where Petrarch wrote his sonnets to Laura. Protected by a low mountain range from the hordes of tourists invading the French Riviera, this region harbored other writers, among them the novelists Giono and Bosco. Camus bought a house in the village of Lourmarin, a house which he furnished beautifully with Spanish austerity. There he planned to spend half the year working. He refused many honors, many invitations to appear as lecturer in France and abroad, in person, on radio or television. But when, in 1959, André Malraux, now in charge of France's artistic activities, offered him the direction of an experimental theater, Camus gladly accepted. "Why am I in the theater? I've often wondered," he commented in a television broadcast following his appointment.[1] "The only answer I can find up to now will no doubt seem to you discouraging in its banality: simply because the theater is one of the spots in the world where I am happiest."

[1] Reproduced in *Le Figaro Littéraire*, May 16, 1959.

Although the Algerian problem weighed heavily on his mind, Camus had attained the freedom which, as a writer, he had for some years felt he so greatly needed. *The First Man*, the novel he was now writing, which was to be neither a "myth" nor a "récit," [2] was progressing. He was thinking of an open-air theater at Lourmarin. The period he was now entering seemed to be similar to that most fertile moment in his career—the mid-thirties. "Do you consider your work finished in its main lines?" an interviewer asked Camus in 1959. [3] "I am forty-five and have a rather consternating vitality," was Camus's answer.

"I recall the letter written to Tolstoi by the dying Turgenev: 'I am writing to tell you how fortunate I was to be your contemporary.' It seems to me that, by the death which struck down Camus and which made us all aware in a secret part of ourselves that we too were dying, we have felt how fortunate we were to be his contemporaries." [4] Better than most these words of the critic Maurice Blanchot reflect the widespread sense of loss and sadness caused by Camus's unexpected death and the general affection and esteem which, unknown to himself perhaps, he commanded in France itself and far beyond the borders of France.

[2] Carl Viggiani, "Camus in 1936," *Symposium* XII, Nos. 1, 2 (Spring-Fall, 1958), p. 18.

[3] Jean-Claude Brisville, *Camus* (Paris: Gallimard, 1959), p. 257.

[4] Maurice Blanchot, "Albert Camus," *N.R.F.*, March 1, 1960, p. 403.

7

The Black Sun of Death

". . . on sait que le soleil est parfois obscur."

"I know now that I shall write . . . I must bear witness
. . . I shall speak of nothing but my love of life. But I shall
speak of it in my way. Others write because of temptations
deferred.[1] And each disappointment in their lives brings them
a work of art. But my works will come out of my happiness.
Even in its cruelty. I must write, just as I must swim, because
my body insists upon it." So speaks Patrice Meursault,
Camus's first fictional hero, who often resembles his creator,
borrowing from Camus's Notebooks at the very moment
he is taking shape in its pages. As early as 1935, at the age of
twenty-two, Camus had made the discovery which Patrice, in
his turn, made a year later, that is, that he must write.

Like most beginners, Camus started out to write a novel.
"We only think in images," he noted; "if you want to be a
philosopher write novels." Typically enough the first novel
he planned, which he at first called *La Vie heureuse*, was conceived as a sort of *Summa*, using and synthesizing the entire
range of the young man's experience: his present and past;
the world around him and the world within him; the people
he loved, among them his mother, and the people he observed
objectively; his illness and confrontation with death; and, not
the least among his themes, the inner progress of his thought,
his own relation to this complex universe. Some twenty years

[1] An allusion, perhaps, to André Gide, who once gave this definition
of his early work.

later he was to speak of the artist's long journeying toward self-knowledge, embodied in successive works of art,[2] but now, at the beginning of his career, in his eagerness to pour into this novel the totality of his life, he failed, like many another writer, to recognize that he could reach his destination only by a slow journey of many stages. It is no wonder that Meursault, the hero of this first novel, found the going so difficult that he had to abandon the task assigned to him. In the course of the writing *La Vie heureuse* became, instead, *La Mort heureuse*. The work, which took two years to write and remains an unpublished manuscript, finally emerged as a curious and revealing autobiography in which there was not only a transposition of facts but a symbolic reordering of them; since the autobiography is, in intent, spiritual, the work is thus something of a revelation.

To say that this first proliferation of *La Vie heureuse* contained in embryo all Camus's future work would be an exaggeration, but it does constitute a matrix where, in themes at least, his future works originated. His first three published works were richly nourished by *La Vie heureuse*; two of its themes, the "world of poverty"—with the figure of his mother at the center—and the beauty of North Africa, were to find expression in two books of personal essays, *L'Envers et l'endroit* and *Noces*, and Meursault, the hero of his novel *L'Etranger*, was a new and lesser role for the Meursault of *La Vie heureuse*, though with one exception these two heroes actually show little resemblance.

La Mort heureuse traces an itinerary, a kind of pilgrim's progress, not toward the City of God but toward death, and toward a certain kind of death, which by its very nature is a comment upon the meaning of life. Its hero, Meursault, a white-collar worker in Algiers, is thrown into this itinerary by a deliberate crime, a murder carefully accomplished in cold.

[2] In his preface to the 1957 edition of *L'Envers et l'endroit*.

blood in the best style of detective fiction. That the crime is symbolic is abundantly clear, and in a sense that is a pity since it weakens the dramatic opening of the story. The victim is one Zagreus and the crime remains unpunished; indeed, much later Meursault recognizes that the shot that killed Zagreus was the beginning of his, Meursault's, conquest of happiness. Zagreus is another name for Dionysus, who symbolizes the forces of the physical universe. To kill Zagreus is apparently equivalent to killing that unconscious animal oneness with the universe which is destroyed when the human being accedes to the world of intellectual consciousness. By his violent gesture Meursault awakens and becomes a free, individually motivated human being.

La Mort heureuse is the story of an individual conquest of happiness, as is also *L'Etranger*, the novel Camus later wrote. It retraces a cyclic experience: a given everyday world, a departure and journey, a return to the same world seen in a new light, and finally an ecstatic and total reintegration with this world at a different level of awareness. And Camus's purpose here is the purpose originally proclaimed by Patrice Meursault, that is, to bear witness to "the joy of life, even in its cruelty."

In the first stage of his life, before he kills Zagreus, Meursault is enslaved by outer routines imposed upon him by the need to "earn a living," those routines which hour by hour lead men to their "natural death." "Natural Death" is, in fact, the title of this part of the story. But Meursault revolts against this servitude to time by attempting to achieve the "impersonality" of natural objects: "a stone in the sun or the rain." His revolt against "natural death" leads to the murder of Zagreus and thereby to the possession of a sum of money by which he is freed from the outer mechanical servitude imposed upon him by his job. He can leave his job, he can leave Algiers, he can live in freedom.

In the dingy solitude of a third-class hotel in Prague he is confronted by the inner void of his own consciousness. Time now stretches around him, vague and amorphous. Anguish fills him, a fear and nausea secreted in the atmosphere of Europe, "that old, wicked and suffering world" heavy with the weight of history and of its awesome Christian God. In the dark streets of Prague he comes upon the body of a man ignominiously lying on the pavement. His anguish gives way to revolt and a long confrontation with himself that leads him back to Algiers, to the fullness of human happiness in the light of the sun and of the sea. "Conscious Death," the title of this second part, is self-explanatory. The consciousness of his mortality leads Meursault to measure fully the values present at every moment in the act of living. Time, which puts its limit upon individual lives, now becomes the present, the miraculous, inexhaustible present, rich in beauty, friendship, and love. It is the present embodied in the innocence of the "house facing the world" that comes straight out of Camus's own life.

The third part of the novel relates the conquest of an even deeper happiness found in solitude and ecstatic "nuptials" with the earth, to which Meursault now returns. Time no longer exists for him until the brutal revelation of sickness confronts him not with the problem of man's mortality in general but with the reality of his own mortality. This imminence of death emphasizes the illusory nature of Meursault's identification with the world. His violent revolt is followed by a last revelation, the revelation that in death alone man accomplishes his human destiny, losing himself at last in the cosmos. "All that accommodates thee, Cosmos, accommodates me." [3] In the full blaze of sun and sea Patrice Meursault goes to his ecstatic death. The human sacrifice is consum-

[3] A quotation from Marcus Aurelius in Camus's Notebooks.

mated, the victim is a willing participant in a tragic and sacred ritual and all is well. Natural and conscious, Meursault's death is also a "happy death." The radiant sun of life and the "black sun" of death are one and the same; the conquest of self and happiness reach their climax in the ecstatic instant when life and death appear as one, and the individual, dying, knows himself as one with the cosmos.

Both the significance and the weakness of the novel can be found in this climax. It is a heroic attempt to come to terms with death, to give death a universal meaning that would make it acceptable by raising it to the level of a great and sacred natural mystery. The pattern followed seems to have been furnished in part by Plotinus. For Plotinus, all beings have fallen from a state of participation in the source of all being and are attempting through various stages of participation to return to this source. Meursault seems to go through the three essential stages of the "procession" from the physical to the intellectual to the spiritual level of awareness. But these stages differ somewhat in nature from the Plotinian stages and are described in a vocabulary that at times recalls Nietzsche and at other times the current "existentialist" vocabulary. The experience of "nausea" and "anguish," for example, the discovery of the "porous" empty quality of consciousness, recall Sartre, whose novel *La Nausée* Camus reviewed in 1938 at the time he had himself almost finished his own first experiment in novel writing. But the framework of *La Mort heureuse* is both too artificial and too grandiose for the experience Camus is trying to relate, and since the climax is, in a sense, an evasion of the real character of that experience, that is, a revolt against death, it carries with it no conviction. Fully aware of this weakness, Camus resolutely turned from this work to the essay, a literary form in which he rapidly achieved mastery and of which he was to make considerable use.

8

The World of Poverty

"Seules les apparences peuvent se dénombrer
et le climat se faire sentir."

Dedicated to Jean Grenier, in 1937 *L'Envers et l'endroit*,
a volume of essays, first appeared in Algiers in a limited edition of 350 copies. When it was edited in 1957 the revised
edition was even more strictly limited, to 100 copies. It was
only in 1958 that, yielding to pressure, Camus published a
larger edition of the essays. Thus it remained for many years
a little-known work, and one toward which Camus's own attitude was ambivalent, as he explained in his preface to the
1957 edition: he considered it artistically weak but nonetheless a sort of touchstone for all that he had since written.

"At twenty-two," he wrote, "unless one has genius, one
hardly knows how to write." Whether a genius or a hard
worker, the young man who extracted from the chaotic mass
of material with which he was wrestling the compact pages of
these essays knew how to write. In fact he showed an unusual
mastery of expression. His models in this area were the great
French stylists, those seventeenth-century French writers who
were always his favorites,[1] Chateaubriand perhaps, and, among
his contemporaries or near-contemporaries, Barrès, Gide, and
Montherlant. His idiom was pure, showing no trace of the
local peculiarities of the French language as it is spoken in
Algiers. Economical in his use of words, scrupulously accurate

[1] Camus often stated that he considered French classical literature
of the seventeenth century the greatest in the world.

in his vocabulary, Camus revealed a gift for constructing concise dramatic situations charged with strong emotion. The pitfall for him was the cultivation of a pathos all the more easy to exploit in essays dealing with his own poverty-stricken childhood. Aware of this danger, the young writer seems to have imposed upon himself a stern discipline, pushing the art of understatement to the point where restraint became constraint. Irony is another means Camus used to free his style from pathos, an irony born of the interplay of fact, emotion, and a sort of common sense. Such as it is, *L'Envers et l'endroit* reveals a unique combination and balance of qualities and bears the stamp of a strong individuality. The young author is merely a little too close to his material, a little too solemn and constrained.

Very early in the first planning of *La Vie heureuse* a certain fragment had refused to fit into the whole, the fragment which in successive projects appears in his Notebooks under the heading "the working-class sections," and with it insistently is the accompanying theme of mother and son. Camus had first intended this fragment to be the core of *La Vie heureuse*, which he was starting to write, and it was from this fragment also that he drew the separate essays of *L'Envers et l'endroit*. The first two essays in this volume are studies of old age, old age in a sordid and small world, in two ordinary, ignorant old people, the one, an old woman, half-paralyzed, the other an old man. The two studies are accompanied by a meditation on the death of a grandmother (Camus's grandmother), unidealized, a petty and unloved tyrant.

In the first essay the old woman sits in a corner with a rosary, a Christ made of lead, and a plaster St. Joseph carrying a child. To the young man, the guest who has come to dinner, she mumbles her eternal litany of boredom and loneliness. When, after dinner, he and the family go out for the evening he feels "confronted by the most terrible misfortune he had ever known, that of an old, crippled woman they were abandoning to go to the movies." In her solitude she is deprived of all comfort. Beyond her leaden Christ there is nothing but a deep, black space—Death. She has been stripped of everything that might mask her human condition. "Nothing would protect her now; and abandoned entirely to the thought of her death, she didn't know exactly what frightened her, but felt she did not wish to be alone. She did not wish to leave the other human beings." [2]

The second essay is a study of an old man seated at a café table with three young men, and talking, talking. He has nothing to say, but "he makes haste to say everything before his audience leaves him." He, too, is "condemned to silence and solitude," and as he walks away he suddenly realizes that "At the end of one's life, old age comes over one like nausea. Everything ends by no one listening. . . . Behind the hills that surrounded the town, there was still a glow of light. . . . The old man closed his eyes. Face to face with the life that carried along with it the roar of the city and the vacuous indifferent smile of the sky, he was alone, helpless, naked, dead already." [3]

As for the grandmother, she was dead now and her death stirred no feeling in the heart of her overscrupulous grandson, who "when he wondered about the sorrow he felt . . . could detect none at all. On the day of the funeral only, because of the general explosion of tears, he cried, but with the fear that he was not being sincere and that he was lying in the face of death. It was a beautiful winter's day, permeated by rays of sunlight. . . . The cemetery lay above the town and one

[2] *L'Envers et l'endroit* (Charlot, 1937), p. 7. Some of the material in these pages appeared first in *French Studies*, Oxford, England, Jan., 1950, pp. 27-37.

[3] *L'Envers et l'endroit* (Charlot, 1937), p. 15.

could see the beautiful transparent sun falling on the bay that trembled with light. . . ." [4]

Three destinies, as banal and undramatic, as mediocre and insignificant as the human beings—the old man, the old woman, the grandmother—who had experienced them. Yet precisely because there is no common measure between the destiny and the individual there is something grandiose about them; the terrible, stark solitude of old age and death is their lot and there is no escape. These first three studies are of "strangers" in the world: strangers among men, in their essential loneliness; strangers also to the "vacuous, indifferent smile of the sky" now that death is at the door. Their destiny also emphasizes the terrible lack of understanding in human beings: only the presence of human beings, they feel, can mask their anguish, but human beings do not stay, do not listen, and thus they are abandoned to their death.

It is all mankind that Camus thus strips bare and contemplates, just as, in the next essay, *"Entre oui et non,"* he contemplates his sick mother "as if she were the immense pity of his heart which had moved outside him, had become endowed with a body, and was conscientiously . . . playing the part of a poor old woman with a moving destiny." This essay, in which Camus recalls his childhood and the silent bond that united him to his strangely silent mother, reaches its climax in the description of the young man's vigil one night at her bedside as she lies sick with fever. As he watches over the silent, indifferent figure, in the quiet of the night, the world loses its habitual, reassuring aspect: "The midnight tramways, as they passed in the distance, drained away all the hope that comes to us from men, all the certainties given us by the noise of the cities. . . . He had never felt so alien. The world had dissolved and with it the illusion that life starts afresh every day. Nothing existed any longer. . . . And yet at this very hour

[4] *Ibid.*, p. 19.

when the world crumbled, he was alive. He had even finally fallen asleep." [5]

The feeling of unreality, of strangeness, in a world stripped of the reassuring forms we meet in our habitual life is the theme of the next essay, *"La Mort dans l'âme."* [6] That world is Prague, where the young man is a "stranger." Traveling for him is no diversion, but a confrontation with oneself. "The curtain of habit, comfortably woven by our habitual gestures and words . . . slowly rises and reveals at last the white face of anguish. Man is face to face with himself. I defy him to be happy." And from the Mediterranean islands of Majorca and Ibiza, to which the next essay *"Amour de vivre"* takes us, the same strangeness arises in a surge of light, of joy, in the splendid dance of a woman in Palma. "For what gives a journey its value is fear." It breaks the kind of inner framework "to which we habitually refer and introduces us into a universe which has no place for us, in which our life makes no sense."

The last essay, *"L'Envers et l'endroit,"* gives the book its title. First meditating on the woman who, having late in her life come into a small sum of money, had a sumptuous tomb built for herself and finished by spending all her time there, Camus then draws together the themes that run through the five essays and thereby gives them their unity.

Poverty, old age, the solitary travels of a young man without money, the silent, helpless night of vigil beside a mother loved but inaccessible, all these forms of life strip the individual bare of illusion, habit, diversion, and bring him face to face with the incomprehensibility of his life and of his death. And in those moments of nakedness, when all rationalization and all protective ideas and beliefs disappear, the beauty of the earth secretly suffuses the soul, reducing to nought the

---

[5] *Ibid.*, p. 29.

[6] Sartre was later to choose the same expression as title for the third volume of *Les Chemins de la liberté*.

"absurd" human being, tempting man away from a wounded humanity into its own indifferent perfection and immortality. "But these are the eyes and the voices which I must love. I belong to the world through all my gestures, to men through all my pity and gratitude. Between these two facets of the world I do not wish to choose. . . . If I listen to the irony slinking behind all things, it slowly emerges, blinking its small clear eye: live as if . . ." [7]

This theme of the essential futility or absurdity of human existence—including human suffering—as revealed in certain stark situations familiar to the young man brought up in Belcourt is not the only link between the five essays. There is the presence of the narrator, who describes the people he observes so pitilessly and yet so compassionately, drawing from them the pathetic though unconscious avowal of their baffled mortality. There is an attempt too at structural unity, a progression from an objective view of the pathos of human life toward an intense personal experience culminating in the formulation of an attitude, an evaluation, and an acceptance. But the structure is weak and does not impose itself, it is an outer rather than an organic unity. In contrast, the voice of the narrator, which speaks throughout the work and gives it its tone, a highly distinctive, clearly recognizable tone, creates a real unity.

The essays are also connected by the common, graceless *décor* of mediocre lives that know no embellishment, by the inner poverty and silence so gently yet so penetratingly portrayed. These people have no recourse to words; the world of the intellect is unknown to them. Unlike Maupassant, Camus has no disdain for their mediocrity. Their poverty is the object of his scrutiny, but not because of poverty itself; in their gestures, their voices, their suffering, unknown to themselves

[7] *L'Envers et l'endroit*, p. 67.

they embody in its purest form the incomprehensible futility and grandeur of human living.

Unlike Malraux, who only late in his career discovered "fundamental man" [8] stripped of intellectual anguish and drive, Camus had from the beginning an acute awareness of his existence: "To be a man, that is what counts. His grandmother will die, then his mother, then he himself. . . . To do one's tasks, and accept being a man leads to being old . . ." This is the wisdom he learned as a child. Where should the writer find the psychological or ideological complexities out of which most novels are forged? To transmit this essential and stark simplicity is, in fact, one of the tasks he set himself. "It is in this life of poverty, among these humble or vain people that I most surely reached what seemed to me the real meaning of life," he wrote in 1935, words which he was to repeat twenty years later.[9]

It is not, therefore, from any textbook that Camus drew his initial conception of the incomprehensibility of the human lot, but from those clear basic "images," as he calls them, that rise straight out of his childhood world. That existentialist philosophies offered him a vocabulary from which he occasionally borrowed is of secondary importance in his case. He had, it is true, been reading the Stoics, Epictetus in particular, and Pascal and Kierkegaard, those descendants of St. Augustine, ancestors of existentialism. But the concrete images and the sensitivity which the essays reveal are essentially his. The scenes he describes and the meditation that envelops them have a dramatic urgency that appeals to the reader directly.

In spite of his philosophical bent, Camus was clearly not interested in the technical vocabulary and logical instruments

[8] Perhaps the "ahistoric peasant" inhabitant of this earth whom Spengler describes.

[9] Notebooks (1935) and the Preface (1957) to *L'Envers et l'endroit.*

of philosophy; he felt no need for these safeguards of thought
or for logical detours of any kind. His thought stemmed directly from a few strong images, bound by a fundamental personal reaction which he elucidated with the common sense
and, on the whole, the vocabulary of the average human being, and this is what differentiated him so completely from
the systematic philosophers, such as Sartre, that controversy
with these men seemed futile.

L'Envers et l'endroit both limits and defines an inner universe: the selection of the initial images or scenes is paramount, personal, and arbitrary; the extension Camus gave
to this inner world necessarily depended upon his power to
renew these basic images. At the outset these images are already voluntarily limited and stylized: intense, sober in line,
allowing for no diversion, no abandon, they are forcefully imposed upon the reader's imagination. The meditation Camus
weaves around them emphasizes both their intensity and their
fundamental similarity and tends to transform them into particular examples of an abstract concept. This imperious and
rigorous handling of what is pictorial and passionate in origin
is quite characteristic of Camus. It is not dogmatic; it seems
rather to arise from an inner uncertainty and the concurrent
need to "make sense."

Young Camus's fascination with the inaneness and yet the
intensity of human existence, gestures, behavior, might well
have led to a wildly satiric view of humanity. But his sensibility was too deeply involved. The essential and dramatic elements of his literary world appear in his first work: a clear
perception of concrete images, situations, people, seen vividly
but felt to be "absurd," that is to say, inexplicable and rationally "meaningless," and a no less insistent, implacable need to
impose meaning upon them.

In spite of his resolution to "be a witness," Camus in
L'Envers et l'endroit also recorded an individual temptation,

a temptation vanquished in the very writing of the essays yet one which made their writing necessary: the insidious urge to renounce all effort at understanding and with it the bonds that tied him to his fellow men. There is a great surge of love in some passages of *L'Envers et l'endroit* and yet a detachment unusual in one so young, a detachment due perhaps to illness and a *tête-à-tête* with death. The irony Camus detected lurking behind all things was also lurking within him, questioning the meaning of his effort. He found himself strongly tempted to yield, to throw himself into a rapturous enjoyment of the beauty of the earth, and it is this temptation that is related in the four essays of *Noces*.

9

Gods of This Earth

"Là était tout mon amour de vivre: une passion silencieuse pour ce qui allait peut-être m'échapper, une amertume sous une flamme . . ."

In *Noces* Camus abandons the city and its human *décor* in favor of the Mediterranean countryside: first come the two contrasting African landscapes, Tipasa and Djémila, on which stand the ruins of two Roman cities. Next, in contrast to the old people in *L'Envers et l'endroit*, he describes the young people on the summer beaches of Algiers. The closing essay, "*Le Désert*," is a long meditation on Italy, more particularly on Florence, and Italian painting.[1] Each of these four essays is a meditation complete in itself, but together they constitute a simple but sumptuously orchestrated spiritual credo: there is no afterlife; each man's life is an end in itself with no significance in terms of a personal God; we die and our only kingdom "is of this earth."

Camus was not the first to question the existence of the silent and ambiguous god who has so large a place in our modern Western literature. Nor was he the first to raise the related question of new ethical values. But this negative credo, which he shared with many around him, is a pretext rather than a motive for these essays; the conscious and deliberate art with which the essays are composed brings to the theme new and

[1] Bernard Berenson's *The Italian Painters of the Renaissance* interested Camus deeply at this time.

appealing overtones. He creates a balance of contrasting land-scapes and emotions far richer in resonance than the muted, almost monotonous style of *L'Envers et l'endroit*. Camus is following great masters, Chateaubriand and Barrès, both of whom are adept at combining landscapes and the emotion they evoke with meditations on man's fate. In respect to Camus, however, the emotion is not sentimental, it is vio-lently sensuous in origin: colors, odors especially, tactile and muscular sensations, acute, simple and precise, are transmit-ted in finely balanced rhythmical paragraphs punctuated by brief, strongly affirmative statements: "In the spring Tipasa is inhabited by the gods"; or, paraphrasing a remark by Barrès,[2] "There are places where the spirit dies in order that a truth be born which is its very negation"; or, again, "The measure of man. Silence and dead stones, all the rest belongs to history."

The last sentence of *Noces* is revealing: "The earth! In that great temple deserted by the gods, all my idols have feet of clay." Yet it is the celebration of these idols that constitutes the real motivating reason for this group of essays, and the language in which they are written is the lyrical language of the ode or hymn. He sings of Tipasa and Djémila, Algiers and Florence, and of death and beauty, revolt and love, and it is these complementary or opposed themes that create the ten-sion and the aesthetic balance in the work.

"*Noces à Tipasa*," the first essay, is the description of a long day of delight spent in the glory and beauty of an African spring: the rich perfume of aromatic plants, the growing heat of the sun, the sea, the ecstatic joy of being alive, and, indeed, the pride of being alive, of accomplishing one's role on this earth:

[2] "*Il est des lieux où souffle l'esprit*," opening line of Barrès's *La Colline inspirée*.

I felt a strange joy in my heart, the joy that comes from a tranquil conscience. There is a feeling familiar to actors who know that they acted their part well or, to be more precise, that they made their gestures coincide with those of the ideal character they embodied, that, in a way, they entered into a preordained plan and suddenly made it live with the beating of their hearts. It was exactly what I felt: I had played my part; I had done my job as a man.

And in the calm of night comes the certainty of the harmony that binds him to the earth, a harmony which is a form of love: "A love that I did not have the weakness to claim for myself alone, conscious and proud of sharing it with an entire race, born of the sun and the sea, alive and rich in savor, drawing its greatness from its simplicity, a race which, from its beaches, exchanges a smile of complicity with the brilliant smile of its skies."

This total surrender of self to the timeless beauty of the world is followed in "*Le Vent à Djémila*" by a contrasted withdrawal of self. On the great desolate plateau of Djémila the wind blows among the ruins, and "In the great confusion of the wind and the sun that merges its light with the ruins, something is forged which gives man the measure of his identity with the solitude and silence of the dead city." Death then becomes the object of meditation: "It does not please me to believe that death opens out upon another life. For me it is a closed door." Why should one wish to be "delivered from the weight of one's own life"? Djémila teaches man to accept without flinching a "death without hope," that "conscious" death to the understanding of which Patrice Meursault had acceded in the second stage of his itinerary: "I wish to carry my clearsightedness to its limit and to look upon my end with all the profusion of my jealousy and horror."

"*L'Eté à Alger*," the third essay, is a meditation on that "race" of men (Camus's compatriots) "born of the sun and the sea" whom Camus rapidly evoked in *"Noces à Tipasa."* Made for the fleeting glory of a youth fast spent, "without a past, without tradition," over whom "no delusive divinity traced the signs of hope or redemption," they represent a species of fundamental man, living outside the realm of Christian "grace." They have erected no screen between themselves and their "human fate." They live against a background of boredom, born of an unconscious nihilism, and by their very being prove that there is no "superhuman joy, no eternity outside the curve of days"—and they die unreconciled with death.

It is Italy that brings the crowning stone to this spiritual edifice. In the Italian landscape, in Italian painting "from Cimabue to Giotto," among the Italian people, Camus saw the celebration of the carnal beauty of life. Beauty, that "magnificent desert," denudes the human being and binds him to a present which is an eternity without change. The monk's cell with its skull and its view of a world charged with beauty is in effect the symbol with which *Noces* closes: "The world is beautiful and outside it there is no salvation. . . . And that world annihilates me." Love—but without hope—for the earth's beauty and the revolt against death, two themes which combine to create an equilibrium from which arises a form of consent: "Florence, one of the only places in Europe where I understood that at the heart of my revolt lay consent. In its sky . . . I learned to consent to the earth and to burn in the dark flame of its celebrations." *Noces* is a celebration of this "dark flame" of nature, and perhaps, at times, it is a kind of exorcism too, for could the No opposed to death have been so insistent if the attraction of death had not been so strong?

There is an unusual vitality in the language of *Noces*, which stems from the direct elemental quality of the images used and the intensity of the sensuous charge these images carry: the sea "in its silver armor," the countryside "black with light," the "yellow and blue" world of Tipasa, and the violent bath of "sun and wind" into which one is plunged at Djémila. Camus's lyricism has its source in a sense of the mystery of life, a mystery evoked in one single and stark symbol, the pagan "dark flame" or "black flame" or "black sun" that contrasts with the smiling, brilliant, real sun of this earth. His imagery is sensuous, drawn entirely from the outer world, an imagery architectural in nature difficult to vary or even renew; but it furnishes the strong lines and colors that delineate a world. Its spatial values served Camus the novelist well; descriptive rather than poetic, it is particularly suited to the rhythms which sustain his prose, a prose based on rhetorical rather than melodic modulations and on the rhythms characteristic of a long line of French prose writers.

The two sets of heterogeneous experiences that Camus describes in *L'Envers et l'endroit* and *Noces* illuminate the same basic thought, a thought that many in his generation share. But Camus gives it a new intensity and makes the content accessible, concrete, and moving. His sense of the mystery of man's life, of its inexplicability, his fascination with that which exists but cannot be explained, are accompanied by pity and admiration rather than, as in the case of Sartre, with "nausea" and rejection of the world. In these essays Camus hesitates between two conflicting attitudes: involvement in the inane tragedy of human suffering or the mystical exaltation of the neophyte indifferent to all except nature, his god. Where either attitude is concerned the impact of the essay comes from the particularly intense urgency with which the dilemma is described, an urgency altogether absent from the discarded earlier novel.

Camus's sensitivity to the world around him was in some ways attuned to his time. In *Noces* he speaks of a new attitude toward the natural world of which our recent widespread habit of passing long hours seminude upon our beaches gives some evidence. Montherlant had spoken of the stadium; Camus speaks of the more generally experienced ease and freedom that every summer comes to thousands upon thousands of tanned bodies from the sun and from the sea. The sense of space, of open horizons, is part of this experience; in an Africa free from the small dimensions of a suffocating Europe Camus saw its geographic and spiritual counterpart. That rather worn abstraction "nature" became a real and intoxicating land.

In direct contrast to this open, spacious world, Camus's human world, reduced to its elementary components, was to find corroboration in the years which opened with the Spanish civil war. The silent figure of the mother asking nothing, answering nothing, moving without complaint through the tedious tasks of a difficult existence, could in itself symbolize what contemporary history was to inflict on a vast majority of human beings. And the sense of immediacy in the face of impending catastrophe that Camus drew from his own experience happened partly to coincide with, partly to precede a more general experience which he had in no way foreseen. It would turn his very limitations to good purpose.

Together these two sets of essays reveal both Camus's strength as a writer and the problems he faced. Following in Malraux's footsteps but going beyond him, he eliminated large zones of human experience from his universe; he also eliminated the vast realm of psychological analysis. Complexities in human motivation and subtle shades of feeling had little place in his universe, which was stripped to the fundamental. He thus made it practically impossible for himself to draw upon the wealth of comedy, tenderness, and infinite variety inherent in human living to which he, himself, was not insensitive. His need to "rethink" the world immediately, to find significance and impose it, gave him a tone of authority, but it constrained the artist, limiting his field of vision.

Scrupulously honest, he started with a world already defined, one from which there could be no ultimate evasion and which, in its main lines, could not be greatly modified or enlarged.

The material with which he was working at this time was the very substance of his own life, markedly different in texture from that of his more self-conscious, purely French contemporaries. It had its geographic correspondents, both real and symbolic: North Africa and its exotic appeal, and in contrast, Europe, reduced to the new and unexpected role of a land of exile, a desert even. Camus's North Africa itself was made up of simple components, carrying a weight of emotion and significance and thus becoming directly symbolic and expressive of an inner life that balked at the language of self-analysis. Freud and his followers had no place at all in this universe.

In answer to an item in one of those questionnaires of dubious value periodically sent to authors, Camus listed his "ten favorite words" as "the world, suffering, the earth, the mother, men, the desert, honor, misery, summer, the sea." [3] These are already the key words in his first essays. But the word "happiness" is missing, happiness, his essential concern and need. That these were key words to him cannot be questioned. They were charged with a rather vague emotion, and though it is difficult to define their specific value in Camus's universe, it is of these that his universe was made and it is of these, and no others, that he wished to speak.

Camus was not the first writer to be shocked by the thought of man's mortality, nor the first to wish to wrest happiness from the present though passing moment. What differentiates Camus is that his need for happiness was associated with another need as strong, as urgent, that is, a feeling of responsibility for the suffering of humanity, a suffering all the more

[3] Notebooks (1951).

intolerable because, in his eyes, it had no compensation, no meaning. This sense of personal responsibility is strangely close to certain Christian attitudes and is thus in conflict with the passionate claim to a happiness savored *hic et nunc*. The young man's world, thus broken apart, refused to be forced into the mold either of a code of ethics or of a novel. His was not so much a limited as a divided awareness. Camus's youthful and generous *élan* to surrender himself to some force greater than himself—often the mark of the artist—was thus held in check.

L'Envers et l'endroit and *Noces*, his two first books, express this division, treating as they do two diametrically opposed moods. It is as though the young author had in each case selected a special tone which governed the choice of vocabulary and the peculiar emotional blending of the two separate and often opposed levels of his experience, feeling, and thought. The unity of tone raises both books above the level of a commonplace expression of the "metaphysical" torment characteristic of the young.

The unification of an experience through the conscious medium of style is an aesthetic solution, not a logical or especially a systematic one. To misunderstand this in the case of Camus is to open the door to quite futile controversy. The fusion of image and thought in both these early books is successful, but the image often seems to be stronger than the thought, for Camus was not impervious to the pleasures of a rhetoric whereby rhythm and image carried meaning beyond the control of thought. Aware of this, he imposed so violent a restraint on his writing that, in these first essays, the tone sometimes seems self-consciously haughty and the sincerity of the feeling is lost.

In his rather pompous language, Spengler writes:

It is Time that is tragic and it is by the meaning it intuitively attaches to Time that one culture is differentiated

from another; and consequently "tragedy" of the grand
order has only developed in the culture which has most
passionately affirmed, and that which has most passionately
denied, Time. The sentiment of the ahistoric soul gives us
a classical tragedy *of the moment* and that of the ultra-
historic soul puts before us Western tragedy that deals
with the development of a whole life. Our tragedy arises
from the feeling of the inexorable logic of becoming, while
the Greek feels the illogical blind accident of the moment.
The life of Lear matures inwardly towards a catastrophe,
and that of Oedipus stumbles without warning upon a
situation.[4]

Camus is "a son" of the Greeks. At the beginning of his life
he stumbled, like Oedipus, upon a situation. This situation
seemed personal to him, so strongly was the feeling of both
the essential meaninglessness of life and the essential desira-
bility of life brought home to him. Many writers before him
had spoken of man's condition, stressing either its futility or
its grandeur or, as with Pascal, both. In its fundamental simplicity what Camus calls *l'absurde* corresponds to facts that
most human beings, if they think at all, vaguely accept. But
Camus started out with a violent personal reaction, then set
himself the task of thinking this absurd situation through to
its conclusion, for himself. The essay proved to be the best
vehicle for such meditation, for it allowed the young author
to speak in the first person yet at the same time indirectly
through the medium of a chosen style.

In the next few years Camus's dialogue with the earth and
with himself was to gain in amplitude till it became a dialogue
between himself and his time.

[4] Oswald Spengler: *Le Déclin de l'occident* (Paris:Gallimard, 1948,
Vol. I, p. 133). Translated from the German by M. Tazerout.

10

Cautionary Tales

"Ce qui caractérise notre siècle, ce n'est peut-
être pas tant d'avoir à reconstruire le monde
que d'avoir à le repenser."

L'Etranger, La Peste, La Chute, L'Exil et le royaume, the
titles of Camus's three novels and one volume of short stories,
capture the imagination. The titles were obviously not chosen
at random for they have a suggestive family resemblance: the
fall is, after all, an exile from the kingdom of grace; the plague,
a fall and exile from the kingdom of health; and a stranger,
an exile from his own country.

To these works more than to any others except, perhaps,
L'Homme révolté, Camus owes his international reputation.
They were published over a period of fifteen years, and each
has a personality and history of its own. *L'Etranger* (1942),
published when Camus was twenty-nine, was widely received
as a masterpiece in spite of a few dissenting critics who re-
proved its "pessimism." That the public during the war years
should be so uncannily responsive to the tone of Meursault's
story is rather curious since the novel definitely belongs to the
prewar period and concerns an emotional and intellectual
climate to which Camus was sensitive in his early twenties.
L'Etranger is more truly the novel of his twenty-fifth than of
his twenty-ninth year.

La Peste (1947), too, achieved a rapid and world-wide success, though it drew some criticism on aesthetic grounds.
Hailed as the one significant French novel to come out of

World War II, it was judged to be more a testimony than a work of fiction. Though it was conceived before the war, it was planned and in great part written during the German occupation of France. It reflected an atmosphere which by 1947 was already dispelled and half forgotten, and its particular mood found less response in the mood of the times than had *L'Etranger*. *La Chute* (1956) was the subject of more passionate argument and much harsher criticism than its two predecessors. Although it sold very well, it could not be said to enjoy the popularity of *L'Etranger* or the high esteem in which *La Peste* was generally held. The volume of short stories. *L'Exil et le royaume* (1957), drew less attention than the three novels, perhaps because these tales, with the exception of "*Le Renégat*," do not raise the controversial issues which, almost to the exclusion of all else, stimulated discussion of the novels.

Fifteen years represents such a short span of time that it may seem idle to attempt to distinguish a separate historical background for each of the three novels, and especially so since Camus carefully avoided the topical as an ingredient of his fictional universe. Each of the novels is illuminated far better by the others than by the outer circumstances which accompanied its elaboration; their very titles show them to have been carefully planned to form together an organic whole. When he was still very young, Camus wrote:

> One may observe a species of creators who proceed by juxtaposition. Their works may seem to have no relation one with the other. In a certain measure they are contradictory. But considered within the framework of the whole, they regain their organic value. And so they draw their final meaning from death. They take the best of their light from the author's life itself.[1]

[1] *Le Mythe de Sisyphe*, p. 155.

He might have been thinking, for example, of Gide, but the description prophetically fitted himself. Each novel is completely objective and individual in form, but each refers back to all the others and, more intensely than is generally the case, to Camus himself. Camus's own life in those fifteen years, however, cannot be divorced from the circumstances of history in which he found himself.

Although Camus was acutely conscious of the bonds that tie a writer to his age, his work, rather paradoxically, developed from within. He knew in what direction he was moving as a writer, regardless of the events taking place around him. His work developed by stages. These stages, outlined in his Notebooks, often indicate plans of many works long before any one of them was written. As one stage draws to its completion, the next is already evolving; the essential symbol of *La Peste*, for example, antedates the outbreak of World War II and coincides with the elaboration of *L'Etranger*.[2] Nonetheless the emotional tone of each novel recalls the atmosphere of the historical period during which it was written, or at least a dominant mood that Camus shared in that period with many others. Like Jean Tarrou, one of the two chroniclers in *La Peste* who observe the onslaught of the pestilence upon the city of Oran, Camus was acutely sensitive to the stuff of which our daily lives—if not our dreams—are made. The atmosphere of day-to-day living in Europe changed rapidly and brutally between 1938 and 1950, and not once but several times. It was only for a short period in the early 1950's that the round of daily existence seemed to Western Euro-

---

[2] See *Cahiers de la Pléiade*, 1947, where Camus published two early fragments of *La Peste* which he did not use in the novel. *La Peste*, as later in the play *L'Etat de siège*, is personified and recalls Jarry's *Ubu-roi*, a monstrous indolent bureaucrat with dirty nails and shoddy, worn, shiny sleeves. There is an element of both lyricism and irony in these passages which Camus eliminated from the novel but integrated into the play. See also R. Quillot: *La Mer et les prisons*, p. 275.

peans to achieve a modicum of stability; by the end of 1956, when the dramatic developments of long-range missiles and exploration of outer space introduced new factors of anxiety into what had been essentially a political uneasiness, even that rather shaky stability seemed very fragile indeed. Camus's novels reflect these shifts in atmosphere.

L'Etranger depicts a prewar private world of secure, apparently indestructible routine broken only by the sea and sun of successive Mediterranean weekends. The basic patterns of existence seem as timeless as the earth itself. *La Peste* installs the temporary but despotically dreary, petty, and deadly round of endless collective regimentation and privation in an atmosphere of weary horror—the atmosphere of the German occupation of France. In *La Peste* the rhythms of living of *L'Etranger* are progressively displaced by the patterns imposed by the ever-increasing obsessive presence of the pestilence. These patterns appear, blend like a musical theme with the rhythms of normal living, become all-embracing, and then, as the basic theme reasserts itself, they disappear. In general the evolution of the plague follows the modalities of feeling in the occupied countries during the war years. The hero of *La Chute*, the "penitent judge," represents a certain aspect of postwar Europe, the postwar Europe of the erstwhile humanitarians, morally shaken, guilt-ridden, and in search of a dubious self-justification. Contemporaneous with the penitent judge, the renegade missionary [3] voices the intellectual confusion and frustrated anguish of an idealistic, Christian "left" upon which Marxism exercises a perpetual fascination.

Camus's novels are thus rooted in the soil—a French soil essentially—of a specific period of time, but through the medium of fiction he frees them from too specific a context. Isolating one of the major ills of the time, as a doctor might

---

[3] "*Le Renégat*," though a short story, belongs by its techniques and spirit to the group of novels with which it will be considered.

isolate the virus of an epidemic, he embodies it in fictional characters who carry it to its ultimate limits, giving it a semi-symbolical expression: the stranger, the penitent judge, the renegade, and, more abstract, the plague. All Camus's novels could, in a sense, be grouped together under one title, which well might read "Parables of the Mid-Twentieth Century" or, better still, "Cautionary Tales for Our Time and All Time."

11

Mid-Century Parables

"Je ne sais pas ce que je cherche, je le nomme
avec prudence, je me dédis, je me répète,
j'avance et je recule."

Of the three novels and one volume of short stories
L'Etranger is closest to that literary form which even after
more than a half century of experimentation we still think
of as a novel. A short novel, it grew out of *La Mort heureuse*,
Camus's first and unpublished story, with which it has many
secret bonds, though its hero, Meursault, is further removed
from his creator than was his predecessor, Patrice Meursault.[1]
Meursault's adventure, although no less strange than that of
Patrice, is easier to follow, and, on the surface, far more
plausible. Meursault's story, which he himself tells from
day to day, more or less as the successive episodes develop
and from no fixed point in time, falls into two parts. The first
part ends with the murder of an Arab on a beach in Algiers;
the second, just before Meursault goes to the guillotine as a
consequence of this act.

Meursault, an office clerk in Algiers, starts telling his story
on the day when he receives a telegram announcing the death
of his mother in the old people's home where she had been
living. He asks for a two-day leave, goes to the old people's
home, vaguely watches over his mother's dead body at night,

[1] Camus indicates in his Notebooks that he had three models in
mind for Meursault: a woman and two men (he, himself, was one of
the two men).

94

as is the custom, and next day follows the funeral convoy to the cemetery. At no time does he manifest any grief nor register any feeling other than a somewhat dazed fatigue caused by the heat. During his night vigil he drinks a couple of cups of coffee, smokes a cigarette, and dozes a little.

On his return to Algiers he realizes that it is Saturday, the beginning of the weekend, the only time which usually matters in a life of pure routine. He goes for a swim. By chance he meets Marie, a girl who once worked in his office. He takes her out to a comic movie then home, where they start a liaison. On Monday he goes back to work as usual and we catch a glimpse of the working-class milieu in which he moves: Céleste, the owner of a little restaurant where he eats; Salamano, an old and lonely man with a scrofulous old dog that he curses and beats, but who cries quietly in his room next to Meursault's when the dog disappears one night; and Raymond, a shady character, reputed to be a pimp.

Raymond has his own primitive sense of honor. When he suspects that his mistress, an Arab woman, is deceiving him, he develops plans for an exemplary though elementary vengeance. As a first step in his plan he asks Meursault to write a letter to his mistress for him and then, after he has caused a scandal by violently beating the woman, he asks Meursault to testify in his favor—and Meursault complies.

The third weekend after the death of Meursault's mother, Raymond asks Meursault and Marie to spend the day with him and his friends, the Massons, at their cabin on the beach. As they leave for their outing they are followed by a group of Arabs with whom at the beach they become engaged in a brief fight during which Raymond is wounded by an Arab knife. Meursault, prudently, had taken Raymond's revolver away from him. The Arabs retreat. After an early and hearty lunch generously washed down with wine, Meursault drifts back along the shore toward a spring, the one shady spot on

the beach. As he advances under the red glare of the midday
sun he sees one of the Arabs lying nonchalantly in the shade:

> I thought that I had only to turn around and it would
> all be ended. But a whole beach vibrating with sun was
> pressing upon me from behind. I took a few steps toward
> the spring. The Arab didn't move. After all, he was still
> quite far away. Perhaps because of the shadows on his face
> he seemed to be laughing. I waited. The flame of the sun
> reached my cheeks and I felt drops of sweat gather in my
> eyebrows. It was the same sun as the day I buried mother
> and now, as then, it was my forehead especially that hurt
> and all the veins throbbed together under my skin. Because
> of the burn that I couldn't stand any longer, I moved for-
> ward. I knew it was stupid, that I wouldn't get rid of the
> sun by taking a step forward. But I took a step, just one step
> forward. And this time, without raising himself, the Arab
> drew his knife and pointed it at me. The light glinted on
> the steel and it was like a long glittering blade that hit me
> full in the forehead.[2] [For a moment everything stood still,
> then] it seemed to me that the entire stretch of sky opened
> and rained fire upon me.

Then the revolver he had taken from Raymond goes off. After
a pause Meursault pours four more bullets into the dead body
of the Arab, "and it was like four brief knocks that I struck
on the door of misfortune."

The second part of Meursault's tale describes his eleven
months in prison, his trial and condemnation to death, and
the days preceding his execution. The long period between
the murder and the trial is interrupted only by interviews
with the prosecutor, with the lawyer, with Marie, with the
prison chaplain. At no time does Meursault attempt to defend himself. Unlike the first part of the story, the second

---

[2] *L'Etranger*, p. 79.

part moves along two levels, the outer level which culminates in the trial and the inner level which reaches its climax at the very end of the novel in a confrontation with the prison chaplain as Meursault waits for the dawning of his day of execution.

La Peste is a chronicle of suffering and struggle which ends in ambiguous victory. It does not contain much of a story. The chronicle is related in the third person by a participant and observer whose identity, though not difficult to guess, is revealed only at the end of the book. It is the record of a collective, not a private, adventure which starts on a certain day in April when rats appear in increasing numbers to die in the streets and in the houses of Oran. Two weeks later come the first cases of the plague; a state of emergency is declared, then the city is closed and virtually in a state of siege. As the ravages of the pestilence increase, a small group of men led by a stranger to the city, one Jean Tarrou, form voluntary ambulance teams to help Dr. Rieux, the most active of the physicians, in his work. The progressive restrictions, the rationing, the lack of communications, the internment or quarantine camps, all call to mind the experiences of World War II.

After an almost absolute reign of ten months the plague disappears. As the citizens of Oran wildly celebrate the end of the siege and the opening of the city gates, Dr. Rieux resolves to write his chronicle:

> Dr. Rieux decided then to write the story which ends here, in order not to be among those who keep silent, in order to testify in favor of the plague-stricken, to leave at least a memory of the injustice and violence done them, and to say simply what one learns in the middle of scourges: that there are more things to admire than things to despise in men.

Yet he knew that this chronicle could not be that of a definite victory. . . . For he knew what the joyous crowd did not know, and which we can read in books, that the bacillus of the plague never disappears . . . and that, perhaps, a day would come when, for the misfortune and instruction of men, the plague would waken its rats and send them to die in a happy town.

La Chute offers even less of a story than *La Peste*. In a rundown bar on the waterfront of Amsterdam, Jean-Baptiste Clamence, formerly a well-known Parisian lawyer now in his forties, imposes his company upon a passing compatriot, a sort of alter ego, a lawyer like himself whom for five consecutive late afternoons and evenings he accompanies in the bar, through the streets of Amsterdam, on an excursion to the Zuyder Zee. In the course of these wanderings Clamence tells the story of his "fall" from the complacency of an unusually self-satisfied human being to the discomforts and pleasures of endlessly discovering the self-illusions and hypocrisy of his ego.

As in the case of Meursault, Clamence's experience begins with a specific incident. Crossing the Pont des Arts in Paris one night he hears behind him the sound of someone laughing. His discomfiture is acute. The rift in his armor has been found. The laughter makes its way inside him, disintegrating the beautiful surface of his life until it reaches the crux of Clamence's latent guilt: two or three years before, again crossing over a bridge at night, he had noticed the slim, black figure of a young woman leaning against the parapet; he had heard her fall, her cries for help; he had hesitated, then had gone on his way. The steady deterioration of his life under the scrutiny of his self-contempt finally brought him to Amsterdam, where he now exercises the self-imposed function of "penitent judge," and, in accusing himself, he accuses all men, the triumphant annunciator of man's total degradation.

At sunrise on the parched plateau beyond the desert city of Taghaza crouches the renegade,[3] an erstwhile missionary to the barbaric people of Taghaza, a gun by his side. He is waiting for his successor in order to shoot him. In a long-drawn-out, silent soliloquy—for his tongue has long been wrenched out—he goes over the events which led to this moment: his harsh upbringing in Auvergne; his conversion to the Catholic faith; his yearning for martyrdom in order to see his faith conquer; his choice of Taghaza, the home of the fiercest of desert tribes, as his particular task of conversion; his flight from the Catholic institution in Algiers; his capture by the natives and his life as their slave; the tortures inflicted upon him in the name of their fetish, whom he learns to serve; his conversion to the malevolent violence and merciless cruelty of their god, the antithesis of the Christian God; the announcement of the arrival of a new missionary and the hatred in his own heart; his resolution to stop the approaching missionary, a hallucination perhaps; the shot fired; the wave of doubt and anguish:

> "Ah! Suppose I was mistaken again! Men, formerly fraternal, the only recourse, Oh solitude, do not abandon me . . . we have made a mistake, we'll begin again, we'll remake the city of mercy, I want to go back home. Yes help me, that's right, stretch out your hand, give . . ."
> A handful of salt filled the mouth of the talkative slave.

It is fairly obvious that each of these tales has an underlying meaning. Camus's comments on the novel, in both *Le Mythe de Sisyphe* and *L'Homme révolté*, are too general to define his own creative processes: in *Le Mythe* he notes that the novel is "a mime" of life, of life seen within the perspectives of *l'absurde*; and in *L'Homme révolté* he describes the novel as that ambiguous act of revolt by which a man both

---

[3] "*Le Renégat*," one of the short stories in *L'Exil et le royaume*.

accepts in part and refuses in part the world around him. The novel is "creation corrected." But the "mime" varies with the writer's experience of life, and what a man accepts and rejects in the world around him is a highly individual matter. It is, therefore, to the novels themselves that we must turn if we are to understand the aesthetic values at work in Camus's fictional universe.

12

Creation Corrected

"Oui, il y avait dans le malheur une part
d'abstraction et d'irréalité. Mais quand l'abstraction se met à vous tuer, il faut bien s'oc-
cuper de l'abstraction."

In form, *L'Etranger*, *La Peste*, *La Chute*, and *"Le Renégat"*
are all strictly objective, with an impressive outer impersonality somewhat reminiscent of Flaubert. Aesthetically, their
effect rests in great part on the creation of a certain "tone"
of voice, the tone of the narrator. Except in the case of *La
Peste*, this fictional narrator is also the semisymbolic character who embodies the emotional and mental mood that the
author is isolating. Camus calls his works *récits* after the manner of Gide. He can truthfully assert, again like Gide, that
they are essentially ironic, since the narrator himself unconsciously exposes the extreme consequences of an attitude that
Camus observes critically.

Dr. Rieux, in *La Peste*, is of a different caliber, he is the
opponent, not the incarnation, of the plague; in his own personality are blended the attitudes of all the other opponents
to the scourge, except that of the priest, Father Paneloux,
whose faith he does not share. Through the use of a very
common literary device—the journal—Camus introduces into
this novel a second voice, that of Jean Tarrou, but since this
second voice blends with that of Dr. Rieux, it is Dr. Rieux's
voice that gives the dominant key to the entire work. *La Peste*,
too, is ironic, but not in the same way as the other *récits* and

only because it records a devastating experience which draws upon all the resources of the human will to live and brings little in return, not even a real added wisdom. All each man derives from this experience is a deeper awareness of what he already knew; the plague, in human terms, is a completely gratuitous form of torment. If the novel succeeds in its purpose, however, it will leave us, too, with a clearer vision of the value of our life as we live it.

The register of the dominant voice in each *récit* is completely different, revealing a deliberate aesthetic intention. Not only was Camus never content to repeat a form of narrative once he had elaborated it successfully, but he carefully created a distinct style for each novel, which may prove bewildering to readers who like an author's works to remain consistently recognizable. This manipulation of style is one of Camus's most effective means of literary creation, one with which he achieved a much broader range of expression than did Gide. It is the means by which he moves from reality into fiction, transforms his own subjective world into an objective universe, and the real people he observes and describes in his Notebooks into the semisymbolic characters who live in his novels. The style unifies and organizes the heterogeneous elements that enter into the making of a novel, welding it into a significant whole. The individual style of each of his works can be seen quite clearly in the opening lines of the four separate tales:

> Today, mother died. Or perhaps yesterday, I don't know. I've just received a wire from the home for the aged: "Mother deceased. Funeral to-morrow. Respectfully yours." That doesn't mean anything. It may have been yesterday.
> The old people's home is at Marengo, eighty kilometers from Algiers. I'll take the two o'clock bus and get there in the afternoon. And so I can watch the body and come back tomorrow night [*L'Etranger*].

The strange events which are the subject of this chronicle took place in 194—, in Oran. In everyone's opinion they did not belong there, being a little out of the ordinary. At first sight it seems obvious that Oran is an ordinary city, and nothing more than a French prefecture on the Algerian coast. The city itself, it has to be admitted, is ugly. Quiet in appearance, one needs a certain time to grasp what makes it different from so many other commercial towns, in all latitudes [*La Peste*].

May I, Monsieur, offer my services, without running the risk of intruding? I fear you may not be able to make yourself understood by the worthy ape who presides over the fate of this establishment. In fact he speaks nothing but Dutch. Unless you authorize me to plead your cause, he will not guess that you want gin [*La Chute*].[1]

What a mess! What a mess! Since they cut off my tongue, another tongue, I don't know, goes without stopping in my cranium, something speaks or someone who falls suddenly silent and then everything begins over again— Oh, I hear too many things and yet I don't say them, what a mess, and if I open my mouth, it's like the noise of pebbles being stirred ["*Le Renégat*"].

The short, juxtaposed, factual sentences of Meursault in *L'Etranger*; the carefully controlled slightly ironic statements and abstract tone of Dr. Rieux, the main chronicler of *La Peste*; the brilliant, contemptuous and sarcastic flow of conversation of Jean-Baptiste Clamence in *La Chute*; the long litany of frustration and woe that rolls in the head of the renegade missionary, although all recognizable modes of contemporary speech, are poles apart, powerful though dangerous instruments in the hands of a very conscious writer.[2] Powerful

---

[1] Justin O'Brien (trans.), *The Fall* (New York: Alfred A. Knopf, 1957).

[2] In his analysis of *L'Etranger*, Sartre related its style to that of the American novelists and Hemingway in particular (Camus also had in

because, from the first paragraph to the last, there is no re-
mission for the reader. Like the character, he is the prisoner
of a closed and consistent world, the particular world of that
one novel which excludes all extraneous materials or moods.
Dangerous, for much the same reasons. Consistency may turn
into monotony and the novel becomes a literary *tour de force*:
to create and maintain a style throughout a novel is a technical
accomplishment of no mean quality which may lead an author
to sacrifice a good deal to form itself. Perhaps the greatest
danger lies in the limits that are drastically imposed on the
development and significance of the story, forcefully molding
it according to a given stylistic pattern. The character who
speaks to us directly may then lose his freedom and three-
dimensional reality, becoming the mere mouthpiece for a text
too obviously prepared for him by his creator; it is then that
fiction moves across the borderline into allegory. Camus was
well aware of these dangers. The search for the exact tone
was one of his main preoccupations as a novelist, a preoccupation which in the writing of *La Peste* was paramount.

Self-contained and shut in upon itself by the use of these
styles, each novel is set in its own, sharply distinct *décor*,
though all share the same basic elements: a city set in a sort
of wilderness, and yet a clearly recognizable city that has its
place upon the map—Algiers, Oran, Amsterdam and, stranger
than these, Taghaza somewhere in the confines of the Sahara

---

mind Cain's *The Postman Always Rings Twice*). The tone of *La Peste,*
some critics have pointed out, recalls Thucydides (in one of the first
versions of the novel, one of the characters is a classics professor who
ponders the work of Thucydides and remarks that he has come to a
complete understanding of it only after he experienced the reality of
the pestilence). The ironic tone of the opening lines of *La Chute* recalls Dostoevsky's *Notes from the Underground.* And the rhythmical
development of the renegade's soliloquy, in which some sentences
are perfect Alexandrines punctuated by the "*ra, ra*" of pain and
anguish, is a very conscious curious stylistic feat.

desert. With the exception of Meursault's Algiers, these cities
all play the role of a prison, and even Meursault will eventually discover Algiers only from behind prison walls. Through
the eyes of his narrators, Camus transfigures each *décor*, inte-
grating it into the story, making of it a significant agent in the
development of his novel. The spiritual value of Algiers and
Oran, as Camus suggested it in several essays, reappears in
the more starkly stylized descriptive passages of *L'Etranger*
and *La Peste*. But in the novels the landscape becomes dramatic, supporting the action. The sun and beaches of Algiers
are the real instigators of Meursault's crime:

> It was the same dazzling red glare. On the sand, the sea
> panted with all the rapid and smothered breathing of its
> little waves. I walked slowly toward the rocks and I felt
> my forehead swell under the sun. All this heat pressed down
> upon me and resisted my advance. And each time I felt its
> great warm breath upon my face, I closed my fists in my
> trousers pockets, I braced every nerve to triumph over the
> sun and to shake off the opaque spell it cast upon me.[3]

The Algerian sun is present at each stage in Meursault's adventure: at his mother's funeral, on the beach where he kills
the Arab, in the courtroom at the time of his trial.

Oran, like Algiers, is a "city without a past," one that
knows no mediators between itself and the impassive beauty
around it. In *La Peste* Oran lives through its tragic year completely closed in upon itself both morally and physically. It
is a modern city ". . . without anything picturesque, without
vegetation and without a soul," [4] incongruously "grafted upon
a landscape unequaled" in beauty. The trials of its captive
population will take place within its dusty streets, under its
pitiless sky, in a closed magic circle.

[3] *L'Etranger*, p. 77.
[4] *La Peste*, pp. 15-16.

"I like these people . . . ," remarks Jean-Baptiste Clamence, as he considers the city of Amsterdam, "wedged into a little space of houses and canal, hemmed in by fogs, cold lands and the sea, steaming like a wet wash. . . . We are at least at the heart of things here. Have you noticed that Amsterdam's concentric canals resemble the circles of hell? The middle-class hell of course, peopled with bad dreams. . . . Here we are in the last circle." [5]

Taghaza, the city that rejects all strangers, the city that blinds, the "city of salt," its walls white under the torrid sun, built in "a white hollow full of white heat" [6] is the active malevolent force that presides over the destiny of the renegade. Taghaza, white upon white: the artistic process by which Camus infused into his *décor* an element of the fantastic is clearly visible here.

And it is largely through the *décor* that an active element of the fantastic enters into the shaping of Camus's tales, a mysterious force in league with the site itself which has the compelling presence of some dark fatality and through which each tale derives its necessity and grandeur. Camus avoids description for the sake of description. Descriptive passages never interrupt the narrative, but emanate directly from it, intensifying the dramatic action without deterring from it, hinting perpetually that, beyond the conscious level of thought and action, primitive forgotten forces, mostly malevolent, hold the human being in their grip.

Algiers and Oran play the same symbolic role as in *L'Envers et l'endroit* and *Noces,* walling their inhabitants inside a present from which the only issue is death. Amsterdam holds captive a different breed of men, a "double" people who are both

---

[5] Justin O'Brien (trans.), *The Fall* (New York: Alfred A. Knopf, 1957), pp. 12-14.
[6] *"Le Renégat," L'Exil et le royaume,* p. 49.

"here and elsewhere": "Their heads in their bronze-tinted clouds they dream, they cycle in circles; they pray, somnambulists, in the fog's gilded incense, they have ceased to be here." [7] Dream-people, living in a dream-world.

As for the barbaric inhabitants of Taghaza, their world is a death-world of evil absolutes: "They reign over their sterile houses, over their black slaves whom they drive to death in the mine, and each slab of salt carved out is worth a man in the southern countries. They pass, silent, covered by their mourning veils [8] in the mineral whiteness of the streets and, at nightfall, when the whole city seems to turn into a milky ghost, they enter, bending forward, into the shadow of houses where the salt walls gleam dimly. They sleep, a sleep without weight, and, on awakening, they order, they strike, they say that they must be obeyed. They are my lords, they know no pity and, like lords, they want to be alone, to advance alone, to reign alone, since they alone had the audacity to build in the salt and the sands a cold, torrid city." They too live in a circle of hell, in fact at the very bottom of the pit of hell.

Camus further stylizes his narrative by using carefully elaborated time patterns. *L'Etranger* takes place in the space of about a year, *La Peste* in about ten months, *La Chute* in five days, "*Le Renégat*" in one long day between sunrise and nightfall. But within this framework and pitted against the even movement of outer time, another time pattern emerges, an inner measure of consciousness or unconsciousness which reflects the emotional value and human content of the events described. Like Proust, Camus is concerned with our indifference to time and for somewhat the same reasons: time manifests our subservience to the material world, our neglect

[7] Justin O'Brien (trans.), *The Fall* (New York: Alfred A. Knopf, 1957), p. 14.

[8] The inhabitants of Taghaza are clad in black robes and their faces are covered with black veils.

of that spiritual content of life which is the only human victory over death.

The tempo of the narrative in *L'Etranger* is an essential feature in its composition. The short, unconnected factual sentences in the opening pages reflect Meursault's relation to time: each successive sensation is registered with each successive moment; time, when Meursault is aware of it, is thus a discontinuous succession of moments, and for days at a stretch it drops out of his consciousness altogether. The shooting of the Arab presents Meursault with a first problem; the death of the Arab binds together a set of unconnected events which become a "past" apparently directed by a malevolent fate. An individual time pattern thus emerges, distinct from the eternal changeless rhythms of the earth. In his prison cell Meursault experiences the empty but continuous presence of his own existence divorced from these outer rhythms. Only with his condemnation to death do the two merge as time seizes Meursault and holds him in its grip, an accelerated time, felt as the ticking of a clock announcing his future annihilation. The ties between the individual and the earth are now severed, for what in nature spells eternity in human beings spells only a sense of their mortality. Meursault now has no future and his life is emptied of content. Only with the certainty of death does Meursault become aware of another dimension of time, an inner coherence, rich in beauty, sensation, and feeling, unique and relative, one which cannot be denied: it is the substance of life just as the relentless rhythms of the earth are now the annunciation of death.

The time patterns and changing tempos in *La Peste* embody the thought that shaped the novel. They transmit the emotional fluctuations which in themselves are direct manifestations of the power of the plague. At the height of its rule, the plague holds in its power a mass of human beings who have lost their past, their future, and all sense of duration.

Their lives are empty of human emotion. The substance of human life, sensuous and diverse, eventually reappears with the flow of a "free time," an inner duration and continuity. Without these there can be neither human joy nor human love. The third and shortest of the five parts of the chronicle, which describes the triumph of the plague, gives an overpowering impression of weight, of a time that has stopped, a time that is dead. The second and third parts of the novel are symmetrical; two tempos meet and clash until finally one almost completely submerges the other: the nonchalant movement of individual life with its yesterdays, todays, and tomorrows, confidently lived as though they were as unmeasured as the air we breathe, and the abstract, empty, mechanical time of the plague that brings only death. The dramatic quality of *La Peste* lies in this antagonism between the mechanical tick of a clock presiding over the monotonous and grotesque hecatombs of human beings and the generous and free flow of a time rich in human emotion. This double perspective is emphasized throughout the novel, and embodies the collective "passion" Camus wished to depict.

In contrast, *La Chute* moves in concentric circles: time is really absent from the universe of Clamence, and with it, life. It is but a shadow of a universe, devoid of the two dimensions of time which support *L'Etranger* and *La Peste*. The first speech of Jean-Baptiste Clamence traces a circle; the second, third, and fourth describe it again but spiral the circle downward: fourteen pages, twenty-six pages, fifty-one pages. The fifth and last part, symmetrical in length with the third, leads us to the very heart of Clamence's distress.

As for the renegade priest, he is caught in an eternal day from which there is no escape.

Within these worlds, the rhythms of seasons and of hours, the rising and setting of the sun, night and day, light and darkness, mark the serene eternity of a nature for which time is essentially rhythm, not the inner nor the outer flow of an individual life. The Holland of *La Chute*, where day and night seem to blend in an eternal twilight, and Taghaza, under the relentless blaze of its sun or its stars, are two extremes between which one can situate Algiers and Oran, where evening brings the relief of a cool breeze rising from the sea. There the timeless rhythms of the sea accompany the timeless rhythms of human life. Here again the contrast between the immobility of a stark landscape and the living movement of the sea emphasizes Camus's preoccupation with the complex time patterns within which human beings move and must maintain a precarious equilibrium.

The apparent realism of Camus's novels is thus somewhat misleading, for by every means at his disposal Camus creates closed worlds which recall the closed, self-contained universe of classical tragedy. Each of these worlds poses a problem, asks a question, which the main characters embody. These are not the well-rounded, carefully observed characters of the traditional novel, and the issues they raise go beyond the problems of individual destiny. Through them Camus sets in motion and questions a number of familiar symbols and myths, many of them connected with the Christian faith. Some of these symbols are timeless: Meursault, the man condemned to death, for example; the plague, the evil of evils, which has had a long career in both history and fiction—a career of which Camus is well aware, having followed its course from the Bible through chronicles, medical books, and other literature. The fall is, after all, the foundation stone of the Judeo-Christian faith. And if all these narratives deal with some sort of trial, they are not unique in that respect. In modern times the romantics had already shaken their fists at heaven, had measured God by human standards and found him wanting. In *L'Homme révolté*, Camus briefly summarizes this trial of God by modern man and traces its evolution as, with Nietzsche, it becomes the trial of man by man. This trial is Camus's central theme, and each one of his novels is, in essence, a refusal of the indictment, a restatement of the problem.

13

Heroes of Our Time:

I. The Stranger

"En tout cas, comment se limiter à l'idée que rien n'a de sens et qu'il faille désespérer de tout?"

Meursault, the hero of *L'Etranger*, is a kind of Adam, a man content just to live and who asks no questions. But, like Melville's Billy Budd, Meursault kills a man. He is then judged to be guilty, but why? The prosecutor, lawyer, and chaplain answer the question in conventional semisocial, semireligious, Occidental terms, but these officials represent abstract entities and their answers mean nothing to Meursault nor to a simple-minded man like Meursault's friend, Céleste; quite obviously their explanations do not apply to the case as Camus devised it.

But as the tale develops it seems clear that Meursault's error lies precisely in his estrangement. He acts in a human situation as though human relationships, and therefore responsibilities, do not exist, and before he knows it he is involved in Raymond's elementary but violent drama. That Meursault killed the Arab is a fact. That his act was not premeditated and that there was provocation also is a fact. But at the trial what both prosecution and defense [1] present to

---

[1] Meursault's trial here recalls that of Dimitri Karamazov with the two parallel and opposed reconstructions of crime, both related to a

the jury are all the unrelated events in Meursault's life between his mother's death and the murder; these events are presented in a logically organized whole as the basis of an interpretation of Meursault's personality. As Meursault sits in bewildered surprise through this reconstruction of his crime, he begins to feel that he is being condemned to death because he was found guilty of not crying at his mother's funeral. And in a sense he is right. In fact he is condemned, according to Camus himself, "because he does not play the game." [2] He is a stranger to society, because he refuses to make any concession whatsoever to its codes and rituals. He sees no relation at all between his mother's death and the fact that he goes to see a comic film two days later, and he establishes none. And, seeing through his eyes, we are almost in complete agreement with him. He is, as Camus himself said, the man who refuses to lie.

Meursault's attitude at first merely reveals how arbitrary and superficial are the codes with which we cover up the stark incomprehensibility of life; for example, we can feel it is enough, in the presence of death, if we simply refrain from smoking a cigarette. With a certain fierce humor Camus uses his hero to shake us out of our complacency and to ridicule our smugness. But when Meursault goes even further, refusing to humor the prosecutor's Christian pathos because he sees no relation between his own act and the crucifix, refusing to take the "leads" of his lawyer, which play on a stock set of conventional emotional values, he becomes a kind of social martyr, a man who "dies rather than lie" in answer to a question. It is not, however, the satire of a society and the miscar-

completely hypothetical and consistent interpretation of the character of the accused. Dimitri Karamazov, of course, is innocent of murder, whereas Meursault did kill the Arab.

[2] Albert Camus: "*Avant-Propos*" to *L'Etranger* (New York: Appleton-Century-Crofts, 1955), p. vii.

riage of justice that give the tale its fundamental significance.
With the shooting of the Arab, Meursault tells us, "everything began," and more specifically still, "everything began"
in the prison after Marie's one and only visit, "everything,"
that is, Meursault's inner transformation.

Once or twice in the course of the tale we catch a glimpse
of an earlier Meursault, for example the student who had
once been to Paris: presumably he had not always lived in the
passive, autonomous state in which we find him. In this respect his precursor, Patrice (*La Mort heureuse*), gives us an
excellent clue to Meursault's adventure which, like his own,
is essentially spiritual in nature. At one stage in his spiritual
career Patrice had aspired to become similar to an object, to
live timelessly and to be one with the world. Meursault seems
to have achieved this state at the beginning of *L'Etranger*.
"Meursault, for me," wrote Camus, is "a poor and naked
man, in love with the sun which leaves no shadows. He is far
from being totally deprived of sensitivity, for he is animated
by a passion, profound because it is tacit, the passion for the
absolute and for truth. It is still a negative truth, the truth of
being and feeling, but a truth without which no conquest of
the self or of the world is possible." [3] That is why, until the
very end, Meursault is the man who answers but never asks
a question, and all his answers alarm a society which cannot
bear to look at the truth.

But the revolver shot jolts Meursault out of his purely negative state. At the time he is aware that he has committed an
irreparable act: "I understood that I had destroyed the equilibrium of the day, the unusual silence of a beach where I
had been happy." [4] As in the case of Dimitri Karamazov, the

[3] *Ibid.*, p. viii.
[4] *L'Etranger*, p. 81. The variants in the manuscript here are illuminating: (1) "I understood that I would be punished for having destroyed on a dazzling beach the unusual silence which was a revelation

real crime is not the one for which Meursault is being tried, but another which he will understand fully at the end when he accedes to a new level of awareness, conquering the world and himself as he grasps the nature of that happiness of which he had had a vague premonition on the beach.

Immediately after his imprisonment, Meursault—like Patrice in Prague after the murder of Zagreus—plunges into a new timeless world, the endless, uniform prison day. There he discovers three inexhaustible but completely closed subjective worlds: the world of memory; the world of sleep; and, as he scans over and over again a newspaper item (a murder story), the world of human solitude. Thus he "kills time," living, as it were, a timeless existence, but an existence which brings him only apathetic sadness. To him in his prison his face is now that of a stranger, an exile.

The final revelation comes like a flash just before Meursault's death. In spite of Meursault, the prison chaplain has come to speak of forgiveness, of an afterlife in which all may be redeemed. For the first time since he shot the Arab Meursault is jolted out of his apathy and in an access of rage he violently shakes the priest. There is no afterlife. There is only one life, his life as he knew it—the swims and the beaches, the evenings and Marie's light dresses and soft body—an intense, glorious life that needs no redeeming, no regrets, no tears. Why cry at his mother's funeral? Why lament his own death? After all, he is no different from any other human being: all are condemned to death just as he is, except that he knows both the glory of life and the unjustifiable nature

that I should have understood and which made me happy" and (2) "I understood that I had done wrong to destroy on a dazzling beach the unusual silence which made me happy." Meursault's "crime" recalls that of Coleridge's *Ancient Mariner*. Like the ancient mariner, Meursault has transgressed a natural, not a human law. Eventually, what frees Meursault (as it frees the ancient mariner) is the awareness of the beauty and, therefore, the sacredness of all living things.

of death. His crime and his revelation are as one. He destroyed and is destroyed. For this destruction there is no explanation, excuse, or compensation. The anguished hours of self-torture in his prison cell are over; he no longer calculates endlessly how he may escape. Defiant and lucid, he will go to his death happy: 'As if my great outburst of anger had purged me of evil, emptied now of all hope, face to face with a night heavy with signs and stars, I abandoned myself to the tender indifference of the world. Feeling it . . . so fraternal at last, I knew I had been happy, and that I was still happy. So that all might be consummated, so that I might feel less alone, all that was left for me to wish was that there should be many spectators the day of my execution and that they should greet me with cries of hatred." [5]

Meursault here becomes a sacrificial victim, his end is an apotheosis, the equivalent of Patrice's "happy death," a descent into the sea and sun, a reintegration into the cosmos. The stranger has in his prison cell, on the brink of death, found his kingdom: the irreplaceable, every-moment life of an ordinary human being who by an inexplicable decree of fate is destined to death. Meursault, as Camus conceived him, must disappear with this revelation.

It is clear that Meursault's initial mental attitude proves

[5] Meursault desires this hatred, no doubt, because it is a sign that the spectators, abandoning for a short time all the myths that mask their human fate, cannot help but see in Meursault the symbol of this fate. Meursault's idea of the ritual of an execution is derived from past practices, in particular from the French Revolution. In *Réflexions sur la guillotine* Camus describes the present, quite different procedures which have been dramatized in a movie called *We Are All Murderers*. He also tells how his own imagination as a child was struck by his mother's account of an execution which his father attended. The shock to the child's imagination resulted in recurrent dreams in which Camus saw himself walking to the scaffold. In the description of Meursault's case there are certainly reminiscences of Stendhal's *Le Rouge et le Noir* and Hugo's *Le dernier jour d'un condamné*.

inadequate to cope with even the simplest of lives. The very essence of *l'absurde* in his case is that out of indifference he linked forces with violence and death, not with love and life. Like Parsifal in the legend of the Fisher-King [6] he fails to ask any question and thereby gravely errs. In *L'Etranger* Camus thus suggests that in the face of the absurd no man can afford passively just to exist. To fail to question the meaning of the spectacle of life is to condemn both ourselves, as individuals, and the whole world to nothingness.

[6] There are many variants on this incident of the legend of Parsifal, one of the most mysterious in the whole cycle. Parsifal is brought to the castle of a wounded king and witnesses a strange procession in which a sacred vase is carried. Parsifal watches the procession in all silence and it disappears from his view. Later he is told that had he asked a question the king would have been cured.

"Perceval is informed by his cousin, a woman, and by his uncle, a hermit, that he did not ask for what purpose the grail was used in the grail castle because of the sin he had committed against his mother. The sin was the following: Perceval rode away from his mother and saw her fall to the ground with grief at his departure. Actually she died. He remained indifferent. Thus he was lacking in charity, compassion, and love, and so would fail to find the grail." (Quoted from Professor Pauline Taylor, medieval scholar, New York University. From a letter.)

14

Heroes of Our Time:

II. The Plague

"Comment dire le lien qui mène de cet amour
dévorant de la vie à ce désespoir secret?"

From the same human indifference of *L'Etranger*, the
plague, as it envelops Oran, draws its pestilential power. Perhaps that is why Camus chose that particular symbol of evil.
The people of Oran, as Dr. Rieux describes them, have little
sense of reality, of either good or evil, and this allows the
plague to make rapid progress among them. Unopposed, it
organizes all that is bad in human life into a coherent and
independent system: pain, death, separation, fear, and solitude. And it disorganizes and destroys all that is good: freedom, hope, and most particularly love. The people of Oran
are easily led to accept the plague as the very form of reality.
It does not develop as would any living organism, it spreads,
monotonous, rigid, inhuman, occupying a city which, because
of its lack of awareness, is already conquered.

The plague is not the symbol of an outer abstract evil; it
merely applies and carries to their logical limits the values
implicit in the unconscious attitudes of the citizens of Oran.
It is monstrous, monstrous as the acts of destruction into
which in this twentieth century we have all been collectively
plunged: war, mass repressions, concentration camps, evils all
seemingly produced without our participation, the result of

some invisible all-powerful mechanism. Had Camus merely chosen a group of human beings as the symbol of this evil of our times, the deeper intent of his novel would have been lost.

It was in the little-known book of essays, *Le Théâtre et son double*,[1] by the rather esoteric writer Antonin Artaud that Camus found the ancient symbol of the plague used in a manner which suited the theme he was pondering. It suggested the double symbolism which had satisfied him aesthetically in Melville's works, especially *Moby Dick*, one of his favorite books. For Artaud, the plague is the concrete equivalent of a spiritual illness, both an individual and a collective illness. After quoting at length from chronicles which describe the pestilence, Artaud concludes: "Thus the plague seems to show up in certain places, preferring all the parts of the body, all the sites in physical space *in which human will and conscience and thought are close by and likely to manifest themselves.* . . . If we are willing to accept this spiritual image of the plague, we shall consider the physical disturbances manifested by the victim of the plague as the concrete and

---

[1] Antonin Artaud, *Le Théâtre et son double* (Paris: Gallimard, 1938). A surrealist at the beginning of his career as poet, Artaud broke with André Breton, the chief of the surrealists. He was a tormented writer who plunged into occultism and finally went mad. It was he who propounded the theory of a theater of cruelty, which was to have some influence over the *avant-garde* dramatists (Adamov in particular) of the 1950's. Camus himself took an interest in Artaud's ideas on the drama. Before Artaud, Kleist in an unfinished play, "Robert Guiscard," had used the plague to symbolize simultaneously a spiritual and a physical evil, and an individual and a collective evil, emphasizing the connection between an individual spiritual illness and its outer, evil effects. In the numerous works Camus read when preparing his novel, the plague is generally considered (because of its mysterious epidemic character) as Father Paneloux considers it—the punishment meted out by God as a consequence of man's collective sinfulness. This is particularly true of Daniel Defoe's *Journal of the Plague Year*, which Camus read in a 1923 translation (*Journal de l'année de la peste*, Dr. Albert Nast and Andrée Nast. Paris: Crés, 1923).

material form of a disorder equal, on other levels, to conflicts, struggles, cataclysm and collapse all brought about by events. *. . . And . . . we can agree that external events, political conflicts, natural disasters . . . are shot into the onlooker's sensitivity with the force of an epidemic.*" [2] From whatever point of view we consider it—individual, political, social, metaphysical—the symbol of the pestilence thus used establishes a direct connection between evil and a paralysis of our human conscience, intelligence, and will.

In spite of abundant documentation,[3] it did not prove easy for Camus to draw from this ambiguous symbol, powerful though it may be, the novel he wished to write. It was not so much the general collective movement of the plague that caused the difficulties—its appearance, its short tussle with a somnolent and abstract administration unable to cope with so concrete an evil, its metamorphosis from invader into an omnipresent form of government—but how to create characters who, taking position in relation to the plague, could carry the main themes of the novel and give to it the deeper significance of the symbol.

In the Notebooks, Dr. Rieux and Father Paneloux, Tarrou, Grand, Cottard, and last of all Rambert, slowly emerge after the main themes have been stated: they are voices and atti-

---

[2] "*Le Théâtre et son double*" (1944 Gallimard edition), pp. 22-26 (my italics).

[3] Camus, as he started work on his novel, listed in his Notebooks: Thucydides: *History of the Peloponnesian War*; Boccaccio: "The Plague in Florence" (no doubt in the *Decameron*); Manzoni: *The Betrothed*; Daniel Defoe: *Journal of the Plague Year*; H. de Manfred and Jack London, each with the note "The Scarlet Plague." And he listed innumerable others, including memoirs by Mathurin Marais; accounts by Michelet, Pushkin, Charles Nicole and others; history, statistics, and symptoms culled from the works of doctors such as Antonin Proust; passages in the Bible (particularly as he started on his second version and admonished himself "use the Bible") and principally from Deuteronomy, Leviticus, Exodus, Jeremiah, and Ezekiel.

tudes before they are individuals, yet each one is clearly differentiated by the particular form of sensitivity his suffering
reveals. In the background is the silent figure of Mme. Rieux,
the doctor's mother. In his notes Camus attaches a greater
importance to her presence than her role in the novel seems
to warrant, but she is closely linked to his main characters
through whose eyes we follow the story, that is, to her son
Dr. Rieux and to his friend Tarrou, over whom she exercises
a strong attraction. These three characters are at the heart
of the novel. Mme. Rieux's fragile presence beside her son
throughout the epidemic and at Tarrou's bedside at the hour
of his death is far more indomitable in its serenity than the
baroque autocracy of the epidemic itself. It is through her
that Camus introduces a human perspective essential to his
novel which none of his other characters convey to us in quite
the same way.

Of all the characters in this novel Dr. Rieux is, in a sense,
the least complicated. He has devoted his life to fighting illness and death; the pestilence is only an acute manifestation
of his daily enemy, man's mortality. Rieux knows the hopelessness of his undertaking and the epidemic only emphasizes
it: as a doctor he can diagnose, not cure. What normally he
can bring to his fellow men—hope and temporary alleviation
from pain—the plague snatches from him. His ethics are clear:
a doctor fights illness, and to fight an illness one must first
recognize what that illness is. Like his friend, Dr. Castel, he
quickly realizes the full implications of the situation in which
the city of Oran finds itself and, with no illusions, he does to
the limit of his strength what it is his function to do. He is
one of two or three men who realize at once that the nature of
the evil appearing in Oran is unusual and must be fought by
new methods. He looks on the scene with the same unwaver-
ing eyes as does his mother. But in the meantime his own
wife, sick of tuberculosis, dies in a sanatorium, alone and re-

moved from the scene of his struggle. When she leaves for the
sanatorium at the beginning of the book we sense that, even
before the advent of the plague, Rieux has allowed one dimension of life to slip from his hands, that is, the personal,
total love that links two human beings. He survives the
plague, but alone, dehumanized. As he watches the exuberant
crowd on the night when the gates of Oran finally open, he
realizes that he will always be a prisoner of the plague. For
him the plague is, in essence, the clear inner awareness of
man's accidental and transitory presence on the earth, an
awareness that is the source of all metaphysical torment, a
torment which in Camus's eyes is one of the characteristics of
our time.

Tarrou lives this anguish in a more concrete way. He is far
more preoccupied than Rieux by the material, visible substance of the world. It is from Tarrou's notebooks that we
get the sensuous and physical description of both the city and
its inhabitants, and a sense of the changes that take place in
the moods, rhythms, and outer appearance of Oran. His own
inner adventure had begun long before his arrival in Oran.
It began when Tarrou realized (like young Albert Camus)
that men condemn other men to death; the judge, in this
instance, had been Tarrou's father and the shock of the revelation threw Tarrou out of his normal human orbit. He left
his home, the father he could no longer tolerate, the mother
he loved. He broke all ties with a society he condemned for
coldly killing men in the name of justice. He now felt he
could not ever judge his fellow men. When seeking to act
in revolutionary political causes in favor of social reform, he
found this form of action made him once again a witness to
the execution of a human being in the name of justice. Tarrou
then comes to the realization that no doctrine is worth killing
for: "my affair," he says, "was that hole in the chest" of the
man shot down. When he settled in Oran before the advent

of the plague Tarrou withdrew from all action, apparently seeking through observation and meditation a road toward the selfless purity of the saint; he wanted no part in any evil. During the plague he becomes the animating spirit of the volunteer teams fighting the pestilence which in the end takes his own life.

Unlike Rieux, Tarrou cannot come to terms with the reality of man's metaphysical condition nor accept man's participation in its cruel rites. He is touched more deeply perhaps than Rieux at the very source of life, in his sensitivity. He experiences the compassion we see in Mme. Rieux's eyes but not the intellectual serenity that accompanies it. In his notebooks Tarrou carefully records the actions of two old men whom he observes: the first automatically appears every day at the balcony of his room, wheedles the cats in the courtyard into coming under his windows and then, when they do, energetically spits on them; the second old man, an asthmatic patient of Dr. Rieux's, spends his time in bed, a veritable hourglass of a man, who transfers chick-peas one by one from one receptacle to another. The life of the first man is entirely disrupted by the plague, since the cats disappear; the second triumphantly and imperturbably survives. These two men, in a mechanical, unconscious way, are crude replicas of Tarrou and Rieux.[4] In his essential absurdity, the first needs to establish a relation with a living being; the second reduces life to the most elementary and indifferent automatism. Tarrou wonders whether this second man is a saint, and we realize that what distinguishes Tarrou from Dr. Rieux is that Tarrou is trying to purge himself of all evil, trying to transcend his human condition.

Upon Rieux and Tarrou, Camus puts the burden of a full awareness of the nature and significance of the plague; but

[4] Camus describes the real prototypes of both these characters in his Notebooks.

to them also he gives the one rich moment of escape from the pestilence. Leaving the plague-ridden city behind them one night, Rieux and Tarrou take a long swim in the sea. The human nightmare is dissipated and the joy and beauty of life flood their entire beings as they move side by side in the buoyant waters. For a few moments they emerge into the greater cosmos of sea and night, freed from their obsession with human suffering and the prison walls the plague has built around them. (For Rieux and Tarrou, the plague is first and foremost a certain metaphysical and intellectual view of life, a part of themselves which, if it goes unchallenged, will dominate and kill the sense of oneness with others, the feeling of harmony with the earth, the physical freedom and enjoyment which are life itself.

Rambert and Grand, both allies of Rieux and Tarrou in the fight against the pestilence, are less involved intellectually. Rambert, the journalist, is concerned not with understanding but with living. Physically sturdy and characteristically generous, he discovered before coming to Oran that the only remedy against human anguish is love and the happiness it brings. For ideologies he has no use. Having fought in the Spanish civil war, he knows how murderous heroism can be even in the best of causes.[5] He is in Oran by accident, on a special assignment—reminiscent of one of Camus's own a few years earlier—and he has no sense of belonging to the city. The woman he loves is in Europe and all he wants is to join her there. More than either Rieux or Tarrou he carries the fundamental theme of the book: the suffering the plague causes by separating and isolating all who—consciously or not —love each other. Whether the separation is temporary, as in the case of Rambert, or final, as in the case of Judge Othon and his son, it kills hope and joy, the sense of duration, faith in the future, the value of human life. Rambert's efforts to

[5] Rambert has little use for the hero "*à la Malraux*."

flee the closed city prove useless, but it becomes clear to him that he who values happiness cannot allow the plague to reign around him. When, on the station platform at the end of the book, Rambert opens his arms to the slim figure of the woman he loves, he is, in contrast with Rieux, one with the crowd around him. (For all these individuals separately life is in essense what the plague destroys, that is, the freedom to love as though both love and lovers were eternal: "They now knew that if there is any one thing that one can always wish for and sometimes get, it is the tenderness of human beings.)

Grand had lost the love that is precious to Rambert, for he had let it be stifled by the dreary routines of his insignificant life as clerk in the city administration.[6] In its stead he has undertaken to write a perfect novel; although after many years of work he has not been able to formulate to his own satisfaction the first and only extant sentence, he dreams that eventually his book will make editors stand up and cry "Hats off, gentlemen!" It is his form of rebellion against the bureaucratic pettiness of his life. The plague merely accentuates all the routines and servitudes with which Grand deals, for it is his role to keep the endless files and records that Rieux needs, and Grand does this unquestioningly: "The plague is here, obviously . . . we must defend ourselves. Ah, if only everything were as simple." Grand eventually falls sick of the plague and then recovers; but he burns the sheets and sheets of paper covered with successive versions of his one and only sentence. What he finds alive again in his heart is the memory of Jeanne, the wife whom he loved and had lost.

Grand and Rambert, who come out of the plague with a greater degree of humanity than before, are the most touching figures in the novel. Rieux, Tarrou, Rambert, and Grand all fight the plague for different reasons but essentially be-

[6] Grand's story of his youthful love for Jeanne appears in Camus's *Notebooks* at a very early period.

cause each in his way is already, as Tarrou admits, plague-stricken, accustomed to living with the plague and to dealing with it more or less consciously but honestly in his private life.

In the lives of Father Paneloux and Cottard, however, the plague plays a very different role. At the beginning of the book, when Rieux begins to organize his medical service, the church also prepares to bring its consolations to the citizens of Oran. Father Paneloux preaches a first sermon [7] in front of a crowded audience. He develops traditional Christian themes: the people of Oran have sinned and God is striking them as he struck the people of Egypt. The trials they suffer are a purification, gratefully to be accepted, for they will lead to a reconciliation with God in this or the next world: "My brothers, you have fallen into misfortune; my brothers, you deserved it." When Paneloux joins the team of voluntary workers it is because, like Rieux, he considers it his duty to tend those that suffer. But his mental attitude toward the plague is entirely different from that of Rieux. In his eyes human suffering is willed by God and justified by man's guilt. The plague poses no new problem for him until that moment when he witnesses the long and excruciating agony of a little boy, the son of Judge Othon. After that experience he can no longer justify the ravages of the plague, and he withdraws into a somber meditation out of which emerges a second tragic sermon. Bowing to the mystery of God's will, like Christ at Gethsemane, Paneloux takes upon himself the ills of the earth and, reliving the Passion, dies alone, consciously draining to its dregs the same cup of suffering as Christ's, accepting that God's will be done.

[7] This sermon recalls some of the exhortations made in 1940, which called on France to consider the defeat and occupation as the natural punishment for its sins and to accept it therefore as such, to repent and trust in God; it also recalls the exhortations of the prophets calling upon the children of Israel to repent in the midst of the disasters that struck them.

Heroic though he be, Father Paneloux is the only person with whom Dr. Rieux in his humanity comes to no understanding, though Paneloux, too, abandons the attempt to understand: "My brothers, the moment has come. We must believe all or deny all. And who, among you, would dare to deny all?" Unwilling to deny his God, he accepts what he takes to be God's will in its totality. If we judge by his death, he has given a negative answer to the question he had been debating in an unpublished treatise: "Can a priest consult a doctor?" But the conclusions the two men draw from their encounter with the plague are irreconcilable: for Rieux, a doctor cannot accept consolation from a priest; for Paneloux, a priest cannot accept the ministrations of a doctor, since the doctor is the enemy of a God who permits evil to reign in this world. "Since the order of the world is governed by death," Rieux says, "it is better perhaps for God that one should not believe in Him and should fight with all one's strength against death."

Cottard is an ambiguous character. A criminal, he is at ease in pestilence-ridden Oran where death threatens everyone and where, as a consequence, he enjoys a reprieve. Upon him Camus accumulates every form of violent death—except death by the plague: Cottard is a condemned man; he first attempts to commit suicide and then, shooting wildly at all who approach him, he is finally shot down by the police to whom he refuses to surrender. Whatever his crime may have been, he wanted above all to escape from its consequences: he prefers suicide to judgment. While the plague was rampant, he strove to build up a solid front of respectability. Tarrou immediately understands Cottard's latent anxiety and his complicity with the Oran plague, which frees him from that other form of evil, man's brutal justice. The plague at least leaves Cottard with a chance, a loophole of hope for the future, which is all he needs. There is something quite pathetic about

Cottard's blind attempts to acquire respectability, his angry discussion of the trial of Meursault—an account of which he reads in the papers—and his irritated denial of the statistics which show that the power of the plague is receding and that, consequently, his own reprieve is at an end. Some critics have thought of Cottard as the embodiment of evil itself, a somewhat questionable interpretation, perhaps, given the anxious humanity of the little man himself. Unlike Rambert, the journalist, who seeks to escape from the oppressive atmosphere of the plague into normal living, Cottard finds refuge from the consequences of his past life in the stifling oppressiveness of Oran.

It is essentially that stifling atmosphere which Camus sought to convey: "I wish to express, by means of the plague, the feeling of suffocation from which we all suffered and the atmosphere of threat and exile in which we lived. At the same time I want to extend my interpretation to the notion of existence in general. . . . The plague will give an image of those whose share during the war was meditation, silence, and moral suffering." [8] The plague, therefore, in whatever context we consider it, symbolizes any force which systematically cuts human beings off from the living breath of life: the physical joy of moving freely on this earth, the inner joy of love, the freedom to plan our tomorrows. In a very general way it is death and, in human terms, all that enters into complicity with death: metaphysical or political systems, bureaucratic abstractions, and even Tarrou's and Paneloux's efforts to transcend their humanity. In the fight against the plague there are neither heroes nor victories, there are merely men who, like Dr. Rieux and Grand, refuse to submit to evidence. However useless their actions, however insignificant, they continue to perform them. It matters little for what reason so long as

[8] Notebooks.

they testify to man's allegiance to men and not to abstractions or absolutes.

(The main characters do not alone carry the full power of this theme; it is woven into the substance of the novel as Rieux describes the effects of the plague on the inhabitants of Oran: lovers and families separated in life and in death, "immigrants" thrown out of the stream of human feeling by the plague, passive collaborators "exiled" upon the arid shores of a collective fate.) To consider the main characters of *La Peste* apart from the collective life of Oran is to mutilate them; if we examine them only in relation to the fate meted out, a little too neatly perhaps, the novel loses an essential dimension and becomes more nearly an allegory. Considered in its totality the novel transmits a personal experience lived in depth and which Camus could express in no other way. Camus spoke of the novel as a confession; Dr. Rieux speaks of his chronicle as a testimony. The confession takes us back directly to Camus's main preoccupation: his need to rethink the fundamental problems of life. The war years had apparently brought the massive evidence of what Camus, in *Le Mythe de Sisyphe*, had set out to deny: the insignificance of the individual human being, the absurdity of human aspirations. That these years almost succeeded in plunging Camus into silence and despair, *La Peste* is there to prove. Nowhere has Camus more starkly depicted his reaction to the total unintelligibility of man's condition, nor his protestation against the amount of suffering inflicted on human bodies and human feelings. No religion, no ideology, he tells us, can justify the spectacle of the collective suffering inflicted upon man. Our minds waver, and Tarrou and Paneloux both die.

In this context *La Peste* marks a change in emphasis; leaving the universe to itself, Camus turns to men. And here the testimony begins. Against all the intellectual evidence in the world stands man with his indomitable needs, his love of life, his will to live. Camus observes him with confidence and this in spite of man's indifference to what he represents, in spite of his depreciation of what he most values, in spite of the facility with which he enters into complicity with the plague. It would have been difficult for Camus to express directly what he felt so deeply within him: the compassion for human beings, the respect for man's fragile joys. Neither sentimental nor blind, his humanism would have been meaningless had he attempted to abstract it from the experience that nourished it. This is why *La Peste* is, within its limits, a great novel, the most disturbing, most moving novel yet to have come out of the chaos of the mid-century.

15

Heroes of Our Time:

III. The Fall and The Renegade

"Laissez donc ceux qui veulent tourner le dos
au monde."

La Chute and *"Le Renégat"* are rude and violent attacks
upon the human beings so gently—almost tenderly—treated
in *La Peste*, though neither of these tales should be considered
as a comment on *La Peste* or as an attack upon the values
implicit in that novel. Camus took his public by surprise with
these two satires, so bitter in their brilliance that they discon-
cert, ferocious and partial indictments to which the epigraph
in the English edition of *La Chute* gives the key in a quotation from the Russian novelist Lermontov: "Some were dread-
fully insulted, and quite seriously, to have held up as a model
such an immoral character as a 'hero of our time,' others
shrewdly noticed that the author had portrayed himself and
his acquaintances . . . *A Hero of Our Time*, gentlemen, is in
fact a portrait, but not of an individual; it is the aggregate of
the vices of our whole generation in their fullest expression." [1]
Clamence, the mock spiritual dictator, masquerading as
Pope in a Tunisian concentration camp, and the renegade,
prostrate before the powerfully evil idol of his tormentors, are
semimythical creatures, the products of a satiric imagination

[1] Mihail Lermontov, *A Hero of Our Time* (Garden City, N. Y.:
Doubleday Anchor Books, 1958). Translated from the Russian by
Vladimir Nabokov.

latent in all Camus's work but one which he had held in check.
Both Clamence and the renegade remain unattached and
roving beings, freer even than Meursault from normal human
ties; they are not essentially individuals but rather embodi-
ments of an attitude. Of the two, Clamence has had the wid-
est notoriety, and he certainly exposes himself to attack, glee-
fully encouraging the reader by the zest of his self-accusation.

Clamence, before the "fall" he so dramatically describes, is
a perfect example of all bourgeois virtues; indeed, in his own
bearing he is the very advocate of man's inherent goodness,
the almost—but not quite—ideal gentleman and good citizen,
"almost but not quite" because we feel his inner emptiness and
a restlessness which becomes apparent in his Don Juanesque
approach to women. This is at least the image of himself
which, from his present hell, he proposes to us, and for which
he now substitutes a bloated, satanic image of perversion and
guilt, a real image of himself and—he would have us think—
of all humanity.

Clamence's fall begins, at least in his eyes, with the derisive
laughter that echoed around him and within him that night
as he was crossing the Pont des Arts. Through layer upon layer
it penetrates his whole being, corroding it progressively, to
reach at last the hidden core of his guilt, a memory: the image
of a shadowy figure in black leaning over a parapet, a scream,
a splash; his own hesitation and abstention. Upon this memory he seizes with a masochistic eagerness; the "high altitudes"
of his past, the "just" causes and "noble attitudes" are emptied of meaning and content as Clamence propels himself
triumphantly into the last "soggy" circle of hell.

The advocate is now the advocate of guilt. He still must fill
the world with his own image, the center of the spectacle he
evokes. He must talk and convince and see himself mirrored
in our eyes. False penitent and self-appointed judge, Clamence, the modern Adam, exhibits his nakedness, calling

upon us to do likewise, justifying by his own disintegration his onslaught on all mankind.

How close we are to Clamence in our moral self-consciousness, our latent feelings of guilt, and our desire to shed our responsibilities, is brought home to us by one brilliant thrust after another. The form Camus uses here is peculiarly fitting to his purpose. Clamence's ferociously cynical wit is highly entertaining to the sophisticated reader who enjoys his own cleverness through Clamence and enters into Clamence's scheme of complicity as Clamence's Sir turns into My Dear Sir, My Dear Compatriot, My Dear Friend, and the insidious voice becomes more and more insistent. Clamence's unerring choice of familiar, quite comical, easily recognizable incidents of everyday experience tightens this web of complicity, for example the description of his satisfaction on yielding a seat in the bus, of his irritation over his maid's ill humor, or of the dispute over a motorcycle stalled at a green light. Yet this very complicity puts us in the uncomfortable position of the medieval prisoner in the narrow cell of "little-ease" or the "spitting-cell" of twentieth-century invention which Clamence describes with a monotonous and passionate insistency. Clamence pursues his "last judgment" of humanity, destroying every shred of belief in man's value and dignity, transmitting to us something of the despair that underlies his orgy of self-indictment.

La Chute can be understood only as a parable, still ringing with bitter personal controversy, still burning with bitter personal experience. It is addressed to only a part of ourselves, the Sadducee in us, as Clamence warns. The Sadducees, those high-class, highly literate Jews, who at the time of Christ held to the *status quo* and the pure application of the books of the law, were detached, untormented, and righteous men. Of these Clamence, before his fall, is the modern counterpart, more self-conscious perhaps than his predecessors, the inheritor of a century of exploration of the "I."

Through Clamence, Camus once again is fighting his enemy nihilism, an inner nihilism this time which has reduced man's "conscience" to an endless, formless, chaotic parade of inner consciousness, a fascinating show upon which the outer law of a disintegrating society has no control because the distance is too great between the inner "I" and the mirror held up to it from outside. Clamence, like the Sadducees, wants a savior but not the one who proposed that one inner law "love." Love, in fact, is what he cannot feel, as all his relations show, relations with his clients, with the women he encounters, with that "primeval ape," his present patron. In his attempts to escape from his "I, I, I," the only real link with his fellow men that he can establish is his feeling of guilt. He cannot love; he can only judge and find guilty. In the secret recess of his apartment—and also of his mind—he keeps a stolen panel of a van Eyck altarpiece, "The Just Judges." As a whole, the painting, "The Adoration of the Lamb," would mean little to him, for he adores only himself. What he yearns for is the judge, the outer law, a new rigorous distribution of punishment and reward which will hold up to him a mirror in which he, Jean-Baptiste Clamence, the prophet of man's worthlessness, will see once again the image of his own righteousness.

In "*Le Renégat*," one of the six stories of *L'Exil et le royaume*, the renegade priest goes one step further. Tormented by his own need to impose himself upon the world through martyrdom, he abandons the Man-God who "never strikes, nor kills." Because his new masters beat and mutilate him in the name of their monstrous blind fetish, he accepts their law of hatred and violence with masochistic fervor. Like Clamence, he is the victim of a terrible fall, and at the source of his disaster is the same Promethean desire to be equal to the gods, the *hubris* always followed in the Greek cosmos by a swift and awful appearance of the sphinxlike Nemesis.

The five remaining short stories in *L'Exil et le royaume* show a complete change in technique. The stories are told directly, objectively. The *décor* carries no symbolic values, the plots—with the exception of *"La Pierre qui pousse"*—are almost conventional in structure. Each story builds up simply and rapidly to an inevitable, final climax as surely as does a story by Maupassant or O. Henry, with no loose strands or hidden meanings.

Of these, one, "Jonas," stands apart; it is a satire, though more gentle in tone than *La Chute* or "Le Renégat," and it is a little too long, a little too local in its Parisian connotations. The misadventures of the painter Jonas constitute an obvious little fable, a humorous comment on Camus's own quite serious view of the artist's dilemma in our modern world. The connection with the biblical Jonah is clearly and amusingly made by the recall of one verse: "Cast me forth into the sea . . . for I know that for my sake this great tempest is upon you." [2]

The four other stories in the volume, *"La Femme adultère,"* *"Les Muets,"* *"L'Hôte,"* and *"La Pierre qui pousse"* counterbalance the bitter sarcasm of *La Chute* and "Le Renégat." [3] The theme in each story is one of a more or less fleeting reintegration into the kingdom of man. The situations are simple: in *"La Femme adultère,"* the journey into South Algeria by Janine and Marcel, a married couple, in search of clients for their small business; in *"Les Muets,"* the relations between

---

[2] "Jonas" calls to mind the last part of Gide's satire, *Le Prométhée mal enchaîné*, and the dilemma of Tityrus. Tityrus, instead of reclining happily in the shade (as in Virgil), plants a tree; he must then tend the tree, make alleys and a garden, and finally he finds himself as completely hedged in by outside obligations as Jonas.

[3] *La Chute* was planned as one of the stories in this volume but in the writing it outgrew the original plan.

a small manufacturer and his workmen—Yvars in particular—
who go back to work after an unsuccessful strike; in *"L'Hôte,"*
an incident in the life of a schoolmaster living in isolation in
the high plateaus of Algeria. The African *décor* appears but
with no symbolic overtones. The last tale, *"La Pierre qui
pousse,"* the most mysterious, relates the experience of D'Arrast, a French engineer, in Iguape on the day of a religious
festival.

Each story leads to a revelation: for Janine, it is the grandeur and mystery of the immense African night which releases
her from the prison of her small, sterile life; for Yvars, who
like his comrades in the strike has refused to exchange a single
word with the boss, it is the depth of human solidarity in the
face of death and with it a renewed contact with the beauty
of earth and sea around him, with his wife and the son he
loves.

More powerful is *"L'Hôte,"* in which the themes of human
solitude and exile stand out in tragic starkness. An Arab,
arrested for murder, is left in the charge of a schoolteacher
who the next morning must take him to the nearest village to
be judged. By every means short of words—for he cannot
speak the Arab's language—the schoolteacher attempts to give
the Arab a freedom he does not take. Finally the schoolteacher
takes his charge to a place where two paths lead in divergent
directions, one to the village and judgment, the other to freedom. There the schoolteacher leaves his prisoner, and turns
back toward the schoolhouse but not before he has caught
sight of the Arab doggedly moving along the path to the village. In the meantime, on the blackboard in the schoolhouse,
an unknown hand has traced the ominous words: "You delivered up our brother. . . . You shall pay." The reader's imagination is held by the inscrutable figure of the prisoner, the
silence that reigns between the two men, and the tragic ambiguity of the schoolteacher's position. But there is a dignity in

their silence, a mutual respect in their attitude which takes us far away from the desperate world of *Le Malentendu*, for example, with which the story can be compared.

But it is in the last story of this volume, "*La Pierre qui pousse*," that Camus's theme of human communication appears in its greatest strength. D'Arrast, a French engineer, is commissioned to build a barrage at Iguape; he arrives at Iguape on the eve of a religious festival, a stranger, rather suspect to the population. In the course of the celebrations preceding the religious ritual he strikes up an acquaintance with the mulatto "Coq," the cook of a ship which had foundered off the coast of Iguape. In his gratitude for the miracle that saved his life when his ship foundered, the Coq has taken an absurd vow: he will carry an unbearably heavy slab of stone in the next day's procession and lay it at the feet of Christ, his Savior. Next day as D'Arrast watches the Coq staggering under the weight of the stone he is filled with a deep concern. He walks alongside the Coq with the Coq's own brother and when the Coq finally collapses D'Arrast lifts the stone and carries it past the cathedral door; he does not stop until he reaches the Coq's house, where he throws the slab on the hearth. "Then the brother led the Coq to the stone and the Coq slid down to the ground. The brother too sat down, beckoning to the others. The old woman joined him but no one looked at D'Arrast. . . ." Finally, "the brother moved away a little from the Coq and half turning toward D'Arrast, but without looking at him, showed him the empty space: 'sit down with us.' " There the Coq's story ends, but it is linked to another, more disconcerting, the story of the miraculous statue of Christ, the "stone that grows," brought to Iguape in another shipwreck, from which "*La Pierre qui pousse*" derives its title. Each year the inhabitants take chips from the statue to bring them happiness, and each year the stone grows back and the statue is whole.

The happiness which D'Arrast derives from his act is of a different nature. As D'Arrast stands in the doorway of the Coq's hut, an immense joy floods his heart: "D'Arrast, standing in the shadow, listened, without seeing anything, and the noise of the water filled him with a tumultuous happiness. His eyes closed, he joyfully recognized his own strength, and once again, a life beginning over again."

The reader is left to ponder the full meaning of *"La Pierre qui pousse"* and the two approaches to happiness that it describes, but in itself it exemplifies the tendencies which prevail in *"La Femme adultère," "Les Muets,"* and *"L'Hôte"*: the silence that envelops the story, a welcome relief from the insistent strident voices of Clamence and the renegade; the weight of human feeling expressed in attention to others, to the world around; the presence of a night as palpable, as all-enveloping, as pervasive as soft, still water. Man once more is rooted in the cosmos, suffused with its mystery, strong in a dignity he draws both from the vastness in which he moves and from the silence within him. The wide desert stretches, the high empty plateaus, the sea, the thick tropical forest, are in harmony with his vast inner world. There is dignity and gravity in the link that binds D'Arrast to the Coq, the schoolmaster to the Arab, Janine to the nomad Bedouins. The folly and heroism of the Coq's absurd vow is given its full significance by D'Arrast's gesture as he carries the stone, that symbol of gratitude for a life saved, to the Coq himself. To such human bonds felt and acted upon and not eternally analyzed, all these stories refer. The life Camus deals with is still dark and violent, but despite the violence it is illuminated by a new approach to the figure of man.

It is easy to read into these stories allusions to the figure of Christ: D'Arrast has been compared to Simon who carried the cross for the Savior. But one must stop short of any metaphysical implication. The Coq and D'Arrast are human and

Camus indicates once more that man's kingdom is within him and "of this earth." In fact one still senses in Camus's writing a fundamental hostility to that humiliating image of man which Christianity presents, man incapable of goodness unless he be sustained by supernatural grace, an image which seems as dangerous to him as the ideal, rationalist image of man incarnated by Clamence before his fall.

In these short stories Camus sharpened his instruments and increased his scope. Through satire and the medium of the short story he seemed to be seeking a form of aesthetic equilibrium, weighting his fictional world, rooting it in a cosmic reality which sustains rather than negates that essential though enigmatic quality of man himself upon which Camus had so long meditated.

16

Tragic Themes and the Theater

"O lumière! C'est le cri de tous les person-
nages placés, dans le drame antique, devant
leur destin."

Four plays, produced in rapid succession within five years
(1944-1949), placed Camus—along with Henri de Montherlant
and Jean-Paul Sartre—among the playwrights who, in the
postwar period, seemed destined to fill the void left by the
deaths of such impressive figures as Jean Giraudoux and Paul
Claudel. But after Les Justes (1949) Camus appeared to
abandon the theater—at least temporarily—as a personal medium of expression. The Don Juan [1] who haunted his imagination and the pages of his Notebooks for many years was to
remain a disembodied hero.

None of his own plays ever enjoyed the immediate box-
office success which his adaptation of Faulkner's Requiem for
a Nun (1957) and Dostoevsky's The Possessed (1959) commanded. Caligula in 1945 came closest to it. L'Etat de siège
(1948) was a failure. Le Malentendu (1944) ran for one year,
but was not overenthusiastically acclaimed. Camus's dramatic
output is sometimes considered slim and his incursion into
the theater merely a brief episode in his literary career, one
of secondary importance in terms of his work. Yet his plays
continue to live in Little Theaters throughout the world, are
frequently discussed in scholarly essays, and seem more alive

[1] Don Juan made his first official appearance in Camus's work as
one of the heroes of l'absurde in Le Mythe de Sisyphe.

in many minds than other more resoundingly successful
dramas. Immediate popularity is not by itself a very serious
criterion of dramatic merit, and though Camus's plays may
not be judged dramatic masterpieces, they still merit serious
consideration. Never since the days of *Le Théâtre de l'équipe*
did the theater absorb so great a portion of his time as in
the last years of his life. Between 1953 and 1959 he bril-
liantly adapted six plays or novels, which were very different
in spirit and technique, and successfully directed their production. "People have often asked, with a solicitude to which,
you may be sure, I am most sensitive," he commented ironically in a television broadcast in 1959, " 'Why do you adapt
plays when you could write plays yourself?' Of course! And,
after all, I have written plays. And I'll write others, prepared in advance to find that they give these same people
a pretext to regret my adaptations!" [2] He went on to distinguish between the activity of the writer working on his
plays according to a "vast and carefully thought-out plan"
and the activity of the adapter and producer working in line
with a certain "idea" he has of the stage. It was Camus's
thought that from this double activity would eventually come
a "total spectacle, conceived, inspired and directed by the
same mind, written and produced by the same man, which
would thus attain that unity of time, rhythm, and style
which is for me one of the essential values of a production."

Besides this ultimate value, the theater, Camus explained,
freed him from the solitude and self-questioning of the writer,
from the pettiness of literary rivalries. Like football, like journalism, the theater is a profession that calls for teamwork,
for a collective effort. One works long hours, the play is produced, it succeeds or fails. But for the cast, as well as for
the producer, something concrete has been accomplished.
". . . theater helps me to get away from the abstraction

[2] "Camus vous parle," *Le Figaro littéraire*, May 16, 1959.

which threatens all writers. Even in my profession as journalist, I preferred the work of laying out the pages on the marble at the printer's to those sorts of sermons we call editorials. In the same way, what I like in the theater is to see the production taking root among the sets, the projectors, the backdrops, and other objects. Someone said that to produce a play well one must have known the weight of the stage sets in one's own arms. It's a great rule of art, and, as for me, I like this job which obliges me to consider simultaneously the psychology of characters and the place of a lamp or a pot of geraniums."

A close observation of Camus's career as a dramatist cannot fail to reveal that it has a consistency and a continuity which the outer pattern of production somewhat masks. The war years delayed the production of *Caligula*, the first of Camus's plays, a version of which had been completed in the late 1930's. *Le Malentendu* was in the making before 1939, though it was not written until 1942-1943. Of the adaptations, one, *Les Esprits*,[3] harks back to Algiers and *Le Théâtre de l'équipe*. Among Camus's favorite playwrights are Calderón and Lope de Vega, whose *La devoción de la cruz* and *El caballero de Olmedo* Camus adapted (*La Dévotion à la croix* and *Le Chevalier d'Olmédo*) in 1953 and 1957, respectively. As for *The Possessed:* "In many ways," Camus wrote in his foreword to the English translation, "I can claim that I grew up on it. . . . For almost twenty years . . . I have visualized its characters on the stage."

Very early in his career Camus came to think, with most

---

[3] Camus's *Les Esprits* is an adaptation of Larivey's comedy (*Les Esprits, ca.* 1579), which was itself an adaptation of Lorenzo de Medici's *L'Aridoso*. Camus said that his adaptation dated back to 1940 and was destined for the group "movement for popular culture and education" in Algeria; it was played in Algeria in 1946 and later reworked for the 1953 production at the Angers summer festival (see the preface to the 1953 Gallimard edition).

of his contemporaries, that there have been only two great periods in Western drama: the century of Pericles in Greece, which produced Aeschylus, Sophocles, and Euripides; and the Renaissance and post-Renaissance period out of which came the Elizabethan theater, the Spanish drama of the *siglo d'oro*, and the French classical theater. It was to these periods that he turned when he embarked upon his career as playwright— adapting Aeschylus's *Prometheus Bound* and translating Shakespeare's *Othello*—and he never abandoned them. Nor did his interest in the problems of the theater in our time ever lessen.

In his Notebooks now and then over the years he jotted down outlines of projected articles on the theater. They cast some light on the ideas that directed both the writing of his original plays and his adaptations. Many of these ideas he inherited, though not from any one source exclusively. In the early days in Algiers his theories were, to some extent, fashioned by his political beliefs; he thought somewhat in terms of the sociorealist drama of communist inspiration. But even at that early stage of his career his point of view was more complex than that of the Marxist.

Camus was well aware of the movement which in the 1920's and 1930's had rejuvenated the French theater, though what he knew he could only glean from magazines, books, and discussion. In respect to the theater Algiers was pretty far away from Paris, from Copeau and the Vieux Colombier; the great four—Dullin, Jouvet, Baty, and Pitoëff [4]—could be little more

---

[4] The opening of the theater of the Vieux Colombier by Jacques Copeau in 1913 marked the beginning in France of a renaissance of the theater which had been slowly shaping in all of Europe since the end of the century. Familiar with the theories and innovations in staging and acting of Stanislavsky, Gordon Craig, Appia, Max Reinhardt, and the Kunstler theater of Georg Fuchs and Fritz Erler, to say nothing of Antoine and Lugné-Poe, Copeau brought to his enterprise his own severe literary tastes, high artistic standards, and the principle that

than revered names to the young amateurs of *Le Théâtre de l'équipe*.

The man who at this time seems to have influenced Camus most directly was Antonin Artaud. Connected with Dullin and with the master of the renascent pantomime, Etienne Decroux, Artaud, a former actor and surrealist, was a mystic imbued with theories drawn from the Upanishads and the doctrine of yoga. He pushed to their limits certain views expressed by Nietzsche concerning the Dionysian collective, ritualistic, and sacred character of drama. These he applied both to the kind of play he considered desirable and to the nature of its staging, going further even than the British dramatic critic Gordon Craig in the wild impracticality of some of his theories.[5] Artaud's articles on the theater (*"Le Théâtre et la peste"* and *"Le Théâtre de la cruauté"* [6]) seem to have stimulated Camus's imagination, counterbalancing the flatness of the sociorealist approach, satisfying his youthful intransigence, his aesthetic sensitivity, and his social consciousness.

Artaud considered a dramatic performance as a mass experience in which the spectator was the essential participant

staging is subordinate to the play itself. He had an almost religious conception of drama as the most difficult, the highest form of art, a collective art of communion and participation involving authors, actors, decorators, and spectators alike. After his withdrawal from Paris in the early 1920's, his work as director was continued by his two pupils, Jouvet and Dullin, and two other great and selfless directors, Baty and Pitoëff. The *avant-garde* theater made great strides; it conquered the public and rapidly transformed both the commercial theater and, to a certain extent, the traditional state-subsidized Comédie-Française.

[5] Artaud was fascinated by Oriental forms of theater, the Bali theater in particular, which he considered as far purer, far more efficacious than our Occidental drama which, in his eyes, was still crude and barbaric. For a description of Artaud, see Jean Louis Barrault's *Réflexions sur le théâtre*, chapter 6.

[6] These texts were later grouped and published by Gallimard under the over-all title *Le Théâtre et son double*.

upon whom the drama must act as violently as a surgical operation, tearing away the complacent mask of security and everyday somnolence. He envisaged a kind of theater-in-the-round in the center of which a magic, daemonic ceremony would be performed through music, dance, mime, cries, and sometimes even words. The dark forces of sexuality, death, and life thus unleashed would then produce a kind of passionate purification of our subconscious drives. Camus, at the time of *Le Théâtre de l'équipe*, was drawn to the concept of dramatic "violence" and "cruelty" [7] that Artaud described, to the "shock technique" that he advocated. Camus also shared Artaud's conviction that significant drama is a form of transcendency, existing only on the metaphysical level.

From the very outset it was clear that Camus's explicit intent as playwright was to give a serious interpretation of life, to reach down to the roots of our very existence. But because of both his social consciousness and his practical experience with the stage, Camus was too involved in the human side of drama,[8] too conscious of the rich humanity present in his great models, to be tempted by abstraction, or to adopt the abstract spatial schemes in which Artaud delighted, or Artaud's overemphasis on sexual symbolism. Violent and extreme characters, passions, and situations, these he could accept, and a "cruel" action but human, concrete, and direct, projected through a fitting language. And though his thought

[7] The "cruelty" envisaged by Artaud has little in common with the lurid horror theater of the Grand Guignol type. He thinks in the same terms as Craig in many ways: marionette-like actors, performing a set of highly stylized, ritualistic movements evoke pain, terror, madness, and death, and culminate in a kind of controlled rhythmical paroxysm.

[8] In 1955, in his preface to the adaptation of Dino Buzzati's play, *Un Caso clinico*, Camus praises the "generosity, warmth of heart and simplicity" of contemporary Italian writing and the "carnal weight" of humanity which it carries (*Un Cas intéressant*, Stage Version, edited by *L'Avant-scène*, 1955).

concerning the drama matured considerably after the 1930's, its general orientation never changed.

As a playwright Camus always thought mainly in terms of tragedy. Like many of his contemporaries—in fact, like most serious playwrights since the end of the eighteenth century—he was fascinated by the problem of tragedy: how to create a tragedy in terms of our time, *"la tragédie en veston"* ("tragedy in modern dress"),[9] unsupported by the great tragic figures of the past, the Antigones, Orestes, or even, as he himself noted later, the Caligulas. Seriously concerned with the role and significance of the theater in our times, he was dissatisfied with his brilliant French predecessors and with Giraudoux in particular. He quite rudely denounced the "Byzantine" fantasy of the Giraldian theater, its ornate, often diffuse flow of poetic language. This opinion he was later in part to modify, admitting that Giraudoux's *La Guerre de Troie*[10] came close to being great tragedy. Claudel's Catholic universe, steeped in religious symbolism, always remained a little alien to him, in spite of its grandeur. Though attracted in the 1940's by Montherlant's neoclassical style, he found Montherlant's plays lacking in substance. Unquestionably, however, he benefited from the unusual richness of the French theater in the 1920's and 1930's and from the many discussions that accompanied its renascence.

A rather simplified view of the theater, apparently derived directly or indirectly from Hebbel, sustains Camus's point of view. Tragedy, he maintains, emerges in great transitional periods, *des époques-charnières*[11] he calls them; at such times individualistic attitudes develop within what had been a

[9] For a brilliant review and exposé of this theme, see Eric Bentley, "Tragedy in Modern Dress," chapter 2 in *The Playwright as Thinker* (New York: Harcourt, Brace, 1946).

[10] *La Guerre de Troie n'aura pas lieu* was translated by Christopher Fry under the title "Tiger at the Gates."

[11] *Une charnière* means a hinge.

homogeneous society and the individual comes into conflict with the group in an atmosphere of social disorder and violence. Ours is just such an epoch and thus, he reasons, we are ripe for tragedy.[12]

Camus drew his conceptions of the fundamental nature of tragedy from the Greeks, but within the Nietzschean perspective: tragedy is born of the conflict between two equally strong, equally valid antagonistic forces (as in Oedipus, for example), man's passionate assertion of his freedom and will to live, and the irreducible natural order to which he must submit. Since there can be no real final reconciliation between these forces, man inevitably goes down to his doom. But tragedy contains a revelation: in the tragic universe man, the victim of a fate incomprehensible to him in rational terms, becomes through his struggle with death and suffering the conscious participant in a higher order of greatness which surpasses him. The hour of death in which tragedy culminates is, therefore, for hero and audience alike, the hour of truth. Camus was quite familiar with the Apollo-Dionysus opposition and its meaning in Nietzschean terms.

For a young writer such as Camus, so conscious of the greatness both of the models of the past and of past themes, so imbued with the grandeur of a dramatic form (tragedy) the elevation of which seduced and satisfied him, the fashioning of a play could only be a difficult and indeed a perilous enterprise. What, in a modern context, is the real core of tragic experience in our time? What form does our *hubris* take and what is the nature of the antagonistic forces which tear our

[12] This view can be challenged. It has also been maintained with some plausibility that tragedy appears in periods of social stability and order, the very periods Camus uses to illustrate his theory—the century of Pericles, the prosperous dynamic reign of Elizabeth, the stable first years of Louis XIV's massive reign. It is conceivable, therefore, that our time is not particularly well suited to the resurgence of great tragedy.

humanity apart? In what terms can we formulate the great
spiritual battles of our time? In what elevated language, natural yet worthy of tragedy, can these struggles be expressed?
In what great new characters and situations, devoid of strain
and posturing, can they be embodied? Camus seems always to
have felt that the answers must be sought in an experience
that he as an author widely shared with the humblest of
men around him: personal, therefore, and collective, immediate, yet universal and timeless. Unquestionably he considered each of his plays as an experiment, a search in the direction of tragedy, not merely as an end in itself.

In this connection, Camus's adaptations, with the one exception of *Les Esprits*,[13] a gay and essentially "theatrical" spectacle, have a particular significance. Though very different in
origin—Spanish baroque, contemporary Italian, and American
—these adaptations are all serious in theme. The two Spanish
plays, *La devoción de la cruz* and *El caballero de Olmedo*,
were probably selected in part because of their peculiar adap-
tability to the outdoor stage of the Château of Angers where
they were produced. Though completely different in their
dramaturgy, the adaptation of Faulkner's *Requiem for a Nun*
and Buzzati's *Un Caso clinico* show a striking resemblance in
theme to the two Spanish plays. *The Possessed*, because it is
the last work Camus completed, because it "summarized,"
he said, "what at this point I believe and what I know about

---

[13] *Les Esprits*, as Camus points out in his preface, is a traditional
comedy "halfway between Italian comedy and [French] classical comedy." Camus's adaptation is felicitous. He simplified the cast, stream-
lined the action, eliminated a certain clumsiness in the plot, and accelerated the tempo considerably. "Two fathers, four lovers, a few liars
and the joy of everyone, that is enough, isn't it, to summarize a life,
enough in any case to make a comedy," announces Fortin, one of the
valets. The use of masques, of mimic, dance, and pantomime, accentu-
ate this poetic fantasy and give Camus's version an elegance, lightness
of touch, and rhythm which the original only suggests.

the theater," will be considered apart, somewhat as the cul-
mination of his work as playwright.

In all four plays Camus deals with a situation wherein from
the beginning the hero is marked for destruction, the victim
of a form of collective murder; and in this murder, consciously
or not, he is a willing participant. *Requiem pour une nonne* [14]
is particularly revealing. Nancy Mannigoe, the central character in the play, desires her doom. She is a willing sacrificial
victim—though not an innocent one any more than Meursault
was—and she is killed according to all the sacred rituals of
society. In his original plays, too, Camus's main characters
suffer this same doom: the Emperor Caligula, Diego in *L'Etat
de siège*, Kaliayev in *Les Justes*, and, in a more private context, Jan in *Le Malentendu*. The fundamental schema is the
same, more or less explicitly one which, as Eric Bentley points
out,[15] often recurs in twentieth-century drama: the stage is a
court of law, where human beings are tried, questions are
asked, depositions are made, verdicts are given—and where
only death sentences are pronounced, sentences from which
there is no appeal. Though this symbolism is central to all
Camus's literary work—obvious in *L'Etranger*, implicit in *La
Chute*, latent in *La Peste*—it is particularly well suited to the
stage.

Camus's dramatic adaptations are not, therefore, merely a
marginal part of his work; they are connected more or less
closely with his search for both a tragic substance and a tragic
form indigenous to our time. In the prefaces to these adaptations Camus stresses that his role consists essentially in his
search for a certain form of language. Therein lies their creative value in his eyes. The search for the language of modern

---

[14] Camus adapted Faulkner's novel with the help of the French
translation by M. E. Coindreau, for which he wrote a very enlightening preface (*Requiem pour une nonne*; Paris: Gallimard, 1957).

[15] *Op. cit.*

tragedy [16] was one of Camus's main preoccupations as dramatist, and that is another reason why his adaptations have a
place in the pattern of his work as a playwright: they are ex-
periments in style. Among them, *Requiem pour une nonne*
stands apart, so great is its transformation in Camus's hands.
In this instance Camus has somewhat taken the place of
Faulkner. *Requiem pour une nonne*, therefore, will be discussed more fully in relation with Camus's four original
plays.

The plots of Camus's plays are starkly simple, reduced to
bare essentials. They all deal with forms of revolt: a revolt
against death and the arbitrary, irrational nature of man's fate
in *Caligula* and *Le Malentendu*; a revolt against tyranny and
injustice in *L'Etat de siège* and *Les Justes*.

The setting of *Caligula* is imperial Rome, but, as Camus
indicates, a poetic Rome and not the historic Rome.[17] Caligula, the young and benevolent Emperor, disappears for three
days after the sudden death of his beloved sister-mistress Drusilla. When he comes back he is transformed. He attempts to

[16] Camus here comes fairly close to Jean Giraudoux, for whom our
time suffers because it has not as yet found an adequate "language";
in other words, it still has no clear understanding of its own significance, it gropes in the dark, unable to control forces which it cannot
name. Camus's concern with the language of tragedy is more purely
aesthetic in nature but it is nonetheless linked to the same preoccupation as that of Giraudoux.

[17] Caius Caesar Augustus Germanicus, known as Caligula, was born
in A.D. 12 and became emperor of Rome at age 25. He was assassinated
four years later by a certain Cassius Cherea. Suetonius gives a detailed
account of Caligula's madness and ferocity in his *Lives of the Caesars*,
from which Camus culled a certain amount of information: the Emperor's youthful age; the change which transformed a kind and pleasant ruler into a viciously murderous tyrant, a change wrought—according to Suetonius, though not to Camus—by illness; a few of
Caligula's mad ideas and the power which enabled him to realize
them; some of his remarks; and his murder at the hands of Cherea.
But Camus's interpretation of the character is entirely his own and
quite modern.

impose upon his court and his people a tyrannical, capricious, and murderous will, alienating even his closest friends until, at last, all join in revolt and kill him.

As the curtain rises we await the return of the Emperor, and the end of the first act heralds Caligula's own "play within a play," announced by the ringing of a gong. In the next three acts Caligula becomes the director of a grim and farcical tragedy in which he has cast himself as a central figure, a play through which, emulating Hamlet, he claims he will "catch the conscience" of his subjects. His "play" ends only with his violent death.

Le Malentendu, long entitled *Budojuvice* (the name of a small town in Czechoslovakia) in Camus's Notebooks, is set somewhere in the center of Czechoslovakia. For a while Camus considered making a comedy of it, but in the grim atmosphere of the 1940's this proved an impossible enterprise. The story is the one which Meursault reads in prison on the yellow scrap of newspaper he found under his mattress, a story that is part of the folklore of all Europe. The setting is always an isolated inn where the innkeeper and his family kill and rob the unwary travelers who stop there. In *L'Etranger,* through Meursault, Camus gives a melodramatic version of the story; in *Le Malentendu* he seeks its tragic meaning:

A man left his Czechoslovakian village to make his fortune. At the end of twenty-five years, rich now, he returned with a wife and child. In order to take his mother and sister, who ran a hotel in his native village, by surprise, he left his wife and child in one establishment and went to his mother's inn. When his mother failed to recognize him as he came in, as a joke he took a room without enlightening her. But he had shown his money, and during the night his mother and sister murdered him with a hammer in order to steal the money and threw his body into the river. In the morning his wife arrived and, not knowing what had happened, revealed his identity. The mother hanged herself. The sister threw herself into the well.[18]

Camus's play follows the pattern given by Meursault except in a couple of details: Jan, the son, has no child and he is drugged by the two women and not brutally murdered with a hammer.

L'Etat de siège takes us to Spain, to Cadiz. It presents the collective experience of the entire population of the city, as a bureaucratic tyranny, incarnated in the symbolic figure of the Plague, takes over the government, until, led by the student-hero Diego, the citizens of Cadiz revolt and drive away the tyrant.

Unlike the three other plays, *Les Justes* is a historical play set in Moscow in 1905. A small group of terrorists prepare and carry out the assassination of Grand Duke Sergei Alexandrovitch. Yanek, the man who throws the bomb, is made prisoner and executed.

But what counts in these plays is not the plot in itself, but the atmosphere which sustains the drama and in great part conveys its meaning.

[18] *L'Etranger*, p. 106.

17

Poetic Fantasy and the Stage

"Ces déments obstinés, accrochés à des
planches, jetés sur la crinière des océans im-
menses à la poursuite d'îles en derive . . ."

Caligula [1] is a young man's play. When Camus finished the
first version in 1938, he was just twenty-five; all the main
characters in the play are thirty or under, including the Emperor himself, and all share the Emperor's disdain for the
older group of Patricians—straw men as much in the young
author's eyes, we feel, as in Caligula's. When Caligula, with
not a trace of irony, tranquilly assumes that, at thirty, his
mistress, Caesonia, is "an old woman," we gain a pleasurable
sense of perspective and enjoy Camus's play with a certain
sympathetic detachment and perhaps a grain of humor. Not
that it is not a serious, moving play, although it does express
clearly and loudly the rebellion of a very young man. A
Caligula has lived perhaps more or less faintly in all of us
and disappeared at the hands of an inner Cherea, Caligula's
challenger, when we turned thirty. And we all must have at
some time made Caligula's simple discovery that "life as it is
is not tolerable" and that "men die and are not happy."

Caligula moves on the wing of a dark inner lyricism shot
through with irony, which reveals how closely this play is tied
to its creator. No other play of Camus's captured the same

[1] There are three main versions of *Caligula*: the 1938 manuscript
version; the current 1945 version; and the modified 1958 version
adopted in the 1960 Sidney Lumet production on Broadway.

warmth of tone, the nonchalant and fierce humor, the overtones of pathos, and the imaginative inventiveness of this
first drama. *Caligula* is not, as it appeared to many in 1945,
primarily a comment upon political tyranny and terror; it is
a highly audacious poetic fantasy, projected in "cruelly" concrete terms. In the Notebooks it originally carried the subtitle
"*Le Sens de la mort* [The Meaning of Death]." "Topic:
Death—time limit, one minute," so rings Caligula's voice
throughout the play, and this, his favorite topic, is the one he
proposes for the great poetic contest to which he has invited
all the poets. Death and poetry are old partners, but Caligula
will make short shrift of a certain kind of poetic pathos, preferring the cruel poignancy of a certain kind of lucidity.

Caligula, like his friend and enemy, Scipio, that shadow of
his younger self, is essentially a poet, a poet who is also a playwright. It is he who engineers the spectacle which takes place
before our eyes, the play within a play. We can watch Caligula's own play with the complex feelings of those other spectators not so safely detached as we: the Emperor himself, for
example, or the Patricians, or that spectator *par excellence,*
the cool and detached Helicon, who can watch the Emperor's
murderous show without its costing even so much as a meal.[2]
Spectators and actors all, it might be said, off stage and on,
at least at the rising of the curtain when with the Patricians
we await the return of the Emperor and the later ringing of
the gong which announces the beginning of Caligula's own
play.

Camus, as a poet, is free to test and carry to its furthest
limit an idea and a mood which must needs kill his Caligula.
To Caligula he gives the mission of trying out, within the
freedom of the stage, an experiment so violent and yet so logi-

[2] In the 1958 version of the play the role of Helicon is enlarged and
modified. He is killed just before the Emperor is killed at the end of
the play.

cal that its full implications can reach us only later, when the
"show" is at an end. This is also true of Camus's other plays.
The full impact of his plays cannot be immediate, which perhaps partly explains the hesitancy in the public's first response
to any one of them. They carry us toward a "point of no return," but we can reach that point only if we abandon the
safe limits of common-sense reality and accept the suggestions
of an unusually concrete and rigorous imagination. This departure into a world so real in concrete terms yet so alien to
us, so estranged, cannot be as easy for spectators as it might be
for readers.

This feeling of estrangement is particularly marked for
many spectators confronted with Camus's second play, *Le
Malentendu,* and it proves particularly hard to bridge. In its
bleak dreariness *Le Malentendu* offers a violent contrast to
Caligula. The lavish sensuousness and the ferocious intellectual play upon life and death have gone, and with them the
stage properties and devices, the gongs and the mirror, the
feasts and pageantry, the brusque and macabre displays of his-
trionism and brutality. And, though death is in the making,
it is a slow, cold, difficult death. An isolated inn, a mother and
a daughter, an old, deaf servant, and a stage set since all time
for murder. These are the ingredients of the plot, the necessary ingredients, it might seem, of pure melodrama. The curtain rises on a scene suitable for a play of "black" mystery.
A traveler has appeared, or rather a victim, since all travelers,
if they are rich enough, are victims in the eyes of the two
women. This one is rich enough, rich enough too to be the
last. At this point we move out of the realm of melodrama,
for this is murder only in view of a high purpose. It is to lead
to freedom beyond the inn on the shores of a sunlit sea, to
an Eden of sensuous innocence and delight.

But the victim has written a script of his own and within
the same *décor* he has set his own stage not for murder but

for love and reunion. He is the savior, the son and brother, and he expects the open arms, the ring upon the finger, the rejoicing, and the fatted calf. He too has a purpose, he too is playing a part: he wants to be recognized. The two scripts thus written in advance tug at one another as the characters meet, while an undertow strong as the current in the nearby river beats against the barrage of misunderstanding which the cross-purposes of the characters have set up. With cold disbelief and a kind of horror, the spectator watches a slow masquerade, a reluctant dance of death: deaf, blind, and dumb, under the inscrutable gaze of the old servant all three characters move toward the cold black waters of annihilation.

"I must have read this story thousands of times," comments Meursault, speaking, in *L'Etranger*, of the Czechoslovakian traveler. "From one point of view it was unbelievable. From another, it was natural. Anyway, it seemed to me that the traveler had deserved it a little and that one must never gamble." [3] *Le Malentendu* is a glacial play, devoid of any comfort, an almost desperate modulation on the finality of death and silence.

With *L'Etat de siège* we emerge out of death into life. A whole city moves and lives in the golden light of summer: the Mediterranean city Cadiz, a poetic artificial city heavy with fruit, rich with the fishes drawn from the sea; Cadiz, surrounded by medieval walls but with open gates, with its crowds in the market place, its soothsayers, churches, alcaldes, governor, and judge—and its lovers, Diego and Victoria. From the very beginning of the play, over the city moves a sign, a comet slowly approaching across the heavens in the light of dawn, accompanied by a steady buzzing sound. Like the citizens of Cadiz, we are fairly warned; the stage is set for a collective disaster. When the curtain rises we are all spectators,

---

[3] *L'Etranger*, p. 106.

we and the inhabitants of Cadiz, waiting in suspense to discover the meaning of the comet. But, far more than in *Caligula*, we participate in the action from one point of view only: as the spectators on the stage are transformed into participants —victims, collaborators, or combatants—we follow their individual and collective reactions and destinies. The action is not focused on the curious personalities of King Plague, its principal character, and his secretary, it is focused on the crowd.

L'Etat de siège, Camus warns us in a brief preface, is not so much a play as a spectacle, a dramatic narration which uses "all the forms of dramatic expression, from the lyrical soliloquy to the collective chorus." The spectacular sets by the painter Balthus and the music by Honegger; the simultaneous projections of scenes taking place in the square, the governor's palace, the judge's house, the church; the mass, seesawing movements of the crowds, from which collective or alternating individual voices arise—all these are features which we connect with Bertolt Brecht and his "epic theater," a type of theater which Barrault, going back to Wagner, prefers to call "total" theater. Nothing, it seems, could be further removed from the glacial atmosphere of *Le Malentendu.* But after an almost operatic opening, when at the sound of two tremendously reverberating thuds a market-place comedian falls dead upon his platform, we know the play is going to deal fundamentally with the same theme as *Le Malentendu,* the same theme as *Caligula:* it is a play with death. This time, however, death alone does not hold sway, for *L'Etat de siège* also concerns love and life.

The theme "Death—time limit, one minute" appears again with the entrance of the nonchalant Ubuesque [4] figure of the

---

[4] King Ubu is a creation of the fiercely satirical, esoteric French writer, Alfred Jarry. Ubu impersonates the greed, stupidity, cowardice, and cruelty which Jarry sensed was latent in the particularly inhuman institutions of our times, our irresponsible, petty bureaucracies.

Plague, a burlesque, complacent, but nonetheless terrifying Caligula. In the end, at the challenging sound of Diego's voice, when the fresh, free wind of the sea blows over Cadiz once more, he hastily deflates and withdraws. "I am the Plague," Caligula had proclaimed, and in many ways *L'Etat de siège* is closer in spirit to *Caligula* than to Camus's novel *La Peste*,[5] or to his two other plays, *Le Malentendu* and *Les Justes*.

In his preface to the French edition of *L'Etat de siège*, Camus gave us the story of its genesis: Barrault's wish, in 1941, to create a dramatic spectacle around the "myth" of the plague, as Artaud had discussed it, using Defoe's *Journal of the Plague Year*; Barrault's interest in Camus's novel *La Peste* and his suggestion that Camus write the script for his preliminary canvass; then, after discussion, a new departure that set Defoe aside. "The problem was . . . to imagine a myth which could be understood by all the spectators in 1948," an "allegorical spectacle" comparable to a "morality" or a Spanish "*auto-sacramentales*," that is, a play containing a positive ethical point of view. Hopefully addressed to the masses, it is, Camus told us, a hymn to freedom, "the only religion which is still alive," a poetico-didactic spectacle.

Les Justes, with its small tight cast, its stark linear action, tense dialogue, and austere stage sets, recalls *Le Malentendu*. If, in *L'Etat de siège*, Camus to a certain extent wrote a script for a scenario devised by Barrault, in *Les Justes* he provided

---

[5] Although *La Peste* was published in June, 1947, and it was only a year later that *L'Etat de siège* opened at the Marigny Theater, on Oct. 27, 1948, *La Peste* had been finished quite some time before June, 1947, and Camus had in the meantime been hard at work on his essay, *L'Homme révolté*, and on *Les Justes*. *L'Etat de siège*, of which he himself was very fond, nevertheless seems a little outside the main line of development of his work. Camus definitely and truthfully stated that *L'Etat de siège* is not an adaptation of his novel.

a scenario for a script written by the Russian terrorist, Boris Savinkov. Savinkov in *Souvenirs d'un terroriste* [6] describes the activities of the combat organization of the Socialist party during the first years of the century. In particular he describes the assassination of the Grand Duke Sergei Alexandrovitch. The facts, respected by Camus, are briefly the following: after the usual lengthy and hazardous preliminaries, the organization decided that two terrorists, Yanek Kaliayev and Alexandrovitch, were to throw a bomb into the carriage of the Grand Duke as he went to the theater on February 2. The carriage rolled by, but Kaliayev, the one who was supposed actually to throw the bomb, failed to do so, explaining later to his fellow conspirators that he had been stopped by the sight of the Grand Duchess and two children, nephew and niece, riding in the carriage with the Grand Duke. "I think I acted as I should. Can one kill children?" he asked. After a brief discussion all agreed with him: children must be spared. Two days later Kaliayev killed the Grand Duke as planned.

In prison Kaliayev refused a pardon offered in exchange for information concerning his accomplices; he received a visit from the Grand Duchess, Elizabeth Fedorovna: "We looked at one another, I assure you, with a mystical feeling, like two beings who remained alive: myself, by chance, and she, by the will of the combat group, by my own will," wrote Kaliayev. Refusing to be moved by her appeal to Christian repentance and atonement, Kaliayev, who, Savinkov notes, had crossed himself piously when, bomb in hand, he passed an icon on the day of the assassination, went to his trial bravely, not as a man accused but as a prisoner of war, an avenger of the people.

[6] Boris Savinkov, *Souvenirs d'un terroriste* (Paris: Payot, 1931), pp. 112-166. Translated from the Russian by Bernard Taft. For a discussion of the group, and its action and significance according to Camus, see "*Les meurtriers délicats,*" chapter 3, in *L'Homme révolté,* and the first version of this chapter in *La Table ronde,* January, 1948, pp. 42-5ᵉ

"I recognize neither you nor your law," he proclaimed, and died satisfied that justice had been done: he took a life in a just cause and, in exchange, he paid with his own.

Of *Les Justes*, Camus said that he never felt himself so little the author of a play. And indeed he did follow Savinkov closely in both the scenario and the dialogue. This was not without its disadvantages. Savinkov's style, in the French translation at least, seems lacking in imaginative scope. And though Camus himself understood the ideological background and deeply felt the moral predicament of the "scrupulous" 1905 Russian terrorists, his audience may feel emotionally very distant from them. Historical figures, left to themselves, seldom create the kind of conflict and dialogue needed to convey the fullness of a life necessarily limited on the stage to this one projection through a play. The mere record of what the characters said, as it is given by Savinkov and reproduced and concentrated by Camus, sounds a little stiff and lifeless. A re-creation rather than a recording might have given the play a poetic truth and an emotional impact which it somewhat lacks, and it might have developed more fully the dramatic potentialities latent in Savinkov's Memoirs. Though Camus does tighten the action, centering it in certain characters, he still keeps a little too close to his source throughout.

Savinkov gave Camus three important characters with almost all the words they speak. Two become the main characters in Camus's play, the "poet" Kaliayev and the woman terrorist, Dora Brillant; the third is the Grand Duchess. The other characters in the play are subsidiary, embodying attitudes and types suggested by brief episodes in the Memoirs of Savinkov or others: Boris Annenkov, leader of the group, is drawn from Savinkov himself; Alexis Voinov's counterpart in real life was the young terrorist Alexandrovitch, who, filled with fervor on February 2, found himself unable to stand the suspense caused by the postponement of the murder and left the organization though only temporarily; Stepan, already the systematic terrorist who feels the lives of two children should not weigh in the balance when considered in the light of the ultimate justice to be established; Skouratov, the chief of police, the guardian of the prison; and the lurid Foka, a former criminal turned hangman.

Camus focuses our attention primarily on Dora and Kaliayev. Dora, Savinkov relates, passionate and silent, was in love with the Revolution, "suffering deeply from its failures yet dreading murder. She could not get used to the idea of blood." She seldom laughed and "relived with intensity the inner suffering that filled her soul . . . For her, terrorist action was the Revolution incarnate and the combat group was the whole universe." But it is Dora who speaks first to approve Kaliayev's abstention on February 2: "The poet acted as he should." And later, when the Grand Duke is killed, it is Dora who, when she hears the explosion of the bomb, cries out in anguish, "It is we who have killed him! It is I who have killed him," revealing a deep distress and sense of guilt. Kaliayev, as Savinkov describes him, was twenty-six, young and enthusiastic. Generous, he loved life and yet, like Dora, thought in terms of the total sacrifice of his life to the revolutionary cause. He was animated by a spirit of fraternal devotion to his brothers of the combat group.

Although Camus's characters are essentially the same as Savinkov's (except that Camus tightens the link between Dora and Kaliayev), because of the tenseness of the dramatic action something of their flesh and blood reality is sacrificed with the weight of their everyday personality and of their past. They tend to become voices, not human beings, to designate positions taken, parts recited.

Curiously enough, it is in the fourth act, the prison act, that the play seems to acquire a certain human dimension. In the first three acts the main dramatic center seems to lie in the Dora-Kaliayev relationship—to each other, to the group, to the action undertaken. In the fourth act Dora does not appear and the dramatic center lies in Kaliayev's confrontation with the forces of social order and justice: the chief of police, the Christian believer, the guardian of the prison, and, most gruesome of all, the hangman. Structurally, or so it seems to this spectator and reader, the play would have been stronger if Camus, instead of following the successive episodes of the murder, had concentrated our attention on one of these episodes, focusing the conflict either on Kaliayev alone or on both Dora and Kaliayev. At any one of its crucial moments— the bomb not thrown, the bomb thrown, the debate in the prison—the action described would have yielded its full potentialities and significance, and allowed for a fuller development of the characters. Indeed both plot and characters suffer from the episodic nature of the action as Camus faithfully follows its outer line of development.

For *Requiem pour une nonne* Camus also drew directly from a text already written, but a far more complex, a far more opaque piece of writing in terms of its symbolic potentialities. Faulkner's *Requiem for a Nun* is the sequel to his *Sanctuary*, and Faulkner deliberately uses *Sanctuary* [7] as a

[7] In *Sanctuary*, Temple Drake, the daughter of a Jackson judge, is taken to a baseball game by Gowan Stevens, a young Virginia gentleman. Stevens gets drunk, wrecks his car, and he and Temple land at a run-down farm, a hangout for crooks and moonshiners. During a terrifying night, Temple witnesses a murder and is raped in a rather singular manner by Popeye, the sinister murderer, who then carries her off to a brothel in Memphis. Six weeks later she testifies in Popeye's favor and another man is condemned to death for the murder she witnessed. Rescued by her family, she eventually marries Gowan Stevens.

In *Requiem for a Nun*, Nancy Mannigoe, a colored woman and a former prostitute, is on trial for having murdered the Gowan Stevenses' little daughter. The defense lawyer is Gavin Stevens, their uncle. Nancy background and framework of reference for the drama that unfolds in the courthouse, the office of the governor of Mississippi, and the jail in Jackson.

As Faulkner wrote it, *Requiem for a Nun* is not a play, though it is divided into three acts. The setting of each act is described at length in long introductory chapters both epic and lyric in character, which create an atmosphere that gives Nancy Mannigoe's trial and Temple's bitter encounter with the past a fatal, symbolic quality embedded in all the long history of the South. Behind the conflict lies the dark world of Faulkner, striking deep roots in a racial and religious soil which means little to Albert Camus. "I modified the last scene considerably," he writes, "one can see . . . that it consists mainly in Nancy Mannigoe's and Gavin Stevens's long speeches on faith and Christ. There Faulkner expounds his strange religion, which he developed further in *A Fable* and which is strange, less by its content than by the symbols he presents." [8] To this discomfort when confronted with Faulkner's religious beliefs—an integral part of a certain religious heritage—is added Camus's quite natural ignorance concerning the relationship of these beliefs with the complex historical past and no less complex present of the American scene in the South. The strange brand of puritanical, racial, erotic, and atavistic guilt and pride which go into the shaping of Faulkner's story either does not interest Camus or escapes him. What he draws from Faulkner's novel is a more clear-cut, less murky, but also more abstract form of symbolism: "Faulkner's

is condemned to death, but between the trial and the execution, act by act, the real connection (prostitution) between Temple and Nancy is discovered and the path whereby Nancy's action leads back to Temple's past. Nancy's murder of the child becomes a sacrifice, the price of Temple's guilt. *Requiem for a Nun* is the story of a strange atonement and a purification.

[8] Preface to M. E. Coindreau's translation of Faulkner's novel, *Requiem pour une nonne* (Paris: Gallimard, 1957), p. 14.

intention is obvious. He wishes the drama of the Stevenses to unfold in the temples raised by man to a painful justice the origin of which, according to Faulkner, is not human. From this point of view the courthouse is the equivalent of a temple, the governor's office of a confessional, and the jail of a convent where the negress, destined to die, atones for her crime and Temple's."

Camus further transforms this fairly simple interpretation of Faulkner's novel by introducing into its framework his own, quite different conception of justice. His play is shrouded in suspense, but stripped of the perspectives inherent in the novel, it moves somewhat disconcertingly between two levels of drama: the stark poetic unreality of fearful, somber legends of crime and atonement such as surround the semilegendary royal families of Greece, for example the famous Atrides of Mycenae, and the melodramatic tenseness and triviality of the conventional middle-class psychoanalytic play so thoroughly alien to Camus. In Camus's adaptation, the clinking of whisky glasses, the allusions to the baseball game or to the local geographic setting, and some of the dialogue seem extraneous, and the implications of the play have shifted. The tragedy of Temple Drake as it slowly comes to light in *Requiem pour une nonne* seems insignificant, fussy, and trivial, too unbelievable to stand beside the grandeur of the opening scene: a single dark figure, a death sentence meted out and accepted.

It is Nancy Mannigoe and not the Stevenses who caught Camus's imagination. She belongs to his world. Without her, his *Requiem* would be a rather dubious, somewhat tiresome morality play. In her heavy carnal reality she is that very mystery with which all Camus's characters contend, a dark divinity brooding over his theatrical world. She is the mute, mysterious, "quivering flesh of humanity," with which Camus in his own plays had been most deeply concerned. His essential dramatic theme so far had been that of the fall incurred by individuals and societies who, in some manner, lose touch with the mystery of man's concrete presence and incarnation in the flesh, that "truth of the body" which escapes all reason.

Camus's plays all follow a basic common pattern: the "natural" order of human life is dislocated; a system takes over which is the very negation of order, a systematized disorder, a perversion in which the notions of good and evil are inverted; life is drained of its substance, then comes a struggle and a final resolution in which, temporarily, the natural order reasserts itself. This pattern reappears in *Les Possédés*, but in a very different context. It was no small task to project Dostoevsky's intricate novel onto the stage, to keep it within bounds without mutilating it. Camus.had lived "for almost twenty years" visualizing "its characters on the stage." He knew the novel thoroughly, had studied Dostoevsky's *Notebooks* and worked with the complete version of *The Possessed*, keeping in mind the "confession" which Stavrogin, one of the main characters—the main character perhaps—writes before he commits suicide, a confession which did not appear in the novel as published. In Dostoevsky's novel, through a large number of intricate episodes one follows the terribly destructive impact upon the society of a small Russian town of a group of young men "possessed" by revolutionary demons of various sorts, ranging from the desperate nihilism of the young aristocrat Stavrogin to the cynical cruelty of Peter Verhovensky, the sinister and despicable character in whose hands everything turns into violence, humiliation, and destruction, the instigator of the deliberate murder of an innocent man.

Camus's experience as producer and adapter served him well in this enterprise. Taking one of the minor characters as narrator, Anton Grigoriev, he linked together, through short introductory speeches the twenty-two "tableaux" or scenes of the play, focusing them far more strongly than was the case in the novel on the character of Stavrogin.[9] All the other forms of "possession," Shatov's, Kirillov's, Shigalov's, Peter Verhovensky's, are subordinated to Stavrogin's, emanate from his. The play acquires therefore a basic unity not so apparent in the novel.

Through his contact with Dostoevsky, Camus in this play succeeded in putting on stage characters entirely human, more varied, more living than ever before. The action is broader in scope and mood: comedy, satire, melodrama, cruelty, despair, tenderness, and suffering are mingled in the fast-moving dramatic situations and dialogue. "I merely tried to follow the book's undercurrent and to proceed as it does from satiric comedy to drama then to tragedy," wrote Camus,[10] thereby introducing into the development of the plot a wealth of emotion which had been absent from the preceding plays.

In many ways, however, Dostoevsky's novel has clearly become Camus's play. In his foreword Camus links the two main and shocking events in the play: the murder of an honest, innocent young man, Shatov, and the suicide of Stavrogin. Suicide and murder are, in his eyes, as they were in *Caligula* and in *Le Malentendu*, two facets of the same sickness which already in Dostoevsky's world was ravaging a humanity which "prefigures" our own: by its nihilism; by its incapacity to feel compassion; by its scorn for moral standards which in its eyes are nothing but the chains forged for themselves by frightened men. The hope that Dostoevsky put in God, Camus,

---

[9] In Dostoevsky's novel, Stavrogin is a young and handsome aristocrat, obsessed by the nothingness of life. After a life of debauch he commits an act for which there is no pardon in his eyes: he takes advantage of an innocent child, drives her to hang herself, and sits coldly by without intervening while she commits suicide. Eventually he too hangs himself.

[10] *Les Possédés*, Foreword.

in his play, seems to place in man, in the love of Shatov for his wife, in the affection that links Stepan Trofimovich to Varvara Stavrogin. Compassion, weak though it may be in *Les Possédés*, negates the scornful image of man which inspires Verhovensky's acts. Compassion, humor, characters that are both human and varied—these characteristics of *Les Possédés*, though not new in Camus's work, seemed to point to a new orientation in his work as dramatist.

18

Dialogues of the Mind

"Il y a pour les hommes d'aujourd'hui un chemin intérieur . . . qui va des collines de l'esprit aux capitales du crime."

The Emperor, Caligula, is the first of the forces of perversion Camus unleashed on the stage. *Rien* (nothing) is the leitmotiv of the play, and Caligula is the man who carries this theme to its ultimate limits, a privilege that only an all-powerful emperor enjoys, as he himself recognizes. In *Caligula*, Camus chose to project upon the stage the extreme consequences of the nihilism with which he grappled in his first works. His emperor is a victim, not a hero, of *l'absurde*, suffering from a form of *hubris* which in Camus's eyes is peculiarly modern and at the heart of much evil in our time.

The Emperor's fall really takes place before the curtain rises. Until the death of his beloved sister Drusilla, Caligula was a perfect emperor, a man who spoke of love, justice, and friendship, a man who aspired to be a just man. When he returns after Drusilla's death and his three-day disappearance —a symbolic descent into hell—he returns a man possessed. He has struggled with the meaning of death and comes back transformed. He sees that death negates life, love, friendship, justice, human beings, human values; that death delivers up the human being to an arbitrary, impersonal, mechanical fate. From this powerfully simple, negative, intellectual vision, Caligula draws extreme consequences: everyday living, individual habits and social institutions, are shams, contemptible

forms of mockery with which human beings delude themselves. From his detached vantage point he looks down on life
and sees around him only hypocrisy, dissembling, cowardice,
a worthless and miserable "play."

Since he is emperor and since he is in possession of an incontrovertible truth he is doubly free; he is free to impose the
truth upon his subjects, he is free to tear away the mask of
their false security as he pleases. In the name of truth he
undertakes a peculiar form of ruthless and disinterested mental warfare upon his subjects. Caligula is now a man with a
purpose—an educator, not a tyrant—the would-be savior of
humanity.

This is the easiest level of action for the spectator to follow,
and the richest in theatrical effects. Camus gives full play to
a macabre, inventive form of "black" humor, using for its
maximum effect the strange mad acts Suetonius records. The
dramatic situation is simple and its dynamism authentic. On
the one hand are the Patricians, types rather than characters,
straw men who incarnate the complacent, righteous attitudes
of good citizens; on the other is the all-powerful Emperor,
who sets out to challenge the authenticity of their attitudes
and to introduce them to the truth. At the beginning the spectator is likely to be on the side of the Emperor, on the side of
his truth against their shams. But as the perspective changes
the spectator reluctantly abandons Caligula, though not to
join the Patricians.

Caligula's educational method is direct. Like Hamlet, he
deliberately stages a play within a play; he reserves the main
part for himself, impersonating his own truth, taking upon
himself "the stupid and incomprehensible" aspect of "the
gods." To his subjects he leaves only one role, that of victim,
and in their anguished faces he eagerly searches for the horror
he himself wishes to escape. In one scene after another he acts
out a wild and murderous double parody: the parody of the

absurd working of social institutions, the parody of the no less absurd workings of fate. He violates all the rules of both games as he applies his system arbitrarily in all realms of life from table manners to religious ritual. All men, in terms of the natural order of things, are condemned to death: therefore all men, according to the legal language of society, are guilty.[1] This is the first axiom on which Caligula works. Caligula, the Emperor, represents the natural order of things, therefore all Caligula's subjects are guilty, therefore Caligula can treat them as he wishes. The "Treatise on Execution" he claims he is writing develops this amiable theme.

In the capricious scheme of humiliation, cruelty, and murder that Caligula then works out for the practical application of his theory, he sets the stage, calls the tune, changes the rules at will; he takes the wife of a Patrician under the man's eyes as he might take a glass of wine; he confiscates possessions, imposes humiliating duties upon the Patricians, creates an artificial famine in his empire, impersonates Venus in a burlesque religious ceremony, and ever and always tortures and condemns to death.

On the stage, act by act, we watch Caligula unconcernedly destroy the Patrician's unconscious assumption: if life is conducted according to certain rules, life will be righteous and secure. But whereas before the Emperor's revelation the Patricians lived in a perhaps harmless enough state of complacent blindness with regard to their ultimate fate, they are now plunged into a world so deadly in its arbitrary mechanisms that they cannot tolerate its existence. From the beginning of Act II in *Caligula* a wave of revolt arises; refusing the role of victim allotted to them, not by nature but by a fellow man, their emperor, the Patricians at last become rebels. Their

[1] This is, in fact, a drastic simplification of the reasoning behind the Judeo-Christian assumption of man's original sin and guilt.

complacency is destroyed; Caligula's rule is intolerable and Caligula's pedagogical career is at an end.

This is, however, only an outer line of action and it is, perhaps, a weakness in an otherwise powerful and original play that there is a disproportion between the theatrical force of the outer spectacle—the somewhat too facile *reductio ad absurdum* and re-education of the Patricians—and the tragic inner drama of which it is only a counterpart. One tends to lose sight of the real conflict and the real tragedy, which is personal and not essentially social in kind. The real center of the play must be sought in Caligula's relationship with himself and with the people of his own race: his friends, Helicon, Scipio, and Cherea; his mistress, Caesonia. They alone participate in his inner drama and each at some point will leave Caligula,[2] who moves beyond them until he faces only his own immeasurable solitude. Caligula's inner tragedy is marked by two symbolic gestures: at the end of Act I he wipes from the mirror the past image of himself; at the end of the play he breaks the mirror and the intolerable image it reflects.[3] Thus before his assassination at the hands of both his subjects and his former friends he admits his self-destruction.

"You have not recognized your real enemy," says Cherea at the beginning of Act II, as the Patricians begin to plot Caligula's death. It is to Caligula's friends that we must turn for the real action and intent of the play. Drusilla's death revealed to Caligula that men die and are not happy. In a world ruled by death human happiness is an illusion, since human life has lost its value. In order to live at all Caligula must, therefore, have something beyond life—the moon, the

[2] In the 1958 version of the play Helicon remains faithful to the Emperor to the very end.

[3] In the Broadway production the mirror was smashed at the end of Act I, and not at the end of Act IV as in the 1945 version.

impossible—and to Helicon he entrusts the mission of getting the moon. The Patrician's real enemy is in the very logic of this conclusion; Caligula, Cherea warns, is a man moved by the highest and most mortal passion, a "philosophy without objections," negating man and the world. And Caligula is "the only artist who has brought his thought and his action into harmony." Therein lies his power, the attraction which emanates from him, and his significance. He is the mad Emperor who, in Camus's eyes, holds sway over a time—our time—which tends to consider an individual life as nothing compared to the moon, that symbol of any ideal state lying beyond the limits of our present lives.

Caligula's problem—how to live without hope—is solved in different ways by Helicon, Caesonia, Scipio, and Cherea, those alter egos with whom he can, to a certain limit, converse. Helicon is the "spectator" of Caligula, he who fails to get the moon for the Emperor and who with Caesonia is the Emperor's henchman. In the 1958 version of the play Camus etched his figure more clearly than before. A former slave, freed by Caligula, he despises the futility, selfishness, and cowardice of the "free men" who run the state. For Helicon the Emperor's experiment is perfectly legitimate; anything is better than insignificance and the *status quo*.

Caesonia knows no truth other than that of her body and to this truth she is faithful unto death—as she is faithful to Caligula. Her body tells her quite early in the game what Caligula discovers only in the end: that the Emperor's enterprise is useless. "If evil is on this earth, why wish to add to it?" she asks. And to the Emperor's contention that he must "give the impossible a chance," she opposes the suggestion that "what is possible also deserves to have its chance." Inevitably Caligula's revolt against death leads him to destroy this voice too purely of the flesh, that flesh which he hates because it is marked for death. His last act will be to strangle Caesonia deliberately.

Scipio, the seventeen-year-old poet, is carried forward in life on a great tide of love—love for the beauty of the earth, love for others, love for Caligula. Caligula, who cold-bloodedly murders Scipio's father, will teach him the value of hatred. "Pure in good" as Caligula is "pure in evil," Scipio draws from his initiation into the dark injustices of life a powerful commitment on the side of all that lives against all that kills. It obliges him to take sides against the Emperor.[4]

Like Caligula, Cherea "lives within the truth" without delusion and without hope, and it is he alone who can confront the Emperor and come out unharmed. For he lives in an intermediate zone between Caligula and Caesonia; he has accepted not only the "meaning of death" but also the certainty of life. He has no need for the moon, and it is he who challenges the wisdom of Caligula's attempt to bring one's thought and actions into harmony. For he recognizes a realm superior to the realm of thought, the relative human order in which reign those "truths of the flesh" that are lived and not demonstrated. These Caligula bypasses or destroys in his longing for the absolute. Since without these Cherea cannot live, the Emperor becomes his enemy.

Step by step in the play Caligula's being is dislocated, emptied of humanity. For one brief instant at the end Caligula faces what he has become, not a superman but a solitary, desperate, frightened, empty shell: Caligula or the state of inhuman nothingness; "I am nothing . . . Nothing, Caligula, nothing."

All three levels of the drama—the awakening of the Patricians, the rejection of Caligula by his friends, Caligula's own

---

[4] In the 1945 version of the play Scipio is among the murderers of Caligula; in the 1958 version he leaves Rome, wounded deeply but unable to kill his former friend.

self-destruction—reach their climax in Act IV when Caligula calls upon the poets to compete: "Topic: Death—time limit, one minute." After a hilarious parody of various poetic approaches, in which Camus as author takes great delight, Scipio presents his poem on death:

> Pursuit of happiness which makes men pure,
> Sky streaming with sunlight,
> Unique and wild celebrations, my rapture without hope.

And indeed, in its entirety the play is a dramatic interpretation of this theme. Caligula himself, in a subterranean way, is an ally of these expansive forces of life which he negates, releasing them in the Patricians, sparing them when he meets them in Scipio and Cherea. The play itself is a cry of alarm and a call to awareness, as Camus discerns in our apathy a sickness of the heart and mind which may lead us to sell our human birthright for a mental delusion we call certainty. Through Caligula, therefore, Camus challenges us to think. But perhaps it is too much to ask of the average spectator that he move, unprepared, into this fairly complex mental universe. Nonetheless, one cannot easily forget Caligula and his bitter experiment nor the price he pays: "I did not take the right path, I have accomplished nothing. My liberty was not of the right kind." The play, in all its aspects, stands high among contemporary productions. In the years after 1938 the road of history so closely followed the pattern of action of Camus's Caligula that the last words of the Emperor have a prophetic ring: "I am still alive."

L'Etat de siège merely projects upon the stage, in broader perspectives and more massive effects, the outer impact of a Caligula-like social experiment. The themes in the two plays are essentially the same, but whereas in Caligula it is only the action of the individual that matters, the action in *L'Etat de siège* involves a city as an entity, as Camus moves from a metaphysical to a social plane. The inhabitants of Cadiz live as a matter of course in the natural fullness of a life accepted unquestioningly; a vague traditional social order subsists, inefficient and without content, represented by the governor, the judge, the church. The Plague imposes upon Cadiz a rigid bureaucratic collective organization, a theoretical abstract order, a mechanical social order similar to the mechanical laws that govern the universe. From this, Camus draws a number of more or less facile burlesque effects. But, like Caligula's arbitrary government, the rule of the Plague is life-destroying: it eliminates love, freedom, and adventure, the very substance of human life. Justice becomes vengeance; love turns into hatred; honor becomes cowardice; the flow of human words carrying questions, comments, answers, fears, doubts, and delights is stopped, as all mouths are gagged. This until Diego, the young student and lover, out of the excess of his despair shouts the words of revolt which loosen the gags, free the citizens, save his love, and cost him his life.

For in Cadiz—as elsewhere perhaps—justice does not lie primarily in the judge, nor in the law; power is not in the government nor in force; and love is not contained in a word. This Nada sees—Nada, the nihilist, the destructive principle *par excellence*—and he aligns himself wholeheartedly with the Plague in his immeasurable Caligula-like contempt for such irrational imaginary entities. And the devilish parody of social order takes over as the source of order is perverted.

The force of revolt in this play is embodied in the hero, Diego, who becomes a central and unambiguous figure as he escapes from the deadly grip of the Plague. He stirs up the latent forces of energy and freedom among the inhabitants of Cadiz, awakening the citizens from their lethargy, calling them back to life.

The pattern is simple and clear: like the Patricians, the

people of Cadiz have fallen prey to a negative, rationalizing power, a power destructive at its very source, a false god, a false pope, wrought out of their failure to trust the great generous forces of the life they feel within them. Their salvation lies in an attack upon the usurper and depends upon their faith in the expansive energies of love and imagination which assure their victory over the negative, subversive power of the mind divorced from the heart.

More even than in *Caligula*, the spectator must accept the characters not as personalities but as abstract forces incarnate, those very forces whose existence Nada would deny. They are there in their positive form: courage in Diego, pure love in Victoria, for example; and in their negative form they are perverted incarnations: law without justice in the judge, government without power in the governor, power without humanity in the Plague. The movement of the play itself is contained in the images projected on the stage: the imprisonment behind the closed doors of Cadiz, for example; the movement toward sunlight and air; the bursting open of the bonds of slavery which accompanies Diego's rebellion and victory. Two atmospheres struggle, rather than two ideas, rather than two clear-cut conceptions of good and evil.

In *L'Etat de siège*, as in *Caligula*, it is the atmosphere that counts; this is a difficult medium to handle, yet one that Camus had to attempt to master if he was to project upon the stage what he wished to convey. The two dangers he attacks are indifference and abstraction, those two facets of a latent nihilism which, he seems to indicate, are already in control of our institutions. Indifference and abstraction make of our human values empty concepts and shameless parodies, delivering us up as captives to the absurd. The stage in Camus's hands, therefore, becomes the *décor* of a mental universe, and the characters that live their short lives upon it are reasons, emotions, forces, inner and outer attitudes, which try to impose their own form upon the play, creating the situation and the inner dynamism of the action. Allegorical in nature, these two plays have very little connection with the current "well-made" psychological or realistic play, and yet by their very realistic technique they remain outside the realm of the so-called poetic drama.

Both plays deal with a form of alienation, and in each case the alienation is simultaneously individual and social. *Caligula* goes from the individual to the social; *L'Etat de siège* from the social to the individual. In both plays the dramatic difficulty lies in the presence on the stage of two kinds of beings both embodied by actors. Caligula and Cherea embody beings of different caliber: as Caligula becomes stronger Cherea fails to reach the stature he needs to play his part as opponent to Caligula. The Plague and his secretary are distinguished from the rest of the cast by the type of costumes they wear, but their relations with such human beings as Diego are disconcerting, for it is hard to project death on the stage in the form of a secretary with a notebook and keep a coherent dramatic atmosphere. But it is harder still to project a sort of double allegory, to project the plague, for example, simultaneously in the form of a mediocre bureaucrat and as a social disaster incarnating a totalitarian tyranny. Diego himself is essentially the incarnation of an attitude—the force opposed to Nada's nihilism and yet a human being in love with Victoria.

In both these plays through essentially nonhuman characters Camus sets up forms of "logical delirium" to which he gives full rein; he allows them to act at first as though they were autonomous, uninvolved in any reality beyond their own, and then proceeds to show how they mutilate that part of humanity which they ignore and how eventually they are destroyed by it. Beyond the willing suspension of disbelief necessary for the enjoyment of any theater, the two plays consequently require that the spectator be aware that the play, the make-believe on the stage, contains a meaning beyond itself. And here Camus leaves much to the spectator, refusing to state his themes in rational terms—as does, for example, Sartre —within the dialogue of the play. The dialogue consequently has a hieroglyphic quality which is at first puzzling, as this dialogue between Helicon and Caligula on Caligula's return clearly illustrates:

> HELICON: You look tired.
> CALIGULA: I walked a great deal.
> HELICON: Yes, you were away a long time (*silence*).
> CALIGULA: It was difficult to find.
> HELICON: To find what?
> CALIGULA: What I wanted.
> HELICON: And what did you want?
> CALIGULA: (*still in a matter-of-fact tone*) The moon.
> HELICON: What?
> CALIGULA: Yes, I wanted the moon.
> HELICON: Ah!

In its matter-of-fact nonchalance this exchange of remarks is an excellent bit of dialogue, but in terms of its meaning it moves too fast for the unprepared spectator, and for the moment at least both its meaning and its relation to the action on the stage may well be lost to him. To Camus, dialogue is not an explanation of action; it cannot be divorced from action and yet it is not a comment on it. To understand the dialogue the spectator must first grasp the play in its totality and then follow an intellectual path as Camus designates it. This path leads not only toward a discussion of ideas—that is relatively habitual and easy—but it leads also toward the delineation of issues that touch upon an experience of life and cannot be stated in simple terms of right and wrong. In *Caligula* and *L'Etat de siège*, the spectacle itself, disconcerting though it be in terms of our theatrical habits, may be suffi·

ciently rich to hold the attention of the spectators during the performance, but this is not so true of either *Le Malentendu* or *Les Justes*.

Le Malentendu is entirely symbolical. The land-locked inn in the center of Europe where mother and daughter so reluctantly carry out their self-imposed duty of murder; the silent servant; the son Jan, who brings with him a wealth of love and life in his wife, his fortune, and his experience of happiness—all these are symbolic rather than human. But Maria, the son's wife, seems to be an ordinary human being, and Jan himself moves between the two levels or two dimensions of the play, halfway between the human and the symbolic. And yet it is Jan's adventure which furnishes the meaning behind the spectacle—a meaning not easily or quickly grasped.

From the strictly realistic point of view of the psychological play with a well-constructed plot, *Le Malentendu* fails to answer one question: For what reason did the son Jan first abandon the inn, his mother and sister? No psychological play would have left the question unanswered. Camus does not give us any reason for Jan's long absence nor does he explain, very satisfactorily, the reason for Jan's return. Though Jan says that he realized, at his father's death, that he was needed, this hardly tallies with the weary round of murder with which his mother and sister had been so long engaged. And the dead father is artificially introduced, one feels, only to "make sense" in terms of the "well-made" play where all is rationally explained; in the symbolic structure of the play it is no more than an irrelevant detail. Nothing in *Le Malentendu* can or need be rationally explained: it is not a psychological play.

The first act of *Le Malentendu* introduces the two forces that will precipitate all four participants into disaster. First the mechanism of murder set off automatically by the stranger's arrival:

MARTHA: Mother, we must kill him.

MOTHER: No doubt we must kill him.

MARTHA: You speak strangely.

MOTHER: I am tired, it is true. And I wish that he at least could be the last. It is terribly tiring to kill. And though it matters little to me whether I die facing the sea or in the center of our plains, I should like it if, afterwards, we could leave together.

MARTHA: We shall leave and it will be a great moment! Make an effort, mother, there is little to do. You know that it's not even a question of murder. He'll drink his tea, he'll sleep, and while he is still alive we'll carry him to the river.

In the meantime Jan is carrying out a plan of his own. "I came here to bring my fortune and, if I can, happiness." But to the question his wife, Maria, raises, Jan gives no answer. "There is only one way," Maria replies. "It's to do what the first-comer would do, to say, 'Here I am,' to let one's heart speak."

JAN: The heart is not so simple.

MARIA: But it uses only simple words. And it wouldn't be very difficult to say: "I am your son, this is my wife. I've lived with her in a country we loved, facing the sea and the sun. But I was not happy enough and today I need you."

JAN: Don't be unfair, Maria. I don't need them, but I realize that they must need me and that a man is never alone.

Like Martha, his sister, Jan thinks in terms of duty. He has come "to find his mother and country" on the one condition that his family recognize him. Recognition is the key denouement of innumerable plays: recognition of the hero's real situation in tragedy, recognition of identity in drama and comedy. Jan, drugged by the tea his sister serves him, will never know

what his real situation is nor his destiny. And Martha and
the mother will recognize Jan's identity only after he is dead
when, too late, they grasp the tragic irony of their situation.
But here again the recognition by means of an outer sign as
in drama—in this case a passport—seems extraneous to the
spirit of the play, which hesitates, poised halfway between a
suspense based on an inner hazardous progression toward the
discovery of the truth and a chance recognition by outer
material signs.

It is easy enough to follow literally the action of the play.
Martha, without knowing it, sacrifices her brother to her
dream of happiness and loses all: her dream, her brother, her
mother's love, her desire to live. The mother, in a moment of
desperate revelation, discovers love as she follows into death
the son she helped to kill. Jan fails to make the gift of love
and happiness he bore, and destroys the happiness and love
he shared with Maria. It is Martha who, in the end, draws
from that literal level of the play a first and partial "metaphysical" conclusion, as before her suicide she faces a dis-
traught Maria:

> I tell you, we are robbed. What is the use of the great ap-
> peal of our being, the great vigilance in our souls? Why
> this aspiration toward the sea or toward love? It's all de-
> rision. Your husband now knows the answer, that frightful
> home where in the end we'll all be huddled together. . . .
> Understand that your suffering will never equal the in-
> justice done man. And finally, listen to my advice. For I
> owe you some advice at least, since I killed your husband.
> Pray to your god that he make you comparable to stone.
> That's the happiness he reserves for himself, that's the
> only true happiness. Do as he does, make yourself deaf
> to all cries, and be as stone while it is still possible. But
> if you are too cowardly to enter into that blind peace,
> then come and join us in our common home. Good-bye.

my sister! Everything is easy, as you see. You can choose
between the stupid felicity of pebbles and the slimy bed
where we await you.

And as Maria cries to God for help in her distress she gets her
only answer from the old servant who at last finds a voice to
say No!

But this is not the final meaning implicit in the play. The
meaning is contained in the development of the action; it is
obscure and hard to find and it does not entirely support
Martha's interpretation. The end, of course, remains unchanged: Maria's appeal to a miraculous revelation from beyond the human realm is still rejected. The cold and haunting
distress is the same: Martha, Jan, and their mother are dead,
they have been "robbed" of the meaning of their acts. But at
each turn in the play one word could have been said or left
unsaid, one move made or not made, or a decision taken, and
perhaps the course of the action would have changed—in so
far as it could be changed. "Your method is not the right
one," cried Maria to Jan; and neither as a matter of fact is
Martha's. Someone could have looked at the passport; the
mother could have arrived in time to take away the drugged
cup of tea; Martha might have wavered had Jan not mentioned the sunny lands from which he came; and Jan might
have declared his identity.

The very structure of the play is ironical and its real implications are carried in its strange blind movement, the "illogical blind accident" of which Spengler wrote. "I shall count
on the force of things," said Jan at the beginning, strong in
his knowledge that he is the son and brother, that his intentions are generous, and that "with time" the stranger will be
recognized as the son. But the force of things is not to be
counted upon and Jan, who "is in no hurry," is already too
late. The path of murder is a path that can be followed in but
one direction, it allows for no return. Jan ignores the reality

confronting him. The tragedy is obviously conceived as a tragedy of situation, tragic because a third path perhaps could have been found not implicit in "the force of things," the nightmarish force of inertia, nor in the force of Martha's will.

All through the play the "illogical blind accident" is opposed by a "truth of the heart," a muffled truth, half heeded and never quite understood, from which comes an impression of slowness and a sense of frustration. Possibly, it implies, there is another solution besides the two Martha proposes when her enterprise fails, another choice besides the indifference of the stones or a despair which leads to suicide, a choice made from the heart.

Behind the play one senses great personal anguish and the dark years of the 1940's, when Europe had, like Camus's inhospitable inn, become a charnel house, a mother wearily slaughtering her sons, hallucinated by dreams of a future felicity. And to the generous *élan* of her favorite children who brought to her rescue their ideal of love and happiness she could answer only in death. The initial fiction of the inn is left far behind as we fumble toward a meaning veiled in the silence which the dialogue delineates but never breaks—a feat in itself.

The conception of the play is powerful and its atmosphere hallucinating, but the characters and plot never quite give form to the questions it poses. The situation and dialogue do not completely complement each other, though the words spoken—particularly by Martha—often have a resonance and an intensity worthy of tragedy. Jan and, even more, Maria are never completely convincing, and the sense of their conversation at the beginning of the play, referring as it does to a plot behind the plot, seems somewhat artificial. The mother and Martha dominate the play like two great masked figures, reducing Jan and Maria to a stature that is never quite adequate.

Les Justes might almost be called a second *Malentendu* presented in terms of a concrete political action; Yanek in a sense is a second Jan, and Dora another Martha who kills the Maria she might have been. To a normal theatergoing audience the most evident crux of the action may seem highly abstract and academic: Can a man deliberately kill another in view of the future good of all humanity? To this question Savinkov's terrorists gave an answer, an answer which *Les Justes* questions. As in Savinkov's Memoirs, the play follows the destiny of Yanek, his successive choices in successive situations, and each choice is openly debated on the stage: the choice of terrorism itself between Yanek and Stepan and between Dora and Yanek in the opening scenes of the play; the limits of terrorism between the group of terrorists after Yanek's first failure to throw the bomb; the relations of the terrorist to society, law, and religion in the prison scene; and, finally, the rebound, the effect of the terrorist's execution upon his comrades. A problem play without doubt, and a play not of one but of several situations—and therein lies its weakness. Yet there is an underlying theme, which, had it been strong, might possibly have bound the successive situations together and given the play an inner dynamism: Dora's tragic evolution.

Undoubtedly Camus's scrupulous respect for Savinkov's Memoirs hampered his treatment of Dora, yet it is Dora who carries in depth the tragic theme which is not Savinkov's but Camus's. Only at the end of the play, when the fact of Yanek's death really penetrates Dora's being, does this theme break through. Is Yanek's death, accepted and foreseen, really justified by the abstract hope in a better future for Russia? The immediate impact of his death is to empty Dora of hope, to draw her away from Yanek's universe of love and fraternity into Stepan's deadly world of vengeance and hatred. Dora has

entered the grim inn of *Le Malentendu* and will follow in
Martha's footsteps.

But along the way the play, situation by situation, explicitly
raises a number of questions implicit in its title *Les Justes*.
Until the end of the third act and the throwing of the bomb,
the question is debated from the point of view of the terrorists: Russia and her people suffer from injustice and the suffering is intolerable. All agree that the Grand Duke, the incarnation of injustice, must die, for to kill the Grand Duke is
a step toward establishing justice. The "just," therefore, have
judged and condemned: the Grand Duke is guilty and the
sentence of death is justified.

But the problem then shifts from the logical to the ethical:
for Yanek, injustice must be fought in the name of life, love,
and happiness for all. For Stepan, who has just come out of
prison, who has already been a victim of the law, injustice
must be fought in the name of hatred and vengeance. For
Yanek and Dora, though the death of the Grand Duke is
necessary, to kill is evil, thus he who kills enters into a pact
with injustice. The killer is guilty, so he must die, but he is
his own judge and executioner; the double human sacrifice
saves his act from the stigma of human irresponsibility. For
Stepan, the Grand Duke is justly condemned and his death
is a matter not of guilt but of rejoicing. Yanek and Dora respect the human being beneath the abstraction; Stepan has
nothing but contempt for him.

The second debate, centering upon Yanek's refusal to kill
two children, is merely a prolongation of the first: it further
delineates the problem of the individual responsibility of the
"just judges" and the nature of their verdict. To kill children
is, to Yanek, an act of both social and human injustice, which
turns into murder his difficult act of justice. For Stepan, a
couple of children are of no account when they stand in the

path of justice; in his eyes Yanek's sense of responsibility should not be first for human beings but for results.

After the throwing of the bomb the spotlight shifts, as it did in *L'Etranger,* to the existing social forms of justice; the debate continues as various codes of justice clash. First Foka comes face to face with Yanek. Foka, a prisoner and criminal who killed three people in a fit of drunkenness, is now the executioner, and every execution cancels one year of his sentence. The irony is obvious and perhaps a little artificial. Yanek admits that Foka—even in murder—is his brother, but he refuses to admit Foka's contention that they are brother executioners. And his conduct supports his point, for he refuses all alibis and goes voluntarily to his death.

Skouratov, the chief of police, is a Stepan further along in his career. "One begins by wanting justice and one ends by organizing a system of police," he states as he interviews Yanek. The debate with him prepares the audience for the entrance of the Christian Grand Duchess, when Skouratov, setting aside the theoretical aspect of the problem, puts it in terms of the flesh-and-blood destruction of a man:

KALIAYEV: I threw a bomb against tyranny.

SKOURATOV: No doubt. But it's the man who got it. . . .

KALIAYEV: I carried out a verdict.

SKOURATOV: No doubt. No doubt. We've nothing against the verdict. What is a verdict? It's a word around which one can argue through night after night. What we don't like . . . no, you wouldn't care for the word . . . Shall we say that it is the amateurishness of the thing, its slight untidiness. The results are unquestionable. Everybody saw them. Ask the Grand Duchess. There was blood, you understand, a lot of blood.

For Skouratov, justice is a matter of appearances: blood is an "untidy thing" and ideas live in a harmless world all their own. What is essential for Skouratov is that Kaliayev play according to the rules of the game: he must admit he is guilty, and if he repents and atones by giving information to the police concerning his organization, he will obtain his grace. In his system of values the Christian approach to the problem comes merely as a help to the police. His matter-of-fact proposal is violently rejected by Kaliayev, but before he leaves he fires a parting shot: "If your idea is not strong enough to kill children, does it warrant you to kill a Grand Duke for its sake?" Like Stepan, he cannot see the value of a limit.

It is with the Grand Duchess that Yanek Kaliayev first really faces the human consequences of his crime and its essential absurdity, for, as the Duchess tells him, the man he killed was a man who dozed after lunch and who spoke of justice as does Kaliayev, whereas the children he spared are not innocent but already hardhearted and afraid of the poor. The theme of justice is now replaced by the theme of injustice: "Certainly you, too, are unjust. The earth is a desert," says the Grand Duchess. And from this universal guilt of man she appeals to God's forgiveness and justice; but in this universal guilt she drowns Kaliayev's one strength: his sense of personal responsibility. It is the sense of personal responsibility, not of guilt, that carries Kaliayev to a death worthy of a man; his self-respect is the force that gives him faith in his oneness with his group. Kaliayev has escaped from the senseless social machinery of murder and reprisal which Stepan and Skouratov embody; he lives, kills, and dies without contempt. Therein lies the "exemplary" value of the play. As Camus pointed out in an article, there is a world between a Kaliayev and the "complacent" bureaucratic organizers of mass murder in our time.

Les Justes, like *Le Malentendu*, may not seem at first fully to come to life on the stage, but that it lives in its full force in the universe of Albert Camus is unquestionable. In a sense *Les Justes* delineates more clearly than any of the three other plays the issues which Camus raises and which concern him deeply. The greatest tragedy for any man in Camus's theatrical world, whether Caligula, Martha, or even Kaliayev, is to make of this earth "a desert," that is, to destroy that part of life which is joy and love or, in the case of a social tyranny like that of the plague, to make their enjoyment nearly impossible. A second tragic error is to abandon that which gives man his dignity: his sense of responsibility. In each play just such a destruction lies at the source of the action; when the sense of responsibility is perverted it becomes a sense of guilt which in its wake brings the judge and with him collective humiliation and collective irresponsibility. Tragically dangerous also are the forms which revolt can take, in this state of separateness and irresponsibility, as the result of the aspiration of a human being for happiness and coherence, for example such perverted forms as the "logical delirium" of Caligula or Martha's murderous dream of a future Eden. Such revolt ends in the destruction of others and the annihilation of self.

The society attacked by the Plague or challenged by Caligula or Kaliayev seems unaware of the mortal dangers inherent in its own structure. Through these plays Camus obviously attacks a society he sees as using three main forms of persuasion, all conducive to irresponsibility: mystification, miracle, and abstract authority. Of these Caligula makes short shrift.

Camus's characters on the stage move between two limits: the irresponsibility of a Foka and the monstrous perversions of a Caligula or a Martha. The fluctuations of the play project the anguished experience of these individuals as they measure the distance between their aspirations and the realities offered by both society and the cosmos.

Essentially the combat is an inner one, as heart and mind struggle in their attempt to come to terms. And it is the mind in each play that forces the issue that starts the action: the mind with its totalitarian logic that sets up its own tribunal and tries to impose upon reality the coherent world of certainties in which it feels at ease and justified. Caligula or the Plague attempts to operate this transmutation; and, because all men escape in part from irrefutable logic, all men, in their eyes, are guilty.

This intellectual perversion is what Camus fought as he also fought the social solution offered by certain proponents of Christianity, the solution proposed by Dostoevsky's Grand Inquisitor. "You have elevated men and taught them pride," accuses the Grand Inquisitor, judging Christ. The perversion of Christ's message he proposes is to keep men humble and satisfied with simple "permitted joys," to make them deaf to that "great inner aspiration" of which Martha speaks. In contrast, Camus proposes in each of his plays that man "be proud of his revolt," but that the revolt be, like Diego's, one of the heart and not merely of the head. Beyond the order of the universe with its mechanism indifferent to humans, beyond the constructs of logic, and beyond the empty forms of social irresponsibility lies the possibility of reaching a human order conciliating heart and head, truth and aspiration. It cannot be argued, it can be lived, and each play shows that it cannot be denied. That is why, no doubt, Dostoevsky's world furnished Camus with those elements he most needed as playwright and why *Les Possédés* is perhaps, with *Caligula*, his best play.

It may well be that Camus's plays will never be popular as theater; the vision they seek to express is confined too narrowly perhaps to Camus's intimate experience and may not be immediately evident to his spectators. And in his effort to give the theater a language cut down to the essential, Camus may not have always succeeded in creating the perspectives a spectator needs in order to catch the mood of the play and its general orientation, if not its meaning. It may well be, too, that a great tragic theater needs to rely on semilegendary, semihistorical figures which cannot be created and for which the allegorical figure of "any" man cannot be substituted. Dora cannot become the equivalent of an Electra, nor Jan of an Orestes, nor can the spectator accept their situation with the same abandon.

But the nature of the problem raised in Camus's plays, the quality of the language, and the originality of the dramatic situations lift them out of the immediate and the topical. It is quite clear that they are not dictated by a theoretical approach, such as permits the deft handling of the current problem play. They move from the concrete to the abstract and not in the reverse direction. Whether the concrete situation is strong enough to carry the full weight of the thought is debatable. For the larger screen against which these plays—far more than the novels—need to be projected we must turn to Camus's essays, where the inner fluctuations of Camus's thought and experience clarify and define the full implications, tragic scope, and dramatic significance of his theater.

19

Essays in Meditation

"Les mythes n'ont point de vie par eux-mêmes.
Ils attendent que nous les réincarnions."

We can "no longer choose our problems. They choose us,
one after the other. Let us accept being so chosen." [1] Certain
problems rather than others equally pertinent to the time
"elected" Albert Camus. They seemed to him to be the crucial problems of his epoch, and he reflected upon them with
an ardent singleness of mind which found expression in essays
of varying length and importance. So basic to Camus is the
essay or personal meditation as a form of expression that even
his short editorials tend toward it. One may, however, if one
limits one's attention to the major essays—*Le Mythe de
Sisyphe* and *L'Homme révolté*, and the eight separate essays
of *L'Eté*—distinguish two different uses of the form: those
essays in which Camus elucidates certain intellectual attitudes, giving the basic orientation of his thought, and those
in which he pursues the type of lyrical meditation so successfully initiated by *Noces*.

But all Camus's essays are marked by personal emotion,
by the same recurrent imagery, the same intellectual preoccupations. Even as apparently objective an essay as his "*Réflexions sur la guillotine*" [2] is permeated with an emotional content that goes back to his early youth. The guillotine, the condemnation to death, are leitmotivs of his work. His essays

[1] *L'Homme révolté*, introduction, p. 15.
[2] In *Réflexions sur la peine capitale* (Paris: Calmann-Lévy, 1957),
pp. 123-180.

contain a record of the inner life of a man whose passionate reactions to the world around him led him to select certain themes, dramatically reducing all problems to a few "givens." Within the essay an inner conviction establishes the relationships, both logical and imaginative, and drives the thought to a conclusion already implicit in the initial and compelling emotion.

It is fallacious to seek a logical system of abstract reasoning in Camus's works. Camus himself speaks of certainties, convictions. All his meditations are intrinsically lyrical and eloquent in nature, though some tend toward demonstration. If a passionate logic does err, it errs gravely, as Camus himself recognizes. When, at the time of the collaborationist trials following World War II, the discussion on justice versus charity opposed him to François Mauriac, he was able then to justify an attitude which he later admitted was basically passionate, not rational, and one he deplored. A part of his work, particularly his first plays and *L'Homme révolté*, is directly or indirectly concerned with the dangers of this form of logic, revealing, perhaps, how familiar these dangers were to Camus.

But this is also why Camus was able to single out a few basic terms or images, current coinage in the intellectual verbiage of his time, and to charge them with a violence of his own, thus polarizing some of the major intellectual assumptions which feed the often nebulous thought of the average reader. The word "absurd," for example, in all its connotations from its current daily usage to its more specialized meaning—contrary to the requirements of reason—was familiar to a generation brought up on Dostoevsky, Nietzsche, Kierkegaard, and Kafka, a generation which felt at home with the basic assumptions of the phenomenologist and existentialist philosophers. The word "revolt" had been common enough since the romantics; it had become inevitable since the surrealists had made it a key to their world, and Malraux the motivating force of his fictional human universe.

But in Camus's work these words are starkly isolated and accompanied by reiterated images. Some of these images are dominant—Sisyphus, the plague, Prometheus; some merely passing—the Minotaur, Helen of Troy, almond trees, summer. Some are part of Camus's mature vocabulary, interwoven into his demonstrations—the stranger, the exile, the man condemned to death, the prisoner, the prince without a kingdom, the desert, the royal way, the arid, desolate way. Others are more limited in their use but equally eloquent—the gambler, the actor, the conqueror, Don Juan, Don Quixote, the creator. The process here is no different from the stylization, so clearly discernible in *Noces*, whereby Camus coins his personal idiom: simple, easily recognizable entities become charged with a complex, intense suggestiveness rather than with a definite meaning, and play a fixed role in his inner universe— the sun, the sea, Algiers, or Florence, for example. How much more accessible is this idiom to the average reader than the abstract vocabulary thrown into circulation by the followers of Sartre! The readability of Camus's work is one of its assets.

And, indeed, his aim was not to demonstrate but to give thought its legitimate place in our lives. One of his avowed purposes was to break that widespread dichotomy whereby the hyperconscious twentieth-century individual somewhat indecisively lives his daily life according to two often contradictory sets of rules: one set for practical or social purposes, one set for the exercise of his intelligence; and so the "game" of life is eluded. Camus's immediate predecessors—Bernanos, Saint-Exupéry, Malraux—were concerned with wresting from the recalcitrant human being a conduct consistent with a certain mode of thought. Camus was intent on forging a consciousness consistent with a daily mode of life, and this, peremptorily, first for himself.

Critics have sometimes accused Camus of not being a consistent thinker, of tackling problems for which he was ill-equipped; this accusation was current during the controversy that raged around *L'Homme révolté*, where the unfortunate use of the argument *ad hominem* often blurred the issue. But Camus was always at some pains to explain that he was not undertaking either to build or to refute a system of thought. His essays are direct meditations on questions that proved obsessively important to him and which, in his judgment, were also characteristic of a time in which he participated.

One may question the validity of Camus's generalization of his own intellectual experience, but one cannot refute his argument, for it is descriptive in nature. The point of view is admittedly partial, but it is perfectly clear and, within its own system of definition, perfectly consistent. The tone is dictatorial. If he forgets the initial definition, the reader may balk at almost every statement. When Camus says "All sane human beings having thought of their own suicide . . . ,"[3] he has, temporarily, defined "sane" as the characteristic of those who think of their own suicide, and by the sheer force of his statement he rapidly herds all his readers into that category. Upon this imperious and deft manipulation, he then proceeds to build an irrefutable argument. And yet a couple of paragraphs before this, he had written "To begin to think is to begin to be sapped," an apparent contradiction.

What "sane" human being would accept the following conclusion simply as it stands: "The world then will no longer be divided between the just and the unjust, but between the masters and the slaves."[4] When was the world ever "divided between the just and the unjust"? Or again: "All great actions and all great thoughts have insignificant beginnings."[5] Do

[3] *Le Mythe de Sisyphe*, p. 18.
[4] *L'Homme révolté*, p. 16.
[5] *Le Mythe de Sisyphe*, p. 26.

they indeed? Cannot one exception be found to deflate so blatant a generalization? It is very easy to destroy Camus's argumentation, sentence by sentence. But what of it? Rhetoric sometimes opens the way to thought and what matters most is the movement of the essay as a whole, the point of departure, the orientation, the *form* imposed upon the material. The conclusion is not demonstrated, *it* demonstrates. It is implicit in the opening sentence, arrived at beforehand, and proceeds peremptorily to dispose of any denial or hesitation, incontrovertible as a musical theme.

How personal the point of view, how passionate the reasoning, becomes still more evident when we recognize that all Camus's thought inevitably led him to a discussion of the question of art: his own problem as writer. So important is the role he gave to art, as evidenced in many lectures and essays, that it warrants special consideration.[6] All roads lead back to it. Never was a man more deeply and passionately committed in spite of the studied objectivity of the tone he liked to adopt.

Camus sometimes humorously complained that his thought was being detailed out in slogans for the evening papers: "I no longer say, even in a casual way, 'how absurd.' There are other terms, too, that always turn up in reference to me: limit, measure. I'll have to renew my adjectives. A tiring job."[7] Yet this, as we have seen, is an almost inevitable consequence of a certain quality in his idiom.

In the years when Sartre's name was almost always followed by "and Camus," Camus rather ironically disclaimed any connection with existentialism. "Perhaps I'll really have to make up my mind to study existentialism"[8] was an obvious

[6] Discussed in chapter 24.

[7] Frank Josserand, *"Interview avec Albert Camus,"* in *La Gazette de Lausanne*, No. 73, Mar. 27-28, 1954, p. 9.

[8] Jeanine Delpech, *"Interview avec Albert Camus."* In *Les Nouvelles littéraires*, No. 954, Nov. 15, 1945.

quip on the part of a man who, a few moments before, had stated: "the only book concerned with ideas that I have published, *Le Mythe de Sisyphe*, was directed against the so-called existentialist philosophers."

Camus was quite familiar with the main precursors and exponents of existentialist thinking, at least in so far as the broad lines of their respective systems of thought were concerned. Nietzsche he read thoroughly and with passionate attention after 1937, and he was fighting against Nietzsche more than any other philosopher, or at least against certain facets of Nietzsche's thought. Besides Nietzsche one can cite lesser names—Gobineau, Sorel, Spengler—quotations from whom appear in his Notebooks. He was not drawn to Kierkegaard, whom he read with some attention, but was sympathetic to the passionate rhetoric of Chestov. One may wonder if he delved into the works of Husserl, Heidegger, and Jaspers with more than the perfunctory interest required by a university course of study, and he seems, at the very outset, to have inherited Jean Grenier's critical reserve toward Hegel and Marx. But, taken all in all, Camus's philosophical background was much broader than that of the average well-educated reader of his generation, though it was not that of a professional philosopher like Sartre. Camus was instinctively drawn to the nonsystematic philosophers in much the same way as he was attracted to certain novelists: Dostoevsky, for example, whose universe thoroughly permeated his own; [9] Melville,[10] whose *Moby Dick* exercised a powerful hold over his

[9] Some of Dostoevsky's basic themes are also Camus's: Dostoevsky's preoccupation with capital punishment, for example, as exemplified in the person of Prince Muichkine; his characters who play their lives out on desperate intellectual premises carried to their logical extremes, such as Ivan Karamazov, or Kirilov; the sense of the strangeness of life as expressed in, among others, Muichkine. The very form of *La Chute* recalls Dostoevsky's *Notes from the Underground* and the scene on the bridge recalls *The Double*.

[10] The first notes on Melville in Camus's Notebooks appear in 1938.

imagination and whose *Billy Budd* is not unrelated to *L'Etranger*.

Camus seemed to read the works of philosophers much as he read literature, that is, essentially for the light they threw on his own thought. Literature has an advantage here, for it also offers technical suggestions of form and style. Though with a good deal more restraint, Camus was, in a sense, comparable to those partial and implacable logicians of passion, Dimitri and Ivan Karamazov and Raskolnikov. "What did I do but reason about an idea which I found floating around the streets in my time? It goes without saying that I nurtured the idea (and that a part of me still nurtures it) with all my generation. I simply stood at a sufficient distance from it to discuss it and judge its logic." [11] And this as a means to self-discovery, a self-discovery that was never complete: "No man can say what he is. But it sometimes happens that he can say what he isn't. He who is still looking is then judged to have concluded. A thousand voices already announce what he has found, whereas he knows it is not that." [12] Other people's thinking interested him less for its intrinsic values than for those particular moments when it either coincided or entered into conflict with his own. He then took what seemed to him essential, indifferent to its origin and often to its exact connotations within its own system of reference. His essays are literary in nature, not specialized; they are addressed to the layman, not to the professional philosopher.[13]

[11] "*L'Enigme*," in *L'Eté*, p. 133 (allusion to *Le Mythe de Sisyphe*).
[12] *Ibid.*, p. 124.
[13] This was particularly evident in the controversy that opposed Camus to the philosopher Francis Jeanson in 1952. The discussion around *L'Homme révolté* (*Les Temps modernes*, Nos. 79, 82) evolves on two separate planes. The misunderstanding is total.

20

Vies Absurdes

". . . devant cette clarté blanche et noire qui,
pour moi, a toujours été celle de la vérité . . ."

Le Mythe de Sisyphe is the work of a young man. Camus
started to think about an essay on *l'absurde* as early as 1938.
The final work, which is, in fact, a set of essays rather than one
essay, really centers on the problem of happiness, a major
preoccupation of Camus's in the late 1930's, and around
which, as we have seen, he had attempted to organize a first
novel. And the novelist is not absent from the essays, for the
hero of the conquest of happiness in the essays is *l'homme
absurde,* to whom Camus devotes a major portion of the book,
describing with obvious pleasure the different, most revealing
forms *l'homme absurde* takes in his imagination.

But, in the young Camus's eyes, it is not possible to understand *l'homme absurde* until the stage has been swept
clean to prepare for his entrance. The first part of *Le Mythe
de Sisyphe* carries out this drastic operation. For once, the
game of life is to be strictly and truthfully described, its
rules laid down clearly for the first time. There is much
charm in this youthful certainty and determination, so much,
indeed, that this part of the book can overshadow the second
part and the ethics of happiness, which the first part was
designed merely to prepare.

The foreword briefly states that the essays are concerned
with a certain *mal*—a sickness or evil—prevalent in the sensibility of the time. Like Chateaubriand describing the roman-

tic *mal du siècle* in the early 1800's, or Barrès analyzing the dilettantism of the 1880's, Camus had an ethical purpose. The main obstacle to his ethics of happiness that he set out to combat was the "sickness" consisting in a certain attitude toward what Camus calls *"l'absurde,"* a notion he then defines. Camus aimed at nothing less than to operate a radical transmutation of values, to elicit from the notion of the absurd a positive response to life instead of the negative one he discerned around him. Within his limits, he was proceeding much as did Pascal when he addressed the libertine and from the libertine view of the world drew the arguments that led not to the apparently inevitable skepticism of the libertine, but to faith.

It is to a fairly large extent true that many young intellectuals in the late 1920's and 1930's shared the feeling that, in terms of our human intelligence, life was quite incomprehensible. They inherited both the skepticism and the pessimism of the *fin de siècle* with a heightened sense of the instability of all human things. That life was also meaningless was—again in a very general way—a logical conclusion for those who, as Camus put it, "live outside the realm of grace." Since life was both incomprehensible and meaningless, it was, one might conclude, a farce—sinister or gay—in which each man could, at will, refuse to play his part or could play it by rules of his own choosing without regard for their ethical quality. Céline's *Voyage au bout de la nuit* (1932) is a typically bitter denunciation of the senselessness or absurdity of life; Montherlant's works attempt to build a personal set of values upon this nihilism; Malraux and Saint-Exupéry, each in his own way, fight it. The existentialist philosophers, tearing down the beautiful orderly façades built by their rationalist predecessors, establish their thought on the basis of the irreducible absurdity and inexplicability of a life refractory to logic and propose various other paths to understanding. But the minds of the majority did not go beyond the simple axiom that human life made no sense and that, since it was meaningless and without value, it mattered little how a human being lived it.

To these young intellectuals Camus addresses *Le Mythe de Sisyphe*. He not only admits but quite triumphantly demonstrates that human life is incomprehensible to the human being, but he does this only in order to refute the conclusion that it is, therefore, meaningless: "It is not in vain that until now people have played with words and pretended to think that the refusal to give life meaning inevitably leads one to declare that it isn't worth living. In fact, there is no common measure linking these two statements."[1] Life, he forces us to admit, is both absurd and, for each of us, infinitely valuable. Its very value is enhanced by an acute consciousness of its irreducibility to human understanding. In a few short pages, with a wave of the hand, Camus dismisses the existentialist and phenomenologist philosophers who, having established this fact, then proceed to commit "philosophical suicide" by eluding their own definitions, arbitrarily attributing meaning to the meaningless in nonrational if not in rational terms. He addresses the same reproach to Dostoevsky and Kafka in the pages which he devotes to them.[2] In contrast, he accepts as final the limitations of his definition and announces his intent to prove the value of a life that has no meaning beyond itself.

This essentially sane rehabilitation of a life too often decried, however specious the reasoning behind it, puts Camus in the company of many other twentieth-century French writers—Gide, Jules Romains, Giono, among the non-Christians—who reacted violently against the various forms of nihilism

[1] *Le Mythe de Sisyphe*, p. 21.

[2] The essay on Kafka was not included in the first edition of *Le Mythe de Sisyphe*. Published separately in 1943 (Lyons: L'Arbalète), it was included in a later edition of *Sisyphe*, to which it originally belonged.

prevalent since the *fin du siècle*. But Camus's method of approach and his sensibility are markedly personal.

Sisyphe opens with one of those categorical statements so characteristic of Camus: "There is only one really serious philosophical problem: suicide"—but not all suicides; only precisely those which do not usually occur, those suicides which logically should follow the belief that life is meaningless and not worth living. The rapidity and vigor with which this highly debatable argument is presented are typical of Camus: the reader is taken by surprise, jolted out of somnolence by a categorical statement, and confronted with the full implications of the question. "The subject of this essay is precisely the relation between the absurd and suicide, the exact measure in which suicide is a solution to the absurd." An academic question prudently stated, one might think, until one realizes that to associate in this simple way two concepts as complex as the absurd and suicide, and then to speak in terms of an "exact measure," is an example of verbal rather than of intellectual clarity.

Camus then proceeds to clarify the meaning of the term *"l'absurde"* by setting up around us the "walls" of the absurd. In rapid succession he extracts from our daily lives those examples of the absurd already in common use, he freely admits, in current existential analyses. The rapidity of his descriptions and the absence of an abstruse vocabulary are distinct advantages: "It happens that the *décor* of our daily life crumbles. Dress, tramway, four hours in an office or factory, meal, tramway, four hours of work, and Monday, Tuesday, Wednesday, Thursday, Friday and Saturday at the same tempo, the road can be followed easily most of the time. Only one day the Why appears and everything begins in a weariness tinged with surprise." [3]

"Everything"?—the word is well chosen. If we do not sink

[3] *Le Mythe de Sisyphe*, p. 27.

back into our routine and go back to sleep again, we start to look about us with new eyes and we are launched upon a perilous adventure, a confrontation with that disturbing dimension of life, the absurd. We are assailed by a sense of passing time: "We live in the future: 'tomorrow'; 'later on'; 'when you get a job'; 'when you're older, you'll understand it.' This inconsequence is admirable, since after all it is a question of dying." [4] Our revolt at this passing away of our lives is another aspect of the absurd.

On occasion, too, we are assailed by the strangeness of the world of objects around us—beautiful though these may be—assailed by our own strangeness which we see in both others and ourselves: "Our discomfort in the face of the inhumanity of man himself, our incalculable fall in the face of this image of what we are, our 'nausea,' as an author [5] of our time calls it, that also is the absurd. And the stranger who, at certain brief moments, comes toward us in a mirror, the familiar yet disquieting brother we recognize in our own photographs, that too is the absurd." [6]

All these aspects of the absurd culminate in the consciousness not of death in general but of the fact that we die. "No ethics, no effort are *a priori* justifiable in the face of the bloody mathematics that order our condition." [7]

Having thus established our familiarity with the various aspects of the absurd and our anxiety in its presence, Camus then turns to our ways of dealing with the absurd and disposes of them without delay. There is a heightening in his tone and his style becomes rich in imagery as he moves from the concrete to the abstract world. He rapidly affirms that the mind can neither explain nor understand the universe or even

[4] *Ibid.*, p. 28.
[5] Allusion to Jean-Paul Sartre, whose novel *La Nausée* Camus had reviewed in *Alger-Républicain* (Oct. 10, 1938).
[6] *Le Mythe de Sisyphe*, p. 29.
[7] *Ibid.*, p. 31. A Pascalian formula.

the individual human being through whom it works: "This world I can touch and I conclude that it exists. That is the limit of my science and the rest is construction"; "Forever I shall be a stranger to myself. . . . A stranger to myself and to the world." The walls have now closed in around us. Since we die, we are obliged, unlike the immortals, to think in terms of life, and we cannot understand our life, though our reason demands that we reduce its divergent patterns to some logical unity. But this is as far as we can go without cheating, without substituting nostalgia or wishful thinking for fact.

All the avenues of escape are blocked, for all are termed illusory: the hope for an afterlife that religions offer or recourse to any form of explanation through philosophy is a mere projection of the "nostalgia" of the human mind in search of unity. Though the reader of *Le Mythe de Sisyphe* may feel some slight misgivings at the ease with which this young man in his twenties simultaneously discards all the classical problems of philosophy and all the age-old tenets of religion, he must also admit a certain pleasure at finding himself so directly solicited to consider the enigma of life, to which, by the oblique path of suicide, Camus now returns.

The line of reasoning is rapid. We die and we know we die, and that is all we know about our lot. We are obliged, therefore, to think only in terms of life, since so far as we are concerned death can make no sense. To commit suicide, in terms of Camus's conclusions, is to admit tacitly that death does have a meaning: "One can lay down as a principle that, for a man who does not cheat, what he thinks determines his action," but in human terms death *cannot* have a meaning. Our only certainty is our life. Logically, it is precisely because our life has no meaning beyond itself that we must violently reject any thought of coming to terms with death. Revolt against death is the only possible human attitude.

Camus can now move on to what interests him most, the

ethics implicit in his conclusions. *L'homme absurde* can now make his entrance. *L'homme absurde* is a man without nostalgia. He has accepted his prison walls and the logical conclusion of Camus's argument. He is passionately wedded to life; he is the enemy of death. Therein lies the conscious affirmation of his humanity; he is against the natural order of the universe in which the words "life" and "death" are meaningless, against the gods—if there be any.

The revolt of Camus's *homme absurde* is not a revolt against the human lot, it is merely an integral part of the human lot. To forgo this revolt is to forgo a part of one's humanity, the part we are most tempted to abandon because we are solicited by our nostalgia for eternity, our need for total understanding. Camus's *homme absurde* can be said to be without hope only in terms of the two human dreams of eternity and total understanding; he is not without hope in life itself. He is not without faith in the reality of his experience within the prison walls, nor is he without joy. Life offers him inexhaustible possibilities which, within the limits of his mortality, he is free to accept.

This doctrine is not simply a new form of hedonism. At every moment in his life *l'homme absurde* must throw into the balance the full weight of his total existence as a challenge, a refusal to capitulate to the evidence of his insignificance, as an assertion of his intense commitment to life. Camus's ethics at this period of his life might be called a heroic hedonism.

It is something of a surprise when, in the next pages of the essay, the reader suddenly moves into the romantic atmosphere enveloping Camus's gallery of *hommes absurdes*. It is the most revealing part of the book, expressing as it does the young writer's tremendous appetite for life or, better still, aptitude for life. Each of Camus's four "heroes of the absurd" incarnates in his own way one of Camus's own *élans*. Though he warns us that even the most humble person can live *la vie absurde*, Camus does not pause to illustrate this point. Counting perhaps on Meursault as an adequate example, he jumps to what he calls the extremes, to Don Juan, to the actor, to the conqueror, to the creator. In spite of the restraint in Camus's tone, there is more than an echo here of the great figures of the Italian Renaissance.

Camus's Don Juan attempts to exhaust all the inexhaustible possibilities of human love, not through any mystic drive toward the absolute but through a passion for the infinite diversity of each unique and passing face. He lives passionately in this partial and constantly renewed contact with a life which, to the very end, never satiates.

The actor assumes a variety of lives, in rapid succession, living each in its full intensity on a stage, consuming his own substance to give a reality to the life of the person he has temporarily become, though he knows that this reality lasts only for those two hours during which he incarnates it. This he does a hundred times over in a repertory which only his death will exhaust; but no one of the hundred lives and deaths he experiences on the stage is any more or any less significant than his own.

The conqueror, in Camus's idiom, is not that familiar historical figure who by conquest holds peoples and vast geographical spaces in his power. Born, perhaps, after 1940, he speaks to us in the first person, in his own name, and the tone in which he speaks suggests that he may be the youngest of Camus's "models." He is the "lucid" conqueror of the Malraux type, who knows that "action in itself is useless": "There is only one useful action, that which would remake man and the earth," [8] an impossible enterprise. Fully aware of his essential uselessness, this conqueror is the man who throws the

[8] *Ibid.*, p. 119.

weight of his conscious and reiterated action against the fatality of history and in favor of the forever lost cause of humanity.

Don Juan, the actor, and the conqueror are thus examples
not merely of hedonism but of the conquest of life, self, and
happiness by a multiplication of self, which is exhausted only
with death: life is "played out" every day by these "princes
without a kingdom," great exiles who have accepted the challenge of the universe and live and act without logically justifying their existence, giving their lives a significance they cannot substantiate.

The most absurd of all, and therefore the greatest prince,
greatest exile, is the creator. The creator knows that a work
of art is nothing but a means by which, with a heightened
consciousness, he re-enacts his life over and over again as a
protestation, a revolt against his human fate.[9]

Sisyphus, hero of the absurd, now appears, summarizing all
these images for us, appealing directly to our imagination. But,
as a symbol, Sisyphus does not quite correspond to the general climate of Camus's thought, even when Camus stretches
the image by drawing on diverse aspects of the story and personality of Sisyphus.

"The gods," Camus tells us, "had condemned Sisyphus
ceaselessly to roll a rock to the top of a mountain from which
the rock fell by its own weight. They had thought, with some
reason, that no punishment is worse than a task that is useless
and without hope." [10] This was because Sisyphus, after his
death, having obtained from Pluto the right to return to earth
for a short time to wreak a personal vengeance, found life on
earth so desirable that he failed to keep his word, returning
to Hades only when forced by the gods. Sisyphus, in Camus's
eyes, is the hero of the absurd, "as much because of his pas-

[9] For a fuller discussion of the role of the creator as presented in
Sisyphe, see chapter 24.
[10] *Le Mythe de Sisyphe,* p. 164.

sions as because of his torment. His disdain for the gods, his hatred of death, and his passion for life caused the ineffable torment in which all one's being is utilized to achieve nothing. This is the price one must pay for the passions of the earth."

To evoke the torment of Sisyphus is easy. It is more difficult to bring him within the focus of Camus's thought. The torment of Sisyphus seems intolerable because it is eternal, yet in the earlier pages of the essay Camus implies that man's torment arises from the fact that he is mortal. In *Le Mythe de Sisyphe* there are, in reality, two images of Sisyphus and they are a little hard to reconcile. There is the Sisyphus who, having returned from Hades, lives in the glory of the sun and the sea, knowing that he can only temporarily defy the gods; his rock is then simply his knowledge that he is mortal and must die. But there is also the Sisyphus who is condemned for all eternity to his desperate task. Rather surprisingly it is on this second Sisyphus that Camus focuses our attention, holding him up as a symbol of the happiness available to man.

Sisyphus, absorbed in the task imposed upon him by the gods, has moved beyond revolt. As he approaches the summit and the rock starts to roll down to the bottom of the slope, Sisyphus watches it in complete awareness and starts his own descent with even steps: "All the silent joy of Sisyphus is there. His destiny is his own. His rock is his possession." [11] "In the same way, *l'homme absurde*, when he contemplates his torment, silences all idols. In the universe suddenly given back to its silence, the thousand small marveling voices of the world arise." We have obviously left behind us Hades where there are no "small, marveling voices of the world."

And finally the symbol shifts again. "I now leave Sisyphus at the foot of his mountain. One always comes back to one's burden. But Sisyphus teaches us that superior form of loyalty

[11] *Ibid.*, p. 164.

which does not acknowledge the gods and lifts rocks. . . . The struggle toward the summit is sufficient to fill the heart of a man. We must imagine that Sisyphus is happy." [12] What summit? The ethics peculiar to Camus's four preceding heroes are derived from the assertion that there is no "upward" path. But Sisyphus is now a moral hero, a stoic, convinced that, in spite of the gods, man's dignity requires him to "struggle toward the summit."

There are obviously many facets to Camus's symbol and his imagination seems to have carried him beyond the idea he had set out to illustrate, revealing perhaps an inner conviction belied by his meticulous desire to remain within the realm of "evidence." Sisyphus, struggling toward the summit, knowing he will never reach it, could be a symbol of all humanity; in the last analysis, Sisyphus's greatness—as well as his happiness—comes from the fact that he cannot allow the rock to lie at the bottom of the slope.

In the course of the essay the word "absurd," like the symbol of Sisyphus, takes on a number of connotations and not without some degree of ambiguity. The same is true of the word "revolt." Is the absurdity of our condition defined in terms of its incomprehensibility or in terms of our mortality? Against what exactly is man's revolt directed? Against death, or the limits imposed upon his reason, or the inscrutability of the cosmos? What is a revolt that ends in the acceptance of a Sisyphus? Whatever facet of the problem we consider, the essay leads, nevertheless, to one conclusion: life is infinitely valuable to the individual; only by a clear consciousness of the given data of life can the individual reach happiness; happiness, at heart, can only be tragic. The absurd human being is by definition wedded to life; all evasion of life is a capitulation. Life is our rock.

[12] *Ibid.*, p. 168.

With *Le Mythe de Sisyphe* Camus began his fight against nihilism. We can imagine, though with some difficulty, that Sisyphus is happy, but in the course of the essay another image of man appears that goes beyond that of *l'homme absurde*. Perhaps the passionate sense of the absurd which Camus was trying here to master, and not merely to exorcise, was counterbalanced by an instinctive belief in an ethical meaning of life: Don Juan and Sisyphus look questioningly at each other from a distance. The rehabilitation of life and happiness has, unaccountably, turned into the celebration of a certain selfless form of duty.[13]

There is a pleasant vigor in the development of *Sisyphe,* an allegro rhythm that binds the various parts together, counterbalancing the self-imposed restraint and the almost too-conscious sobriety of the vocabulary. Malraux is not far in the background, suggesting the "virility" of tone which Camus proclaims somewhat self-consciously. Perhaps it is the need to maintain both tone and tempo that accounts in part for Camus's indifference to the shifting implications of his vocabulary. Perhaps, too, the ambiguity is deliberate, for the enemy is the absurd in all its forms and it must be mastered.

Question upon question can be raised by the reader, but the essential problem is, nevertheless, there, as is the flash of intuition by which Camus counters a nihilism he is unwilling to accept, proclaiming that the value of life cannot be stated in terms of its meaning and must be stated in terms of the way it is lived. What is essential is a "style" of life worthy of a man. This in itself opens the door to Camus's violent quarrel with all ideologies and to his exploration of the "way" a man worthy of the name can live. The essay is

[13] The idea of an essay on *l'absurde* goes back to about 1936. The essay seems to have gone through several versions. It may well be that "the conqueror" and "Sisyphus" were born of a more mature meditation during the early years of the war.

thus something of a landmark in the history of ideas in our century—and for Camus, a point of departure.

Camus's aim in *Le Mythe de Sisyphe* explains and justifies his method. The essay is addressed to the somewhat passive nihilist to whom the absurdity of the world has often been demonstrated. That "all is given and nothing explained" in this world is the position beyond which Camus wishes to move him. He adopts one term to express all facets of the essential obstacle, the sense of *l'absurde*, whether it be seen in man's mortality coupled with his passionate claim to eternity, or in the irremediable incoherence of his experience and his drive for rational unity, or in the insignificance of his life and his passion for absolute values and meaning.

This distinguishes Camus from both Malraux and Sartre, who frequently use the same term. For Malraux the absurdity of man's condition lies essentially in man's need to transcend his own mortality. Malraux's universe is a universe of torture and strife in which highly conscious and desperate individuals snatch their deaths from the hands of a blind chance by deliberately choosing to die a certain way.

For Sartre, the absurd is more philosophically defined as a consequence of man's total contingency, hence the horror, the nausea, that the Sartrian human being feels in the "viscous," "the full" universe that has no place for him.[14] Sartre clearly distinguishes between his and Camus's use of the term "absurd," stressing, as Camus himself often does, that Camus is not an existentialist but a moralist, in the tradition of the great French moralists of the seventeenth century.

The absurd for Camus requires no other universe than our daily world, our earth as we see it, our fellow men, ourselves. Thus integrated into our daily lives, it can be faced at every moment and, by our action, denied. Our revolt against the absurd begins when our consciousness of its existence is fol-

[14] See *Paru*, December, 1945.

lowed by the refusal to be obsessed and paralyzed by it. It is a state of mind. The emphasis which Malraux puts on death, Camus shifts to life. The emphasis which Sartre puts on the total liberty inherent in man's total contingency, Camus puts on lucidity.

Le Mythe de Sisyphe was finished in 1941 but was not published until 1943, one of the most somber of the somber war years. This was a momentous period for Camus: he became engaged in the pitiless struggle against the German occupation; and 1943 is the date of his first "letter to a German friend." The climate of his life and thought had changed dramatically since the late 1930's when, in the light of the African sun, he had begun to plan *Sisyphe*. His purpose—to rehabilitate life as a value significant in itself—had led him to propose an individual pattern of ethics highly aesthetic in nature. *L'homme absurde* transfers his need for unity and duration from the absolute to the relative, from the universe to his own life. He imposes a style upon his life, a coherence for which Camus offers certain models: a form of love, a form of play, a form of heroism, a form of clearsighted persistence.

The basic amenity of the essay and the evident personal prejudice in favor of heroic moral values were not immediately apparent to a wartime reading public plunged in disaster and thus more drawn to the "sickness" so well described than to the concept of individual happiness offered as a remedy. In 1943 it was Sartre's description of existence, the nausea and anguish he described, that seemed closer to the emotional mood of the times. The limpid atmosphere of *Sisyphe* and its call to happiness were closer to the prewar epoch and, perhaps, to a prewar Camus.

21

Good-by to the Minotaur

"Il y a dans chaque homme un instinct pro-
fond qui n'est ni celui de la destruction, ni
celui de la création. Il s'agit seulement de ne
ressembler à rien."

"Oran, ou la halte du Minotaure," [1] written in 1941, is one
of the most delightful of Camus's shorter essays. Its mood is
close to that of *"L'Eté à Alger"* from *Noces* and the *"Petit
Guide pour les villes sans passé."* [2] All three essays benefit
from that love of Algeria which was perhaps Camus's deepest
and only love: "As far as Algeria is concerned, I'm always
afraid to press upon the inner chord which corresponds to
it inside me and whose blind and grave song I know. But I
can say at least that it is my real country and that I recognize
its sons and my brothers by the laughter of friendship that
seizes me when I meet them anywhere in the world." [3] That
laughter is present in *"Oran, ou la halte du Minotaure."* In
1939 and 1940 Camus attained a certain happy equilibrium
in his writing; it seems less studied than in *Sisyphe*, having
acquired an ease, flexibility, and serenity apparent in *"Les
Amandiers,"* written in 1940 at the time of the defeat of
France.

Oran and its inhabitants are amusingly and quite accurately

[1] First published in a limited edition by Charlot (1950), it is the
opening and longest essay of *L'Eté* (pp. 13-36).

[2] *L'Eté*, pp. 93-104 (written in 1947).

[3] *Ibid.*, p. 102.

described in *"La halte du Minotaure,"* but not for the sake of description alone. They are seen in the light of *l'absurde,* another illustration of Camus's personal spiritual geography. Like Algiers and like Constantine, Oran is one of those "cities without a past," in which, according to Camus, man, without a history, a tradition, or even a religion to which he can refer, is face to face with the stark fact of his inexplicable existence. Oran illustrates a metaphysical situation. The character of the land and of the city heightens this vision, which Camus further transfigures by a semihumorous introduction of the myth of the Minotaur. In Oran one is devoured by the Minotaur, the unfathomable ennui of a physical life untouched by any form of intellectual anxiety. No wonder some Oranese indignantly protested!

Taking as his point of departure the most striking features of the landscape around Oran—the arid rock of mountain cliff and coastline and the peculiar architecture of a city which turns its back upon the sea—Camus sets up a dramatic contrast. In Oran, nature and men, impervious to each other, live back to back as it were. "Obliged to live in front of an admirable landscape, the Oranese have triumphed over this redoubtable trial by protecting themselves with really ugly buildings." With these two elements—the stark beauty of the land, which he can so richly describe, and the dusty ugliness of the city and the peculiar habits of its citizens, which inspire his comic verve—Camus introduces into his description a play of incongruous contrasts. He builds his favorite *décor* of great blocks of stone, light, and color; then he turns a sympathetic but mocking eye upon the strange evolutions of the little human creature in a city imaginatively transformed into a camp fortified against any invasion of the *nonhuman*. The emotional detachment which Camus achieves here is rare in his essays and explains, perhaps, both the humor and the absence of the moral contention and pathos so characteristic of his later work. The imaginative transfiguration of the city takes place before our eyes and yet the city never loses its concrete, clearly recognizable character.

All around Oran we see "the brutal African landscape . . . clad in its flaming glory. It bursts through the clumsy *décor* built upon it, screaming violently between the houses and over the rooftops." A "mineral" sky, the bare jagged cliffs, "squatting in the sea like red monsters," and, beyond, the long solitary dunes of interminable beaches—the landscape is alive and fantastic. Against it, incongruously dusty and bizarre, stands Oran, with its incredible buildings and shop windows, its daily parade of adolescents along the boulevards, its shoe-cleaning rites and boxing matches. The vision is almost surrealist in nature, clear and strong as in a painting, concise in the merciless accuracy of its concrete, ludicrous details. The Minotaur is at home here, with the monstrous beauty and indifference of the land and the equally monstrous unconsciousness of its inhabitants. The evocation of the Minotaur effectively leads to the personal meditation through which Camus integrates Oran into his own spiritual odyssey: in the double desert where nature and man share only their total lack of spirituality, the call of the Minotaur is "one of the rare invitations to sleep that the earth grants us." It is the temptation to abandon that attribute (in Camus's idiom) of Europe as opposed to Africa, the life of the mind. For Camus the halt at Oran was a short one.

In the years immediately following *"Oran, ou la halte du Minotaure"* the tone of Camus's essays changed greatly. The grandiose and harmonious universe exemplified by his African landscapes disappeared. Even in *Le Mythe de Sisyphe,* where description was limited to certain images of man, this universe is implicit: Don Juan, the conqueror, and Sisyphus himself move in an open world, and many latent images recall this emotional landscape. When we consider that this universe was, in Camus's first works, the aesthetic equivalent of happiness and love, its disappearance becomes significant: the exile of Helen [4] has begun. The balance between description and imagination, contemplation and meditation—so nicely achieved in *"Oran, ou la halte du Minotaure"* and *Le Mythe de Sisyphe*—is definitely broken. The twentieth-century man who invades Camus's world, with his harsh disputes and exorbitant demands, is not that fundamental "ahistoric man," the North African "brother" Camus had thus far so gently mocked or so compassionately observed. There is an early Camus who will not again appear even when, much later, the older Camus retraces his itinerary in Algiers and Tipasa.

It has been said that the period between 1940 and 1945 created a deep cleft in the sensibility of the French, and for no writer is this more true than for Albert Camus. It transformed the climate of his essays. During "the year of the war I had planned to make the voyage of Ulysses again . . . but I did as everyone else did: I did not sail. I took my place in the shuffling queue standing in front of the open door of hell. Little by little we entered. And at the first scream of assassinated innocence, the door slammed shut behind us. We were in hell, we have never quite come out of it again." [5]

This was a man-made hell, and Camus's initial confidence in his fellow men suffered greatly, a serious setback for a writer: "Something in us was destroyed by the spectacle of the years through which we have just lived. And that something is the eternal confidence of man which always led him to believe that one could elicit human reactions from another man by speaking the language of humanity." [6] Sartre, discussing *L'Homme révolté*, accused Camus of loving humanity but mistrusting individual men, and there is some truth in this

[4] *L'Exil d'Hélène"* (1948), in *L'Eté.*
[5] *"Prométhée aux enfers,"* in *L'Eté,* p. 84.
[6] *"Ni victimes ni bourreaux,"* *Actuelles I,* p. 144.

accusation. To salvage something from the wreck of the war years, Camus seemed forced in spite of himself to divide humanity, with the rigorous simplicity of a last judgment, between "victims and executioners," the "just and the unjust," "the truthful and the liars." The positions of judge and artist were hard tb reconcile, but *L'Homme révolté* (1951), the next major essay Camus was to write, was an attempt at such a reconciliation.

In the years that separate *Le Mythe de Sisyphe* and *L'Homme révolté*, Camus wrote a number of shorter essays and his *Lettres à un ami allemand*. Most of these essays were, in the end, incorporated into the text of *L'Homme révolté* with only minor changes, indicating that the essay itself is not systematic, spotlighting as it does different facets of the problem as they occurred to Camus. From 1943, the date of his first letter "to a German friend," to 1951 almost all of Camus's essays and editorials thus led to his essay on revolt.[7] Important among these are the pages grouped in *Actuelles I* under the title "*Ni victimes, ni bourreaux*," [8] and two of the essays in *L'Eté*: "*Prométhée aux enfers*" (1940) and "*L'Exil d'Hélène*" (1948). All these one might call "The Promethean Cycle": Prometheus now displaces Sisyphus.

[7] These are: (1) "*Remarque sur la révolte*," *L'Existence*, pp. 10-23, *Collection la métaphysique* (Paris: Gallimard, 1945); (2) "*Les Meurtriers délicats*," *La Table ronde*, No. 1, 1948, pp. 42-50; (3) "*Le Meurtre et l'absurde*," *Empédocle*, No. 1, 1949, pp. 19-27; (4) "*Nietzsche et le nihilisme*," *Les Temps modernes*, August, 1951, pp. 399-407; and (5) "*Lautréamont et la banalité*," *Cahiers du Sud*, No. 37, 1951, pp. 399-407.

[8] These were first published as editorials in *Combat*, Nov. 19-30, 1946, and reproduced in *Caliban*, November, 1947.

22

The Fall of Prometheus

"Nous avons à réinventer le feu . . ."

Among the great mythical figures inherited from the Greeks, Prometheus has been, since the romantic period, a literary favorite. In the twentieth century and particularly in the past thirty years he has haunted European literature and thought. Modern science, modern political theory, and modern literature have all, with various shifts in emphasis, been characterized as Promethean. And, indeed, he who stole the fire of Zeus, the liberator of mankind who triumphed over Zeus's unjust wrath and heralded a new order of justice, is a figure with particularly rich meaning for our age.

Essentially Prometheus came to symbolize man's revolt against the limits imposed upon him by nature; chained to his rock, proudly refusing to accept Zeus's justice, he might, at first thought, seem perfectly to incarnate *l'homme absurde* as he is described in *Le Mythe de Sisyphe*. When the hero of Camus's adaptation of Aeschylus's *Prometheus Bound*, one of the first plays he adapted for *Le Théâtre de l'équipe*, bitterly complains: "The truth is that I can no longer bear to suffer and to be right," [1] he seems cut out to be Camus's *homme absurde*. But Camus prefers at first the figure of Sisyphus, for he wants us to imagine *l'homme absurde* as happy. Prometheus is not a happy hero, and in this respect Sisyphus is to a certain extent anti-Promethean. In the years following 1943, "the winter of the world," Camus often alluded to Prome-

[1] Scene VI, in Camus's unpublished adaptation.

theus, but to a Prometheus who had traveled a long way from Greek mythology and whose modern reincarnation he evoked in *L'Homme révolté*.

L'Homme révolté traces the "amazing itinerary of Prometheus" in a sort of fable entirely invented by Camus and directed toward his contemporaries:

> Proclaiming his hatred of the gods and his love of man, he [Prometheus] turns disdainfully away from Zeus toward the mortals to lead them in an assault against the sky. But men are weak and cowardly; they have to be organized. They love pleasure and immediate happiness. In order that they may grow, they have to be taught to refuse the honey of each day. So Prometheus, in his turn, becomes a master who first teaches, then commands. The struggle continues and becomes exhausting. Men doubt that they will reach the city of the sun, doubt the very existence of the city. They must be saved from themselves. The hero now tells them that he knows the city and that he alone knows it. Those who doubt will be thrown out into the desert, nailed on a rock, offered as prey to cruel birds. All others shall walk in the dark behind the pensive and solitary master. Prometheus, alone, has become god and reigns over the solitude of men. But he has conquered only Zeus's solitude and cruelty; he is no longer Prometheus, he is Caesar.[2]

This is obviously the story of a perversion, a fable all the more significant since it attacks the figure of a rebel in whose favor we are strongly prejudiced. Through this rebel Camus was deliberately attacking one of the powerful traditional idols of a number of his fellow countrymen, the myth of revolution. It would not, however, be fair to either Prometheus or Camus to abandon his fable at this point, for, as Camus well knew, Prometheus is an indestructible figure: "The true, the eternal Prometheus has now assumed the face of one of his victims.

---

[2] *L'Homme révolté*, p. 301.

The same cry, rising from the depths of the centuries, still resounds in the depth of the Scythian desert."

L'Homme révolté is, in effect, the cry of a "son of" the real Prometheus, protesting against the perversion of the hero.[3] Camus calls it a confession, and it is ordered with tremendous certainty according to the highly imaginative perspective of his Promethean parable. However objective the tone of the essay, the experience which impelled Camus to write it is strictly personal. It is not, perhaps, as universal an experience as an encounter with *l'absurde*, because the experience is fairly complex: though linked to an exceptionally violent form of political action, it is intellectual in nature. If the images of hell, flame, blood, the cries of the innocent, and the figure of the executioner occur and recur in the essay with some monotony, it is not simply as a form of rhetoric. "The scream of assassinated innocence," for example, may, as a curious rhetorical abstraction, make us smile, but for Camus it is no verbal convention. The "repulsive" or "hideous" visage of our time—another very general and abstract image; the "thick soil of accumulated iniquities"; the "irrational fury of the brute"; the "skeleton of Europe, peopled with ghosts"; the "clamor" and "the fury"; and many other such images express the genuine distress of a sensitive man haunted by what seems to him the mortal disorder of his age. The revealing context of the essay is not to be found in literature, ideologies, or politics, but essentially in contemporary history.

Camus explained this clearly: "At the root of any work one almost always finds a deep and simple emotion, pondered over at length and which, without justifying it, is enough to explain it. For my own part, I should not have written *L'Homme révolté* if in the forties I had not found myself face to face with men whose acts I did not understand. To put it briefly, I did not understand that men could torture others

---

[3] See *"Prométhée aux enfers."*

without ever ceasing to look at them." The disconcerting
truth which Camus discovered was that "crime . . . could
be reasoned, could turn its system into power, spread its co-
horts over the world, conquer and rule." [4] In other words,
Camus found it impossible to understand that crime could
be not only organized but rationally justified and legalized.

Secondly, in the face of this deliberate, rationalized terrorism he was confronted by his own unreasoned revolt, his commitment to the struggle embodied in the French Resistance
movement: "To a reasoned crime, it was necessary at least
to oppose the reasons for a right . . . for my part I disposed
only of a revolt that was sure of itself, but still not conscious
of its reasons." [5] Camus here meets his old opponent, the intellectual nihilism he defined in *Le Mythe de Sisyphe*. Now
it is negated not by a great surge of life but by a definite action
born of a revolt which made him willing to sacrifice his life
to something beyond itself.

The problem, at its origin, is clearly stated in his *Lettres à
un ami allemand*. In the days before the war Camus and his
German friend had agreed that, in a world which so far as
they were concerned had no recognizable supernatural order,
all criteria of good and evil, formal or individual, were arbitrary. But Camus's own action and the action of many others
were proof to the contrary. That justice exists is the leitmotiv
of the letters. Yet the conviction had no rational basis. "It
seemed to me then, since I knew nothing more and was no
further helped, that I must try to draw a rule of conduct and
perhaps a first value from the only experience with which I
was in agreement and which was our revolt." [6] For if no
rational ethical value could be established by which the violence of the "executioners" could be distinguished from the

[4] Unpublished manuscript, 1952.
[5] *Ibid.*
[6] *Ibid.*

violence of their opponents, then all sacrifices involved would be meaningless. "Is it possible, without referring to absolute principles, to escape from a logic of destruction . . . ?" This was the question which the *"Réflexions sur la violence,"* written in 1945 and incorporated into *L'Homme révolté* with only slight changes, attempts to answer on the basis of an objective examination of Camus's own experience.

But between 1945 and 1951, when *L'Homme révolté* was finished, the context if not the content of Camus's thought changed notably. In 1945 Camus was thinking in terms of the violence and cruelty of the nazi domination; in 1946, with *"Ni victimes ni bourreaux,"* in terms of the cold war; but in 1950 it was the danger of Marxist ideology that he denounced. His essay on revolt thus developed within a shifting political context which, to some degree, seems to have oriented Camus's thought in a direction which he had not foreseen in the initial *"Réflexions sur la violence."* In the course of this development, and because of his own involvement in the political turmoil that followed the liberation of France, Camus went far beyond an intellectual clarification of his own initial position and was led to attack two of the shibboleths of the political left: the doctrine, inherited from Hegel, that there is a predetermined direction to history; and the all-or-nothing character of French political attitudes. His originally apolitical study had turned into a highly inflammable subject.

Camus was not the first to criticize both the theory and the methods of the French political left. In fact there are innumerable contemporary treatises both on the Hegelian-Marxist interpretation of history and on the strength of the revolutionary myth among the French leftist parties.[7] But these were specialized studies that reached a limited audience; their authors, unlike Camus, were not well-known champions

[7] Written by Raymond Aron and Jules Monnerot, among others.

of the liberal left. The reactions of the leftist intelligentsia, from the Communists to the Catholic Progressists—and not forgetting the Sartrian existentialists of *Les Temps modernes* —were, therefore, unusually violent, and opportunities for misunderstanding and hot debate were numerous.

Camus examines the notion of revolt, as he had examined the notion of *l'absurde*, in order to establish the reasons for a position he had already taken and deduce the practical consequences of such a position. When he examined the sources of certain contemporary axioms concerning the nature of history, he obviously did not stop to reread the complete works of Hegel and Marx. What was important to him for his essay was the bearing that certain conclusions or assumptions of these men had upon his own analysis. To misunderstand this, as did his existentialist opponent, M. Jeanson, and reproach Camus for a lack of scholarly thoroughness seems rather pedantic.

Camus begins *L'Homme révolté* with a personal study of the implications of an individual act of revolt: in an act of violence the slave [8] revolts against his master because in a confused way he feels that the master has gone beyond a bearable limit, has violated something essential. Revolt, therefore, becomes the refusal to accept a master's right to absolute freedom and the affirmation that a slave has the right to limit this freedom, even by violence, to obtain a measure of justice for himself. This right of the slave transcends consideration of his individual situation, since he is willing to lose his life in order to assert it. The individual master-slave relationship [9] thus becomes a man-to-man contest centered upon the concept of a right, a limit set to individual freedom, and it is valid

[8] In "*Réflexions sur la violence*," the "functionary" is chosen and not the "slave." In 1945 Camus was closer to the nazi bureaucracy than to Hegel.

[9] *L'Homme révolté.*

for all men. "I revolt, therefore we are" is the much-discussed formula by which Camus summarized this concept.

Revolt is then defined by Camus as the "impulse that drives an individual to the defense of a dignity common to all men." It involves the idea of a measure of liberty and a measure of justice; it contains an affirmation of human solidarity which, in its turn, serves as a limit for revolt itself. The No thrown in the face of a violation that has gone beyond a certain limit is spoken in the name of all men and presupposes that the slave's revolt must stop at the moment when it reaches that limit. If, in his turn, the slave claims absolute freedom, he then becomes the master to some other slave whose right he violates.

Camus's definition thus stresses the double relativity of revolt. The form of revolt he defined is opposed to the all-or-nothing attitude, the attitude most frequently associated with the word, and since this all-or-nothing attitude has been a part of French political ideology—particularly leftist ideology—from the time of the French Revolution, Camus's orientation of the problem contained more dynamite than might at first be evident.[10]

Having set up his definition and oriented the problem, Camus then limited the scope of his essay in time and space; he would consider only our modern Occidental world since the time of the French Revolution. The concept of revolt, as he defined it, seemed to him inseparable from the concept of a society based on the definition of the rights of man es-

[10] Many liberal French thinkers—Péguy and Alain among others—resemble the doctrinaires in that they tend to oppose individual rights and the organized power of the modern state, tacitly assuming that basic morality and political efficacy are of necessity mutually exclusive. Camus inherited this attitude, which Sartre criticized with some justification, though Sartre then begged the issue by assuming that the only alternative to this inefficacy could be found in communism. The old dichotomy of morality versus efficacy is manifest in *Lettres à un ami allemand.*

tablished in human terms without reference to a theological universe. This desacralization[11] of society, heralded in France by the execution of Louis XVI, God's representative on earth, is the medium within which the particular movement of revolt analyzed in the essay develops. Revolt, Camus concluded, is our historic reality.

With the problem defined, oriented, and generalized, Camus set out to examine the intellectual content the word "revolt" has assumed in the past century and a half. He did not claim that he was writing a history of revolt from Rousseau to our time, as some of his highly vociferous critics seemed to think. He chose as exemplary figures those men who make revolt the pivot of their thought and attitudes, pushing the implications of the idea to their ultimate logical limits. Sade, Lautréamont, Rimbaud, and the surrealists, whom he used as examples, may seem a curiously esoteric group, examples only of the strange hagiography peculiar to an *avant-garde* intelligentsia. Netchaiev, Sasanov, or Chigalev, upon whom he dwells, may appear interesting only as madmen moving outside the main currents of European thought, in comparison with those really great and significant figures to whom Camus gives about the same amount of attention— Nietzsche, Marx, and Hegel. But, though Camus's choice may at first seem entirely arbitrary, it is, in fact, entirely consistent: in each case the revolt is systematic, the consequence of an implacable logic. Camus is fascinated by the monomaniacs of revolt.

Camus describes first the "metaphysical" rebels against God and the miserable condition of man in the universe, and then the "historical" rebels against man's injustice to man in society. It is not our purpose to analyze here the development of the essay, but what Camus sets out to demonstrate he dem-

[11] A modern term and a favorite theme of our time (see Jules Monnerot).

onstrates clearly: metaphysical revolt in the name of man's freedom ends in an unlimited claim to freedom which turns into a murderous and unjust tyranny exercised against one's fellow men; historical revolt against social injustice ends in an unlimited claim to justice which turns into a murderous terrorism directed against individual freedom. Revolt in the name of "absolute freedom" and "absolute justice," as opposed to the claim for the "measure of freedom" and the "measure of justice" described by Camus as the source of revolt, is therefore a perversion. When a revolt becomes a political revolution it must renounce absolute ends in favor of just such a relative measure of justice and freedom, otherwise it is on the road to tyranny.

In this context Camus's analysis of communist ideology is provocative. It is marked by his complete inheritance of certain attitudes of the French political left which accepts the decadence and social guilt of the bourgeois capitalist society as an axiom. He does not question the expression "reactionary bourgeois," a term of reprobation. In fact, and this may seem surprising, Camus finds it necessary to defend himself against any allegation that he is tainted with the crime of "bourgeois-ism." The intellectual blackmail associated with the term in France is one of the stumbling blocks in the path of liberal thinkers and a weapon to which the communist press rapidly resorts in any controversy. Camus, as a recipient of this usual treatment, undoubtedly became sensitive on the subject.

Following the thread of his argument in *L'Homme révolté*, Camus distinguished two main forms of revolt culminating in the intellectual justification of two forms of contemporary police states: the nihilistic, individualistic revolt, inherited from a perverted Nietzscheism, in which men, arrogating to themselves the privileges of gods, recognize no limit to their freedom to conquer and destroy—the nazi state, for example;

and the ideological revolt whereby man replaces God by some other absolute. For the men of the French Revolution, who belong to the latter category, reason became God: a rational government, resting on certain uncontested ideological principles was to inaugurate the advent of a happy and innocent humanity living in harmony and absolute agreement. When this failed to happen, a man like Saint-Just could not bring himself to question the validity of an incontrovertible principle; the remedy obviously lay in the elimination of those perverted individuals who were quietly compromising the happiness of the group. Thus capital punishment became a path to perfection.

With Hegel, according to Camus, principles were replaced by history. Each individual life, as Hegel saw it, was oriented in relation to "the direction" of history, since the history of mankind was predetermined and moving toward the ultimate liberation of humanity. Current Marxist ideology accepts this reasoning as an axiom, one on which it bases its contention that the advent of a socialist classless state is the last stage in the evolution toward a "just" society. And this leads to another axiom: all means that favor the advent of the socialist state are justified, and particularly justified is the destruction of all forces which delay so inevitable and desirable a conclusion. In *L'Homme révolté* Camus questions both these axioms. He questions first the prophetism, as he calls it, inherent in the doctrine, and then its justification of the means by the end. He rejects the conclusion that, historically, defeat involves guilt, thus indirectly justifying his own generous prejudice in favor of such groups as the Spanish Republicans. He also points out the fallacy involved in sacrificing the immediate happiness of a human being—for whom justice is sought—to an end which appears both nebulous and problematic.

Camus's criticism of current Marxism is not new. The

twentieth-century background of Marxist thought, its transformation from hypothesis to dogma, the historic developments it failed to foresee, the contradictions between its principles and their application by means of an apparatus of state
terrorism, its irremediable "Caesarism," are all current themes
in the ideological controversies of our time. But the passion
behind Camus's indictment in *L'Homme révolté* is unmis-
takable and somewhat overshadows the main conclusions of
the essay, which are as important at least as his stern criticism
of current "Marxist" thought.

Camus's initial question had been: "Is it possible, without
referring to absolute principles, to escape from a logic of
destruction . . . ?" *L'Homme révolté* is a description of that
"logic of destruction" at work in the thought and practice
of our time as it becomes manifest in, for example, war, concentration camps, political trials, brainwashing. Camus concludes first that we shall not escape from a logic of destruction by the grace of the one ideology—the Marxist—still extant. But his final answer is that escape is possible, escape by
means that are implicit in his initial definition of revolt. Man
the rebel, that is, modern man, must abandon the absolute
and accept the relative, he must think in terms of a measure
of freedom, a measure of justice. But though the end must
be seen as relative and as a form of compromise, the means
by which that compromise is obtained must be subjected to
serious examination. The immediate rights of a human being
as progressively defined by law must be considered inalien-
able. They constitute the only guarantee a human being has
that he can extract from life the daily measure of happiness
which, in Camus's eyes, is man's greatest treasure.

The only rebels who along the way satisfy Camus's ethical
—and perhaps aesthetic—sense are the "scrupulous murderers"
he studied in *Les Justes*. In Camus's eyes the tragic anxiety of
the 1905 Russian anarchists, who never ceased to question

their right to assassinate and who paid for each murder with their own lives, places them at the opposite pole from the "complacent" murderers of bureaucratic oppression who combine mass murder with a sense of moral justification. But the "scrupulous murderers" of 1905 are not presented by Camus as models for imitation, they serve merely to illustrate the extreme and desperate limit which revolt can reach in the use of violence without betraying its initial generous impulse.

The conclusion to *L'Homme révolté* seems eminently sane, defining, as it does, though rather vaguely, the ideal mechanism of a democracy that always seeks to safeguard the means, and, in respect to the ends, recognizes the need to compromise within certain limits. And Camus's intellectual itinerary reveals some of the complexities and crosscurrents that determine the climate of political thought in Europe, pointing sometimes toward a new orientation. His strength seems to lie precisely in what some critics criticized as his weakness: his effort to give his conclusions a reasoned basis in experience, his own experience.

No doubt, with *L'Homme révolté* Camus undertook much, too much perhaps. In substance, the topic was not favorable to artistic expression, and political controversy was not essentially Camus's forte. As Sartre pointed out, Camus was interested in moral not political issues. The only practical suggestion Camus makes in *L'Homme révolté* is to propose a form of action in line with pre-Marxian revolutionary syndicalism. It would seem that he passed over the really fundamental problem that confronts the Western world and France more particularly, and that is not so much how to maintain the basic rights and liberties of the individual as how to reconcile them with the necessities of twentieth-century existence.

It is not our intent here to review the discussions that *L'Homme révolté* stimulated. At their best, they pointed out certain limitations in Camus's analysis, disregarding the main issue; at their worst, they resorted to personal insult, especially in the communist press where Camus was accused of being sold to capitalist America. The most revealing reactions came from the "Progressists"—or Catholic leftists—and the existentialist leftist group of *Les Temps modernes*. The argument centered around the logic of Camus's discussion and the degree of his familiarity with the authors he quoted. In point of fact the real crux of the matter lay elsewhere: Camus had raised a crucial issue for the noncommunist left.

Both the Progressists and Sartre's group accept the theory of the infallible development of history. Both groups assert their responsibility, their "commitment" to their time, and, therefore, to political action. Since the only really efficient working-class party in France is the Communist party, for them the problem of political action can be put in these terms: Is it possible to create outside the Communist party an efficient left-wing party that will serve the working class? After Sartre's attempt failed, the only form of action that remained open to the leftist intellectual seemed to him to be to support the Communist party whenever possible, attempting at the same time to orient it wherever possible from within. Camus challenged this attitude, calling for a new orientation of thought in the leftist groups paralyzed by the deterioration of the ideology of the French Revolution and the even more dangerous degradation of what he called the "Post-Revolutionary" ideology of the Communist party. His preoccupation with the only too evident political stagnation of French politics was thoroughly justified, and his analysis, though incomplete, suggested new avenues of political thinking.

At the end of *L'Homme révolté*, after a very personal study of the relationship of art and revolt, Camus changed his idiom to speak as an artist, and this explains to a certain extent some of the misunderstanding which his essay aroused. His analysis had emphasized the idea of measure: a measure of justice, a measure of liberty; and the idea of limit, of equilibrium. Within this measure and inside these limits, he felt, the daily sum of individual human happiness, that happiness so blithely sacrificed by the prophets of the future Eden, could be preserved. To his own ideal he applied its inner geographic equivalent: "Mediterranean" or "Greek." And the critics continued hot on his trail, accusing him in this part of the essay of regionalism, confusion, intellectual grandiloquence.

Camus, however, had now staked out his own route from Sisyphus to Prometheus, to Nemesis: Nemesis, the goddess of measure who chastises all who attempt to escape from her rule.[12] Having thus explained to himself how it had come about that men "could torture others," examining them meanwhile like objects, Camus was ready to break with some of the obsessions around him, in particular the attitude of perpetual "commitment" advocated by Sartre. In 1951 he felt that the tensions in Europe had temporarily lessened and, rejecting the arid and vain "promised lands" of political controversy, he turned toward the relative fulfillment of a life anchored to the present. "At this hour when each of us must draw the bow and prove himself once again, conquer in and against history what he already possesses, the sparse harvests of his fields, the brief love of the earth, at the hour when a man at last is born, we must take leave of this age and its adolescent fury."

The crisis of the war years was over. *"Retour à Tipasa,"* [13] which followed *L'Homme révolté*, clearly marked this voluntary liberation from an obsession with the "blood, sweat, and tears" of the preceding period. "In the middle of winter, I learned at last that I carried inside me an invincible summer."

[12] "*L'Exil d'Hélène*," in *L'Eté*, p. 108.
[13] In *L'Eté*.

23

The Invincible Summer

"Au centre de notre oeuvre, fût-elle noire, rayonne un soleil inépuisable, le même qui crie aujourd'hui à travers la plaine et les collines."

The last three essays of *L'Eté*—"*L'Enigme*" (1950), "*Retour à Tipasa*" (1952), and "*La Mer au plus près*" (1953)— mark Camus's return to an inner equilibrium. The vast landscape of sun and sea reasserts itself and once again his thoughts turn inward toward himself and toward his work as an artist.

In the center of his work he discerns not the visage of *l'absurde* but the dazzling enigma of life: "In the center of our work, even were it black, shines an inexhaustible sun, the sun that cries out today over the plains and hills." [1] That central enigma, it seems to him, is what the artist must attempt to decipher. "Real despair is agony, tomb or abyss"; in any event it is silence, and there is no such thing as a "literature of despair."

At Tipasa, Camus writes, "I rediscovered that one must keep intact within oneself a freshness, a source of joy, love and light that escapes injustice, and that one must return to the struggle having conquered that light. Here once again I found the old beauty, the young sky, and I measured my good fortune, understanding at last that in the worst years of our madness the memory of this sky had never left me. And that mem-

[1] *L'Eté*, p. 137.

ory had, in the end, protected me against despair." [2] The
obsession with violence and injustice assumed its rightful pro-
portion in his thinking: "Yes, there is beauty and there are
the humiliated. Whatever the difficulties of the enterprise
may be, I should like to be unfaithful to neither the one
nor the other." [3]

One of the most successful of Camus's lyrical essays is *"La
Mer au plus près,"* the last essay in *L'Eté*. Organized around
the great image of the sea, it crystallizes the inner climate of
his life, transposing it through the combined use of rhythm
and image: "I grew up in the sea and for me poverty was
sumptuous, then I lost the sea, all luxuries now seemed gray
to me, misery intolerable. Since then I have been waiting." [4]
In *"La Mer au plus près"* we are once again in the great realm
of literature.

Two voices speak in this essay. The first is the voice of the
exile, of him who is waiting: "Thus I, who possess nothing,
who have given away my fortune, who camp beside all my
houses, yet know fulfillment when I so desire, I weigh anchor
at all hours, despair does not know me. There is no father-
land for the man without hope, whereas I know that the sea
precedes and follows me, I hold a folly ready. Those who love
each other and are separated can live in pain, but it is not
despair: they know that love exists. That is why I suffer with
dry eyes, in exile. I still wait. A day arrives at last . . ."

This theme of exile is followed by the description of a voyage,[5] and now it is the voice of the traveler who speaks in
short vigorous sentences in contrast with the rhythm of the
exile's voice in the opening passage of the essay. A precise,
concrete description, so characteristic of the earlier Camus,

[2] *"Retour à Tipasa,"* p. 159.
[3] *Ibid.*, p. 110.
[4] *L'Eté*, p. 167.
[5] The occasion of this essay was Camus's journey to South America.

launches us on a sea voyage in which day and night, sky and sea, islands and continents, pass before our eyes in a sumptuous succession of moods and images; it is a song of nuptials with the sea and a record of successive spiritual moods translated through fantastic and rich imagery. For the sea itself is life, spacious, beautiful, and magnificently dangerous:

> At midnight, alone on the shore. Waiting again, then I shall leave. The sky itself is motionless with all its stars like those liners covered with lights which, at this very hour, in the entire world, illuminate the dark water of the ports. Space and silence lie with a single weight upon my heart. A sudden love, a decisive act, a thought which transfigures, at certain moments give the same intolerable anxiety accompanied by an irresistible attraction. Delicious anguish of being, exquisite proximity of a danger whose name we do not know, is to live then to run to our death. . . . I have always had the impression that I lived on the high seas, threatened, at the heart of royal happiness.[6]

The voice of the exile and the voice of the traveler are two different voices of the artist, and the essay, as its subtitle, "*Journal de bord*," indicates, is his "logbook." The strife and the anger, the pettiness and the grandeur of the past years are now blended in the song of life which, in his exile, the poet knows he will eventually hear, for he is attuned to this song. In Camus's imagery the sea has superseded the sun and Africa has stretched to the confines of the earth. As the figure of Nemesis, the goddess of measure, now appears to govern the affairs of men, the natural *décor* which incarnates Camus's own spiritual *décor* greatly expands, carrying with it unexpected intonations of infinity. "*La Mer au plus près*" is one of the high peaks in Camus's work.

Camus's essays, both the shorter, more lyrical essays and those which are longer and more intellectual, serve a definite

[6] *L'Eté*, p. 188.

function. For Camus, increasingly involved in the confused turmoil of our time, the essay was an instrument of inner clarification and definition and, therefore, of liberation. The shorter essays express the inner climate, the solitary moods of a sensitivity which, though it finds little outlet in the wear and tear of daily living, is nonetheless the real source of a writer's personality.

The two longer essays are a form of intellectual discipline. Camus systematically applies a certain method of reasoning to the baffling problems of his time in order to consider them in terms of his time. The problem which concerns him chiefly is the ethical nihilism which he considers characteristic of our Occidental world. From this nihilism he sets out to wrest new values, "without the aid of eternal values which, temporarily perhaps, are absent or distorted in contemporary Europe." [7] "For me *The Myth of Sisyphus* marks the beginning of an idea I was to pursue in *The Rebel*"; it consisted in an attempt to discover whether "within the limits of nihilism it is possible to find the means to proceed beyond nihilism." [8] To proceed *logically* beyond nihilism, for nihilism is an intellectual attitude, and Camus's appeal is to the intellect. He first draws from an initial proposition its counterproposition: the proposition that life is not worth living, pushed to its farthest limit in the concept of suicide, reveals consequences that are incompatible with the premises, consequences from which Camus logically deducts "a lucid invitation to live and create in the very midst of the desert." [9] In the same way *L'Homme révolté* draws from the consequences logically implicit in the notion of revolt an ethic of conscious, constructive participation in the political and social life of our times;

[7] Preface to *The Myth of Sisyphus*, translated by Justin O'Brien (New York: Alfred A. Knopf, 1955).
[8] *Ibid.*
[9] *Ibid.*

starting from the initial fact of crime rationally justified, Camus logically proves that crime cannot be rationally justified. Many critics have pointed out "the excessively dialectical cast" [10] of Camus's mind, and one may wonder whether Camus's argumentation is not in fact something of a *tour de force*.

That beliefs can neither be established nor argued away by logic is a truth that sustains Camus's arguments. What characterized Camus, as many of his editorials demonstrate, is that direct *bon sens*, of which Descartes spoke, coupled with a passionate adherence to the principles of liberty and justice. But what characterizes our time—and apparently Camus himself —is that this does not seem to us sufficient in itself. In order to obtain a hearing Camus felt he must establish some intellectual proof of the validity of his principles. There is a scholasticism of the twentieth century, as Sartre's monumental *L'Etre et le néant* shows, to which Camus paid tribute, though he sought to escape from it.

In the great tradition of Pascal's *Pensées*, *l'homme révolté* and *l'homme absurde* are myths constructed to justify conclusions already arrived at. In this context both *Le Mythe de Sisyphe* and *L'Homme révolté* belong to the realm of the history of ideas. Politically, the battle around *L'Homme révolté* has not abated, nor did Camus's position change: [11] "I was born in a political family, the left, where I shall die, but whose decadence it is hard not to see. I am responsible for this, with others," he wrote in answer to one of his progressist attackers.

And once again he discussed the problem, the problem of

[10] Richard Wollheim, "The Political Philosophy of Existentialism," *The Cambridge Journal*, October, 1953. Mr. Wollheim considers Camus's essay as an illustration of the "political philosophy of existentialism," a very questionable position.

[11] See "*Le Refus de la haine*," Camus's preface to *L'Allemagne vue par les écrivains de la résistance française* by Konrad Bieber (Geneva: Droz, 1954). Also in *Témoins*, Spring, 1955.

collaboration with the Communist party debated in *L'Homme révolté*, but this time he discussed it on the level of common sense: "Is there not more vanity, though hidden, in imagining that one can change the enormous communist machine from within than in opposing it from the outside, calmly and without hatred, with what one thinks is true? . . . I believe, for my part, that the idea of revolution will regain its grandeur and efficacy only when it renounces the cynicism and opportunism which it has made its rule in the twentieth century, when it reforms its outworn ideological material corrupted by half a century of compromise, and when, finally, it puts in the center of its movement an irreducible passion for liberty." [12]

Camus's position was clear, his passion for liberty and justice was unquestionable, his concern for the suffering of human beings was real, his dedication to the defense of the oppressed was obvious. Why, then, when he could act directly in editorials, prefaces, and lectures, the logical detours of the essay? It would seem first that Camus had to operate for himself that transmutation of values which the essay permits. Secondly, one of the ills that Camus discerned in our time is our passion for absolutes; it was one of his beliefs that we forge our own ideologies and then chain ourselves down with them. The essay, in itself, invites discussion, and thus, according to Camus, it offers the writer who fulfills his real function in our society a medium with which to fight the latent dogmatism and intolerance of our age.

[12] *Actuelles II*, p. 76.

24

The Role of the Artist

"Je veux délivrer mon univers de ses fantômes
et le peupler seulement des vérités de la chair
dont je ne peux pas nier la présence."

"We all carry within us our prisons, our crimes, our de-
structiveness. But to unleash them in the world is not our
duty. Our duty consists in fighting them in ourselves and in
others."[1] Camus had an almost desperate sense of our immediate need to impose a tolerable pattern upon the violently
haphazard development of our civilization. To him our greatest temptation, obsessed by powerful mechanical forces which
we manipulate and do not control, is to abandon our ethical human standards and needs, identifying ourselves thereby
with a world which denies us our rightful place. Between
these superpowerful forces and the individual he could detect no present intent on the part of the conscious human
community to defend a "kingdom of man" that embodies
in its institutions the aspiration of the individual toward the
undeniable "truths of the flesh."

Our institutions, as Camus saw them, tend either toward
the inefficient routines of the somnolent bureaucracies, satir-
ized in *La Peste* and *L'Etat de siège*, or toward the blind
mechanisms of a world which, impervious to the dictates of
human conscience, is, like the Grand Inquisitor of Dostoevsky,
contemptuous of mankind in general. As individuals we are
exiles, exiles in a universe in which we no longer claim our

[1] *L'Homme révolté*, p. 373.

rightful place, exiles in a social order increasingly powerless to defend our aspirations. Thus estranged and alienated, the individual stands alone, outlawed and in fact accused; he is "guilty" by the very fact that his intellectual aspiration toward understanding and coherence and his aspiration toward love, happiness, and the full enjoyment of living are torn asunder, so incommensurate are the modest needs of an individual human being with the titanic collective ambitions and technical powers of today's societies.

No one of us today, therefore, if he be lucid, can escape the judgments of a double tribunal, the subjective inner tribunal and the outer objective tribunal, and the two refuse to be reconciled. The aspirations of modern man are thus thwarted as he is increasingly subjected to the rhythms of a collective and technical order indifferent to the "truths of the flesh." He has forgotten in his confusion that he carries within him a force—his sense of freedom, his need for justice—which can oppose, control, and destroy the abstract mental or social patterns which oppress him. It is to this force that Camus constantly appealed, calling upon himself and upon us to let the "judge" in us yield to the "creator" in us. The "creator" is that "Prince" in exile in a world of "judges," he who, like Rieux in *La Peste*, "forces . . . himself to understand rather than judge."[2] To understand is to open a path to action; the creator frees, whereas the judge imprisons.

Since our time taxes this power of understanding to the utmost, it offers the artist a challenge that is most desperate yet of the highest order: "For more than twenty years of absolutely insane history, lost hopelessly like all those of my age in the convulsions of the epoch, I derived comfort from the vague impression that writing was an honor today because

[2] Camus's speech of acceptance of the Nobel Prize for literature, Dec. 10, 1957, p. xx. Translated by Justin O'Brien (New York: Alfred A. Knopf, 1958).

the act obligated a man, obligated him to more than just writing. It obligated me in particular, such as I was, to bear—along with all the others living the same history—the tribulation and hope we shared." [3] The task of the men of his generation, a task which for Camus superseded all others, was "to fashion for themselves an art of living in times of catastrophe, in order to be reborn before fighting openly against the death instinct at work in our society." [4]

For the artist this art of living can be reached only through reconciliation: "No great work of genius has ever been founded on hatred or contempt. In some corner of his heart, at some moment in his history, the real creator always ends by reconciling." [5] To reconcile was the first and perhaps the hardest task that confronted Camus, and one may venture to think that art was increasingly the only, the almost desperate means by which he could reconcile his experience and the exigencies of his passionate and often uncompromising temperament.

In the first stage of his career the elements in conflict were normal and inherent in human life: the poverty and suffering of human beings; the magnificence of the natural world; the unremitting presence of death; the passion for life—timeless themes of the artist. But the widespread political terrorism of the war years, the outer violence and the inner anger of the underground struggle against the Nazis, were more difficult to accept: "For men today there is an inner path that I know well because I followed it in both directions and it goes from the hills of the mind to the capitals of crime." [6] But in the grandeur of the struggle, in its tragic inequality, and the

[3] *Ibid.*, p. x.
[4] *Ibid.*, p. xi.
[5] "*L'Artiste en prison*," Camus's preface to *La Ballade de la geôle de Reading* by Oscar Wilde, translated by Jacques Bour (Paris: Falaize, 1952).
[6] "*Retour à Tipasa*," in *L'Eté*, p. 159.

burning certainty that it was justified, there was an element
of coherence that made conciliation possible.

The postliberation period was to present the most difficult
obstacle of all. The black-and-white certainties of the underground, where Camus had been most at ease, were, after the
liberation of France, torn asunder. Camus now had to deal
with men and not with heroes, with opinions and not with
actions. The hothouse atmosphere of Parisian polemics was
alien to him.[7] Unlike Sartre, who wields the weapon of polemics with bland and gleeful mastery, Camus tended to withdraw behind moral retrenchments. He did not immediately
nor easily achieve detachment. His irony often seemed tinged
with that personal resentment which, in his preface to *L'Envers et l'endroit,* he claimed to have conquered.

It was not in the daily round of polemics that he could find
any ground for reconciliation, and naturally enough, for at
that level reconciliation is seldom compatible with integrity,
and in any event Camus was not at home in the world of
political debate. It was perhaps a weakness that in the arena
of political action he could accept no universe other than his
own, one often shaped, at least to some extent, by his own
hands. His vision was both imaginative and relentlessly ethical; a few strong, simple abstractions became concrete, active
participants in its shaping—and then he fought the entities
he had created. Our universe was divided between "victims"
and "hangmen"; or parceled out between "tradesmen" and
"policemen"; or it became *"l'univers du procès"* or *"l'univers
concentrationnaire,"* the scene of a sinister continuous trial of
innocent human beings or a vast torture camp.

The whole human world seems to be animated with a per-

[7] Camus often spoke quite sarcastically about the mores of the
Parisian journalist and man of letters: see in particular the preface to
L'Envers et l'endroit, and the short story "Jonas" in *L'Exil et le
royaume.*

verse will embodied in abstractions: the "century" makes "dupes" of us, "pretending" to run after the "empire of reason whereas it is only searching after the reasons for loving which it has lost"; it "cultivates" a special "species" of hatred, cold hatred. It plays its role as "the century of fear" or as "the century of polemics and insults."

Amid this universal perversity we "fumble" along "dark walls" hunting for the "invisible spots in which doors can open." Truth is "in exile" in a "desert"; the "palaces of oppression" rise in the "capitals of crime" while a "hideous plague" ravages both East and West, engaged in a universal conspiracy against freedom, truth, and love.

And verbal opposition accentuates the stylization: hatred and falsehood strangle love and truth; crime, formerly "solitary as a cry," becomes as "universal as science"; France hesitates between "the tradesmen who possess her" and "the policemen who covet her," and so on interminably.

In the world of literature, Camus moved with greater freedom. Here he was master of a world which he controlled and which responded to his exigencies and certainties, and thus here reconciliation became possible. Camus's essays indicate some of the points of this reconciliation with the universal "monsters" he found in his path, and each of his works is an effort in this difficult direction. Although his works are detached from the everyday universe of contention and disillusionment, they nevertheless proceed directly from it. They are the real expression of Camus's relation to his time.

This effort at reconciliation was deliberate, the basic motivation for his writing. It stemmed from a clear and personal conception of the function of the writer in relation to himself, his time, his art. Camus explained it often and freely.[8] Each

---

[8] For example, in both *Le Mythe de Sisyphe* and *L'Homme révolté* and in many articles and lectures: "*L'Intelligence et l'échafaud,*" *Confluences*, July-August, 1943; introduction to Chamfort's *Maximes*

successive formulation was made in relation to his main theme at that moment—successively in terms of the absurd, of revolt, or of measure—but his basic ideas as they matured remained remarkably consistent. If Camus is one of the most scrupulous among the literary craftsmen in mid-century France, it is because he had an uncompromising and elevated idea of art, an initial advantage over many of his contemporaries.

Literature was for Camus an essential human activity, one of the most fundamental. It expresses and safeguards the aspiration toward freedom, coherence, and beauty, those components of man's relative happiness, an aspiration which alone makes life valuable for each separate transient human being. It defines that part of existence in which each individual is more than a social unit or an insignificant cog in the evolution of history. Camus's anger was instantly awakened by any action, any ideology, that threatened to destroy this aspiration. All his articles gain their real and valuable meaning in that perspective. His quarrel with the Hegelian-Marxist philosophies of history has its source in his despair when confronted with an interpretation of life which "deliberately amputates from the world that which makes its permanence: nature, the sea, the hill, evening meditation," [9] the beauty of the earth.

et anecdotes (Monaco, 1944); his lecture "*Le Témoin de la liberté,*" November, 1948 (*Actuelles I,* p. 25); "*L'Artiste et son temps,*" *Actuelles II,* p. 179, and *Quaderni Aci,* No. 16, Torino, 1955; "*L'Artiste en prison,*" preface to *La Ballade de la geôle de Reading* by Oscar Wilde and translated into French by Jacques Bour; "Melville," *Les Ecrivains célèbres,* III (Paris: Editions d'Art, Mazerod, 1951), pp. 128-129; several essays in *L'Eté* and various prefaces to translations of his work; short book reviews in *Alger-Républicain* (December, 1938-April, 1939); preface to the German edition of *The Poems of René Char* (1952); and preface to the complete works of Roger Martin du Gard (Paris: Editions Pléiade, Gallimard, 1955).

[9] *L'Exil d'Hélène,*" in *L'Eté,* p. 115.

French writers, particularly since the romantic period, have kept up such a steady running debate on the place and function of literature that it is next to impossible for a young French author interested in producing something more than popular reading matter to avoid some form of theoretical approach to his art. The cumulative effect of a century and a half of discussion led with the surrealists to launch what has been defined as literary "terrorism," an onslaught on the values of literature itself. Pushed into its last retrenchments, literature was decried as a vast mystification which, with the help of conventional language, amiably puts us to sleep, masking the terrifying nature of our condition.

Marxists, on the other hand, attacked "bourgeois" writing, justifying literature only as an instrument of social progress, a broad and rapid path to a particularly tiresome species of writing: propaganda. With Proust, Gide, and, in spite of his universal skepticism, Valéry, the last real believers in the values of literature disappeared. Colette seems almost the last of the great French writers to have taken her profession for granted.

The question "What is literature and has it any significant function in our society?" was debated with considerable acuity in the 1940's and 1950's. The writer himself—that idol of French society, particularly Parisian—questioned his profession. This is certainly true of Sartre, whose vigorous advocacy of a "literature of commitment" was an attempt to reinstate literature as an immediately effective force and yet to preserve its freedom, an attempt at justification which seems to have failed—in his eyes at least.

Camus's masters in literature were the Greeks and the French classics, to which he added a chosen gallery of writers: alongside of Molière, Shakespeare, Lope de Vega, and Calderón; accompanying Mme. de Lafayette were Tolstoy and Dostoevsky, Kafka and Melville, Gide and Proust, Malraux and Montherlant. His admiration for these masters taught him to set his goals high. He did not feel the slightest self-consciousness in regard to his profession, which he thought of with "gratitude and pride." [10] Indeed his conception of the function of the creative artist seems to have been a determining factor in the conscious construction of his own personality, compelling him to take action almost in spite of himself: "It is not the struggle that makes us artists, but art that obliges us to be combatants." [11] His stubborn, sometimes irascible defense of his political integrity was really a defense of his artistic integrity. But Camus, unlike Sartre, did not legislate for all artists nor make political commitment a *sine qua non* for artistic achievement in all ages.

"The first choice an artist makes," Camus writes, "is precisely to be an artist, and if he chooses to be an artist it is in consideration of what he is himself and because of a certain idea he has of art." [12] But, he ironically observes, we live in "a time when Racine would blush at having written *Bérénice*, and Rembrandt, in order to apologize for having painted the 'Night Watch,' would run to register at the local communist headquarters." [13] Social consciousness when it is based on an unsufficient understanding of art is, according to Camus, the enemy of the artist and not his safeguard.

Though the first responsibility of the artist is to his art, Camus contended that he could meet it only in the measure that he first met his responsibilities as a man, an ordinary human being comparable to any, facing like any other the current problems of life within his given social framework. Any evasion eventually limits the writer's efficacy. But an artist need not necessarily run after unusual experiences or adventures. Camus disliked Sartre's contention that the artist must

[10] *Actuelles I*, p. 263.
[11] *Ibid.*, p. 264.
[12] "*Le Témoin de la liberté*," *Actuelles I*, p. 254.
[13] *Ibid.*, p. 253.

"commit" himself politically and socially at all times and for all men, in any situation, all over the world, as if he were perpetually on trial. He seemed rather to believe that for the European of the past quarter of a century, issues were raised which required each human being to make drastic and often dangerous decisions if he wished to keep his inner integrity; this was as true for the artist as for all others. But so great is the toll in time, action, and energy that the artist's creative vigor cannot but be greatly impaired. The European writer of the twentieth century thus "walks a tightrope in an uneasy equilibrium between insignificance and silence." [14] And silence, for the artist, is death.

Camus first organized his scattered views on art within the framework of "absurdity" in *Le Mythe de Sisyphe*—an excellent framework which, by definition, disposes of a number of somewhat worn clichés. In a world where all is given and nothing explained no activity needs justification, for all activities are equally arbitrary though not necessarily equally satisfactory. In *l'univers absurde* the artist's "creation" escapes from the most obvious blind alleys followed by theorists of art. *La création absurde* explains nothing, proves nothing; it "cannot be the end, the meaning, nor the consolation of a life." [15] A literature of self-justification, therefore, makes no sense, nor for that matter does a literature of psychological analysis, since both seek to explain or to prove what can be neither explained nor proved.

The creative artist, *l'homme absurde par excellence*, finds an intense delight in the gratuitousness of his work, which is a perpetual challenge to his consciousness; it is "a unique chance to keep his consciousness alert and to fix its adventures." His task requires strict discipline, the will never to

[14] Camus answers questions put to him by Jean Bloch-Michel, *The Reporter*, Nov. 28, 1957.
[15] *Le Mythe de Sisyphe*, p. 134.

yield a fragment of his lucidity. The artist stands, therefore, fully armed in the face of the universe, refusing the somnolence it offers. He knows the limits of his mind, the limits of his life, and the uselessness of an effort which he maintains at its highest level of intensity. Knowing the limits of his mind, the artist does not attempt to "reason the concrete," but through his intelligence he orders a sumptuous "mime" of concrete images that testify to the carnal reality of a universe whose mystery remains intact. This ordering is the second facet of his revolt, for his creation "corrects creation," imposing limits, a coherence—therefore a selection—and a harmony which exists only in the exigencies of man.

There is a Dionysian element in this "mime of life" suggested no doubt by Nietzsche, but it is balanced by the strict injunction that the artist stay within the limits of the reality perceived. Camus, meditating on an idea which came to him perhaps from Spengler, perhaps from Malraux, noted that "the Occident does not retrace its daily life. It unceasingly sets up for itself great images which enervate it, and it pursues them—Manfred or Faust, Don Juan or Narcissus. But the approximation is always in vain." [16] When he made this comment, Camus considered the image to be the essential factor in a work of art, and one which must come out of our "daily life," but it is not a phantom to be pursued nor is it even originally a symbol; it is instead a stylization that illuminates and does not enervate.

Following this line of thought, Camus defined a personal type of "objective" literature which aims at something more than a "realistic" reproduction of life yet emerges from life. The artist must first be *"un grand vivant"* at grips with life itself. Much later Camus clarified this concept of objectivity still further: "The idea that every writer obligatorily writes about himself and depicts himself in his books is one of the

[16] Notebooks. See also *"L'Art et la révolte"* in *L'Homme révolté.*

puerile ideas that we inherit from romanticism. It is not at all impossible that an artist should take interest first in others, or in his age, or in familiar myths . . . , within the measure of possibility I should, on the contrary, have liked to be an objective writer. A writer I consider objective is one who sets himself subjects without ever taking himself as an object. But the contemporary passion to identify the writer with his subject does not permit this relative freedom of the author." [17]

The freedom of the author is in the stylization and the simplification and unity imposed upon the images that he has chosen. *L'Etranger*, Camus's first novel, is an application of this aesthetic, and indeed for Camus the novel is the form best suited to the "mime of life," endlessly re-creating as it does the images of our daily life.

Among all novels, Melville's *Moby Dick* is, according to Camus, the highest form of that particular form of art, *la création absurde*, as is also, though to a lesser extent, Melville's *Billy Budd*.[18] As Camus interprets them, Melville's works "are the record of an experience of the mind unequaled in intensity and are in part symbolic." They create great myths: the myth of man's endless "quest, pursuing and pursued on a limitless ocean." *Moby Dick* is "one of the most disturbing myths ever invented concerning man's fight against evil and the terrible logic which ends by first setting the just man against creation and the creator, then setting him against himself and his fellow men." *Billy Budd* is "youth and beauty," killed "so that an order can be maintained." Melville outdistances Kafka as a creator "because in Kafka's work the reality described is summoned by the symbol, the fact is a consequence of the image, whereas, in Melville, the symbol is born of reality, the image, of perception."

[17] "*L'Enigme*," in *L'Eté*, pp. 131-133.
[18] Albert Camus, "Melville," *Les Ecrivains célèbres*, III (Paris: Editions d'Art, Mazerod, 1953).

Although this basic approach to literature did not change, during the war years the emphasis shifted from man's struggle against the injustice of the cosmos to man's struggle in the world of men, and the freedom Camus generously gave the artist in *Le Mythe de Sisyphe*—with his appetite for every form of life—seemed for a time to disappear. In two articles of literary criticism written in 1943 and 1944, *L'Intelligence et l'échafaud* and an introduction to Chamfort's *Maximes*, he shifted the scene from man's relation to the outer universe to the inner world of human passions and ethical judgments.

In these articles Camus scrutinizes French classical literature, whose greatness lies in its treatment of human passions. It is a literature that carries the logic of human passion to its extreme limit—most often death. The classical artist thus gives each individual passion the unity, coherence, finality, and language that our sensibility demands and does not find in life. He wrests from each passion an ethic both of integrity and of limitation through the aesthetic discipline of form. The contemporary writer, like the French classical writer, must now become the diagnostician and exorcist of the fierce, murderous, human passions of his time, but unlike his great models, he moves among collective, not individual passions:

> To dominate collective passions, one must, it is true, live them and feel them, at least relatively. At the time he feels them, the artist is devoured by them. As a result our age is the age of journalism rather than works of art. Finally, the exercise of these passions carries with it greater chances of death than at the time of love or ambition; the only way to live a collective passion authentically is to accept that one may die for it and through it—the greatest chance for failure in art.[19]

[19] *L'Homme révolté*, p. 339.

classicists, for the emotional texture of Camus's thought is far
removed from theirs. The spirit of refusal is strong within him,
the "corrected creation" of the artist is still, in his eyes, one
that contests and condemns reality, correcting it on ethical
grounds. Camus does not, as is the case with the classics,
"correct creation" in the name of a truer vision of reality,
aesthetic and rational in nature. The "correction" of creation,
as Camus defines it in *L'Homme révolté*, comes perilously
close to mutilation. Camus does, however, break definitely
with a certain trend in French literature that he analyzes in
L'Homme révolté, which culminates in the surrealistic revolt
against all reality.

Camus again uses the modern novel to illustrate his point
of view, the novel which, according to him, developed with
"man's revolt" and with the "literature of dissent" that at the
end of the eighteenth century took the place of a "literature
of consent." "What is the novel, in fact, if not the universe
where action finds its form, where the final words are said, the
human being abandoned to other human beings, where everything bears the mark of destiny?" [20]

Thus Camus required that art fulfill many functions, and
particularly that it have a direct bearing upon the contemporaneous scene. In his article *"L'Artiste et son temps,"* Camus
summarized all his previous themes and stresses more particularly the relation between the writer and the society in which
he lives. Art "is the contrary of silence"; it is rooted in reality,
therefore it is communicable to all men; it is an invitation to
dialogue and therefore to freedom. Because it requires the
artist to create his own order, it is in itself a manifestation of
freedom and cannot submit to any other order; in fact it is a
challenge to any other order. This leads to a direct attack
upon the Marxist and Sartrian positions: valid art is, to these
men, one of the means by which men discern and describe

[20] *Ibid.*, p. 324.

The Role of the Artist

Because he must himself experience these passio
writer, objective though he may attempt to be, is by t
nature of his function called upon to take sides. In *L'F
révolté* Camus defines the artist as the man who must
in that difficult state of equilibrium "between Yes an
which, to Camus, is the only fruitful form of revolt a
deed, of any human activity. For the artist cannot deny
as does the ideologist, who substitutes abstract logic f
"Man can permit himself to denounce the total injus
the world and demand a total justice that he is alone
ate," but "no art can live on a total refusal": even the
abstract art uses line and color. And yet no art can li
a total acceptance of reality, which would mean only e
enumeration. An art that tends toward a total refusal of
is a formal art, the ultimate limit of which is futility a
significance. A "realistic art" tends, by the opposite
toward an equally futile and dismal monotony. The real
uses the substance of reality but "corrects creation." H
fuses to admit the incoherence and perpetual "becoming
human life, and therein lies his revolt and his creativity
gives coherence to the incoherent, form therefore to wh
formless, and value to what is meaningless.

This unification can be carried out in a number of w
The American novelists of the 1930's and 1940's stylize
world from outside in terms of appearances—images, gestu
words, movement—a form of unification Camus consider
be eventually impoverishing. Proust, at the end of a long
meticulous inner odyssey, restores the world of his experie
to its ordered, inner coherence and individual beauty, a
more satisfactory "correction" in Camus's eyes.

This concept of art is not new and hardly seems to warr
the somewhat artificial enrollment of the artist under the b
ner of revolt. In its main lines it takes us back to the sev
teenth century. But there is a world between Camus and t

the real sense and orientation of their time, the "shape of things to come." For Camus "the object of the artist in history is . . . what he can see of history and suffer himself, directly or indirectly; it is the present in the strict sense of the word, that is to say, the men living today, not the relation between this present world and a future which cannot be foreseen by the living artist." Moreover, "the aim of art is not to rule, but first to understand"; the artist "is not a judge but a justifier"—hence his role as conciliator.

There are in Camus's discussion of art some loose ends which are very revealing. In *L'Homme révolté*, distinguishing between the revolutionary and the artist, Camus based the artist's acceptance of the world on his sense of its beauty: the artist "cannot claim that the ugliness of the world is total." Beauty, in Camus's eyes, appeared as the prerogative both of the natural world and of the world of art. To man he attributed only a "common misery." Neither beauty nor joy seemed to emanate from the human visage as he saw it; instead, man apparently experiences beauty and joy only as a reflection of a work of art. In Camus's long analyses of art, in spite of his appeal to the fraternity that binds the artist to all men, one looks in vain for that immense delight in man himself—in his dignity and grandeur—that has always characterized the great creator.

"Each great work of art makes the human visage more admirable and richer, that is its entire secret," wrote Camus, but one sometimes wonders whether the human visage which he observes outside the realm of art had not become for him merely the ravaged visage of our "common misery." Here Camus's experience seems to have weighed heavily upon his sensibility; the times took their toll of the artist. One remark in *L'Homme révolté*, however, reveals an unexpected direction in Camus's thought: "There is perhaps a living transcendency of which beauty is a promise, which may make us love, and prefer to any other, the limited and mortal world." [21]

What is, in truth, the source of the beauty which moved Camus both in the work of art and in nature? Not revolt, certainly; not unity and coherence alone. Rejecting in part both the purely natural and the purely human, and yet at the same time considering each as an autonomous entity, Camus could not completely "reconcile" the elements of his universe: he seemed to be reaching toward that "living transcendency" he mentions and which might be a key to unity.

It is difficult to arrive at a just appreciation of the true significance of Camus's aesthetic thought. *L'Homme révolté* and *"L'Artiste et son temps,"* with their emphasis on the ordering of an experience, on stylization of experience through art, and on human understanding as the main sources of art, seem to define a new classicism. The road Camus followed may appear unnecessarily complicated but this is precisely because—very much of his time—he shared in certain of its fashions, the prisoner sometimes of attitudes and a vocabulary which he himself in part created. To see all things, including the problem of art, even temporarily, in the light of *l'absurde* or *la révolte* is a limitation. One feels that Camus consciously and ferociously imposed this limitation on himself. For him, therefore, it was no doubt a necessity. It was also something more. Each stage in his thought was a struggle toward a certain intellectual grasp of life, an effort to dominate a disorder so great that it tended to reduce freedom to anarchy. And yet freedom was what Camus as an artist most needed, that freedom which is a leitmotiv of his work: freedom in respect to himself and to his age, freedom in respect to his art and to other human beings, a freedom which, at the time of his death, he was just beginning to enjoy.

Camus grappled with the forces that reject and menace

[21] *Ibid.*, p. 319.

freedom. He called these forces to life, incarnated them, and mapped out their violently destructive career. For a young man brought up "in the sunlight, the delight in life, the freedom" of long Algerian summers, the task was hard. "To think," he wrote, "is to learn how to see anew." The outer world thrust upon him a vision he abhorred. Camus recognized at the outset that the "tragic" element in our time was intellectual in character. To look unflinchingly at the world around him, "refusing to lie" to himself or others, was the task he set himself. From *L'Envers et l'endroit* to *La Chute* the existence of the "kingdom of man" that he had sought from the outset was more and more sharply challenged, and Camus felt that it was imperative to integrate into his vision his own violently disruptive experience. He thus delivered his world from the "phantoms" which invaded it, slowly establishing its fundamental unity and its limits in human terms.

With *L'Exil et le royaume* Camus seemed deliberately to have been moving toward the projection of this carefully limited and sharply defined "kingdom of man," and of the "free and naked way of life" which defines an "art of living" with dignity in our time and face to face with ourselves. More than ever, in Camus's eyes, the artist was committed to his task of expressing "the sufferings and joys of all" in the language of all mankind. He is, he must be, on the side of freedom, and of justice against the "dark wind of death" which already blew over the ruins of Djémila. The images of freeing, of breaking open the prison bars, the great sustaining movement of the sea, the confrontation with the terrible enigma of the "dark" sun of life continued to sustain his universe.

Camus slowly came to know a man attuned both to the inner Africa of his youth and to the symbolic, spiritual Europe which he had once discovered with so much misgiving; a man like himself, "vulnerable and stubborn, unjust and eager for justice, constructing his work without shame or pride within sight of all, constantly torn between pain and beauty, and devoted to extracting from his dual nature the creations he obstinately strives to elevate in the destructive fluctuations of history." [22]

In his Notebooks, the Promethean cycle of revolt, which followed the cycle of Sisyphus or "l'absurde," was to be followed by the cycle of Nemesis, or measure. A fourth cycle of works was mentioned: the cycle of "a certain kind of love." *L'Exil et le royaume* and *Les Possédés*, each in its way, seem to foreshadow the direction Camus's work was taking. Among the works Camus was planning to include in the cycle was "a vast novel." In a manner very reminiscent of Gide, Camus, in the last editions of his works that appeared during his lifetime, listed no novels. *L'Etranger, La Peste, La Chute,* and *L'Exil et le royaume* are grouped together under the heading: "récits" (tales) or "récits et nouvelles" (tales and short stories). The "vast novel" was therefore to be different from the preceding fictional tales.

He announced the title of this novel, *Le premier homme;* a novel which, taking him back to his point of departure, would, it seemed, do what *La Mort heureuse* had attempted— and failed. Camus was setting out to "rewrite" that fragment of his first novel, *L'Envers et l'endroit.* "If after so many efforts to build a language and to make myths come alive, I do not succeed, someday, in rewriting *L'Envers et l'endroit,* I shall not have attained anything, that is my obscure conviction," he wrote in 1957.[23] "Nothing in any case prevents me from dreaming that I shall succeed, that I shall still place in the center of this work the admirable silence of a mother and

[22] Camus's speech accepting the Nobel Prize for literature, Dec. 10, 1957, p. xii, translated by Justin O'Brien (New York: Alfred A. Knopf, 1958).

[23] *L'Envers et l'endroit* (Paris: Gallimard, 1958), Preface, p. 33.

the effort of a man to rediscover a justice or a love which could counterbalance that silence."

Camus, after a difficult and long detour imposed upon him by historical events, and more still by his generosity and exacting code of dignity, was returning to the initial source of his writing, the richest, according to some critics, in his work—the world of his Mediterranean childhood. He felt that he still had a long road ahead of him. But, as the work accomplished stands, in its entirety now, before our eyes, although dated perhaps in some of its themes, as is natural and inevitable, it bears all the signs of a literary landmark.

Bibliography

WORKS BY CAMUS

GENERAL EDITIONS

Œuvres complètes. Paris: Bibliothèque de la Pléiade (Gallimard).
I: *Théâtre, récits, nouvelles*, ed. Roger Quilliot, 1962.
Œuvres complètes. Paris: Imprimerie nationale Sauret.
I: *Récits et romans*, 1961. II: *Essais littéraires*, 1962. III:
Essais philosophiques, 1962. IV: *Essais politiques*, 1962. V:
Théâtre, 1962. VI: *Adaptations et traductions*, 1962.
Œuvres complètes. Paris: Bibliothèque de la Pléiade (Gallimard).
II: *Essais*. ed. by Roger Quilliot, 1965. [*L'Envers et l'endroit*;
Le Mythe de Sisyphe; *Actuelles I*; *L'Homme révolté*; *Actuelles
II*; *L'Eté*; *Chroniques algériennes*; *Réflexions sur la guillotine*;
Discours de Suède; *Essais critiques*; *Textes complémentaires par
Albert Camus.*]

NOVELS AND SHORT STORIES:

L'Etranger. Paris: Gallimard, 1942. (*The Stranger*. Tr. by Stuart
Gilbert. New York: Knopf, 1946; Vintage, 1954.)
La Peste. Paris: Gallimard, 1947. (*The Plague*. Tr. by Stuart Gil-
bert. New York: Knopf, 1948.)
La Chute. Paris: Gallimard, 1956. (*The Fall*. Tr. by Justin O'Brien.
New York: Knopf, 1957.)
L'Exil et le royaume. Paris: Gallimard, 1957. (*Exile and the King-
dom*. Tr. by Justin O'Brien. New York: Knopf, 1958.)
La Mort heureuse. Paris: Gallimard, 1970.

PLAYS

La Révolte dans les Asturies: Essai de création collective. Alger:
Charlot, 1936.

"Le Malentendu" suivi de "Caligula." Paris: Gallimard, 1944. (*"Caligula" and "Cross-Purpose."* Tr. by Stuart Gilbert. Norfolk, Conn.: New Directions, 1948; *"Caligula" and Three Other Plays.* Tr. by Stuart Gilbert. Preface by Camus [tr. by Justin O'Brien]. New York: Knopf, 1958.)

L'Etat de siège. Paris: Gallimard, 1948.

Les Justes. Paris: Gallimard, 1950. (*The Just Assassins.* Tr. by Elizabeth Sprigge and Philip Warner. Microfilm, 1957.)

TRANSLATIONS AND ADAPTATIONS

La Dernière Fleur (James Thurber). Translation. Paris: Gallimard, 1952.

La Dévotion à la croix (Pedro Calderón de la Barca). Translation. Paris: Gallimard, 1953.

Les Esprits (Pierre de Larivey). Adaptation. Paris: Gallimard, 1953.

Un Cas intéressant (Dino Buzzati). Translation. Paris: L'Avant-scène, 1955.

Le Chevalier d'Olmédo (Lope de Vega Carpio). Translation. Paris: Gallimard, 1957.

Requiem pour une nonne (William Faulkner). Adaptation. Paris: Gallimard, 1957.

Les Possédés (Feodor Dostoevsky). Adaptation. Paris: Gallimard, 1959. (*The Possessed.* Tr. by Justin O'Brien, with a foreword by Camus. New York: Knopf, 1960.)

ESSAYS

L'Envers et l'endroit. Alger: Charlot, 1937. Reprinted Paris: Gallimard, 1957 and 1958, with preface by Camus.

Noces. Alger: Charlot, 1938. Reprinted Paris: Gallimard, 1947.

Le Mythe de Sisyphe. Paris: Gallimard, 1942. (*The Myth of Sisyphus.* Tr. by Justin O'Brien. New York: Knopf, 1955. *The Myth of Sisyphus and Other Essays.* New York: Vintage, 1960.)

Lettres à un ami allemand. Paris: Gallimard, 1945.

"Remarque sur la révolte," in *L'Existence.* Paris: Gallimard, 1945, pp. 2-23.

Prométhée aux enfers. Paris: Palimugre, 1947.

Actuelles I (*Chroniques 1944-1948*); *II* (*Chroniques 1948-1953*); *III* (*Chroniques algériennes 1939-1958*). Paris: Gallimard, 1950, 1953, 1958. (*Resistance, Rebellion and Death.* Tr. by Justin O'Brien. New York: Knopf, 1961.)

Le Minotaure ou la halte d'Oran. Alger: Charlot, 1950.

L'Homme révolté. Paris: Gallimard, 1951. (*The Rebel*. Tr. by Anthony Bower, with a preface by Sir Herbert Read. New York: Knopf, 1954; Vintage, 1956.)

L'Eté. Paris: Gallimard, 1954.

"*Discours de Suède*" et "*L'Artiste et son temps*." Paris: Gallimard, 1958. (*Speech of Acceptance upon the Award of the Nobel Prize for Literature*. Tr. by Justin O'Brien. New York: Knopf, 1958; *Atlantic*, CCI, No. 5 [May, 1958], 33-34. "The Artist and the World." Tr. by Brian Selby. *Twentieth Century*, CLXVII, No. 996 [1960], 161-62.)

L'Intelligence et l'échafaud. Liège: Dynamo, 1960. Collection: "Brimborions," No. 59.

Méditation sur le théâtre et la vie. Liège: Dynamo, 1961. Collection: "Brimborions," No. 75.

Lettre à Bernanos. Paris: Minard, 1963. Collection: "Bulletin de la Société des Amis de Bernanos," No. 45.

NOTEBOOKS

Carnets: mars 1935-février 1943. Paris: Gallimard, 1962. (*The Notebooks: Volume I, 1935-1942*. Tr. by Philip Thody. New York: Knopf, 1963. *Volume II, 1942-1951*. Tr. by Justin O'Brien. New York: Knopf, 1965.

WORKS WITH PREFACES BY CAMUS

Chamfort, Sébastien. *Maximes et anecdotes*. Monaco: Duc, 1944.

Salvet, André. *Le Combat silencieux*. Paris: Ed. France-Empire (Collection Le Portulan), 1945.

Camp, Jean, and Cassou, Jean. *L'Espagne libre*, Paris: Calmann-Lévy, 1946.

Char, René. *Feuillet d'Hypnos*. Paris: Gallimard, 1946.

Clairin, Pierre-Eugène. *Dix Estampes originales, présentées par Albert Camus*. Paris: Rombaldi, 1946.

Leynaud, René. *Poésies posthumes*. Paris: Gallimard, 1947.

Héon-Canonne, Jeanne. *Devant la mort*. Angers: Siraudeau, 1951; Paris: Amiot-Dumont, 1953.

Char, René. *Das brautliche Antlitz*. Tr. by Johannes Hübner and Lothar Klünner. Frankfurt: K. O. Gotz, 1952. Also *René Char's Poetry*. Ed. de Luca, 1956. Tr. by David Paul.

Mauroc, Daniel. *Contre-Amour*. Paris: Ed. de Minuit, 1952.

Wilde, Oscar. *La Ballade de la geôle de Reading*. Paris: Falaize, 1952.

Guilloux, Louis. *La Maison du peuple*. Paris: Grasset, 1953.

Rosmer, Alfred. *Moscou sous Lénine: Les Origines du Communisme.* Paris: Ed. Flore, Pierre Horay, 1953.

Bieber, Konrad. *L'Allemagne vue par les écrivains de la Résistance française.* Genève: Droz, 1954.

Targuebayre, Claire. *Cordes-en-Albigeois.* Toulouse: E. Privat, 1954.

Camus, Albert. *L'Etranger.* Ed. by Germaine Brée and Carlos Lynes, Jr. New York: Appleton-Century-Crofts, 1955.

Martin du Gard, Roger. *Oeuvres complètes.* Paris: Bibliothèque de la Pléiade (Gallimard), 1955.

Faulkner, William. *Requiem pour une nonne.* Tr. by M. E. Coindreau. Paris: Gallimard, 1957.

La Vérité sur l'affaire Nagy: Les Faits, les documents, les témoignages internationaux. Paris: Plon, 1958.

Grenier, Jean. *Les Iles.* Paris: *La Nouvelle Revue Française,* 1959.

IN COLLABORATION

Désert vivant: Images en couleurs de Walt Disney. Textes de Marcel Aymé, Louis Bromfield, Albert Camus, *et al.* Paris: Société française du livre, 1954.

Koestler, Arthur, and Camus, Albert. *Réflexions sur la peine capitale: Introduction et étude de Jean Bloch-Michel.* Paris: Calmann-Lévy, 1957.

SELECTED ARTICLES

Most of the more important articles written by Camus for newspapers and magazines can be found in *Actuelles I, II,* and *III.*

Alger-Républicain, Oct. 9, 1938-Aug. 18, 1939. Ninety-two articles.

"La Présentation de la revue *Rivages,*" *Rivages,* Algiers, 1939.

Soir-Républicain, Sept. 15, 1939-Jan. 1, 1940. Twelve articles.

"Portrait d'un elu," *Les Cahiers du sud* (Apr., 1943), 306-11.

"Sur une philosophie de l'expression," *Poésie* (Jan., 1944), 15-23.

Combat Clandestin, Mar., 1944-May, 1944. Two articles.

Combat, Aug. 21, 1944-Dec. 25, 1948. One hundred and thirty-two articles written by Camus; twenty-two articles probably written by Camus.

"Préface à une anthologie de l'insignifiance," *Almanach des lettres et des arts* (Summer, 1945).

"Réflexions sur le Christianisme," *La Vie intellectuelle* (Dec. 1, 1946).

"Le Meurtre et l'absurde," *Empédocle,* No. 1 (1949).

"Nietzsche et le nihilisme," *Les Temps modernes* (Aug., 1951).

"Rencontres avec André Gide," in *Hommage à André Gide*. Paris: *La Nouvelle Revue Française*, 1951.

"Herman Melville," *Les Ecrivains célèbres*, III. Paris: Ed. d'Art, Mazerod, 1953.

"Calendrier de la liberté," *Témoins*, No. 5 (Spring, 1954).

"Lettre à Roland Barthès," *Club* (Feb., 1955).

L'Express, May 14, 1955-Aug. 24, 1956. Thirty-three articles.

"My Debt to Spain," *New Leader* (June 9, 1958).

INTERVIEWS
Excluding six interviews reprinted in *Actuelles I* and *II*.

" 'Non, je ne suis pas existentialiste,' nous dit Albert Camus," *Les Nouvelles littéraires*, No. 954 (Nov. 15, 1945), 1.

"Servir," *Revue de Lausanne* (Dec., 1945).

Gazette des lettres (May 10, 1951, and Feb. 15, 1952). The February 15 interview also appears in Jean-Claude Brisville's book, *Camus*, pp. 249-55.

Gazette de Lausanne (Mar. 28, 1954).

"Obstinate Confidence of a Pessimistic Man: Albert Camus Answers Questions Put to Him by Jean Bloch-Michel," *Reporter*, XVII, No. 9 (Nov. 28, 1957), 37-39.

"Camus nous parle," *Le Figaro littéraire* (May 16, 1959), 1, 4.

"Réponses à Jean-Claude Brisville," 1959, in *Camus*, by Jean-Claude Brisville, pp. 256-61.

"Albert Camus (1913-1960): A Final Interview," *Venture*, III, No. 4 (Spring-Summer, 1960), 25-39.

SELECTED ARTICLES ON CAMUS
Ames, Sanford. "From Summitry to Speleology in *La Chute*," *French Review*, XXXIX, 559-66.

Garnham, B. G. "Albert Camus: Metaphysical Revolt and Historical Action," *Modern Language Review*, LXII (1967), 248-55.

Girard, René. "Camus's Stranger Retried," *Publications of the Modern Language Association*, LXXIX (1964), 519-23.

Manly, William M. "Journey to Consciousness: The Symbolic Pattern in Camus's *L'Etranger*," *Publications of the Modern Language Association*, LXXIX (1964), 321-28.

Storzer, Gerald H. "La Genèse du héros de *L'Etranger*," *French Review*, XXXVII (1964), 130-45.

Toenes, Sara. "Public Confession in *La Chute*," *Wisconsin Studies in Contemporary Literature*, IV (1963), 305-18.

SELECTED WORKS ON CAMUS

Bollinger, Renate. *Albert Camus: Eine Bibliographie der Literatur über ihn und sein Werk.* Cologne: Greyn Verlag, 1957. This is a most complete bibliography up to 1957. It lists 549 titles.

Crépin, Simone. *Albert Camus: Essai de bibliographie.* Bruxelles: Commission belge de bibliographie, 1960.

Fitch, Brian T. *Albert Camus: Essai de bibliographie des études en langue française consacrées à Albert Camus.* Paris: Lettres Modernes, 1965.

Roeming, Robert F. *Camus: A Bibliography.* Madison: University of Wisconsin Press, 1968.

FRENCH-LANGUAGE BOOKS ON CAMUS

A Albert Camus, ses amis du livre: Albert Camus au marbre. Paris: Gallimard, 1962.

Albert Camus: *Camus devant la critique anglo-saxonne.* Ed. by J. H. Matthews. Paris: Minard, 1961.

Barrier, M. G. *L'Art du récit dans L'Etranger d'Albert Camus.* Paris: Nizet, 1962.

Bonnier, Henry. *Albert Camus ou la force d'être.* Lyon-Paris: Vitte, 1959.

Brisville, Jean-Claude. *Camus.* Paris: Gallimard, 1959.

Castex, Pierre-Georges. *Albert Camus et 'L'Etranger.'* Paris: Corti, 1965.

Champigny, Robert. *Sur un héros païen.* Paris: Gallimard, 1959.

Coombes, Ilona. *Camus: homme de théâtre.* Paris: Nizet, 1968.

Fitch, Brian. *Narrateur et narration dans L'Etranger d'Albert Camus.* Paris: Minard, 1960.

Ginestier, Paul. *Camus.* Paris: Bordas, 1965.

Luppé, Robert de. *Albert Camus.* Paris: Ed. Universitaires, 1958.

Maquet, Albert. *Albert Camus ou l'invincible été.* Paris: Debresse, 1955. (*Albert Camus: The Invincible Summer.* Tr. by Herma Brissault. New York: Braziller, 1958.)

Nguyen-van-Huy, Pierre. *La Métaphysique du bonheur chez Albert Camus.* Neuchâtel: A la Baconnière, 1962.

Nicolas, André. *Camus.* Paris: Seghers, 1966.

Pinnoy, M. *Albert Camus.* Bruges: Desclée de Brouwer, 1961.

Quilliot, Roger. *La Mer et les prisons: Essai sur Albert Camus.*

Paris: Gallimard, 1956. This contains an extensive bibliography of Camus' work.

Simon, Pierre-Henri. *Présence de Camus.* Bruxelles: Renaissance du livre, 1961.

Thorens, Léon. *A la rencontre d'Albert Camus.* Bruxelles-Paris: La Sixaine, 1946.

ENGLISH-LANGUAGE BOOKS ON CAMUS

Camus: A Collection of Critical Essays. Ed. by Germaine Brée Englewood Cliffs, N.J.: Prentice-Hall, 1962.

Cruickshank, John. *Albert Camus and the Literature of Revolt.* London: Oxford Univ. Press, 1959; New York: Galaxy, 1960. The latter includes a tribute to Albert Camus.

Hanna, Thomas. *The Thought and Art of Albert Camus.* Chicago: Regnery, 1958; Gateway, 1959.

SPECIAL ISSUES OF REVIEWS EXCLUSIVELY ON CAMUS

"Albert Camus," *Preuves,* No. 110 (Apr., 1960).

"Albert Camus," *La Table Ronde,* No. 146 (Feb., 1960).

"Albert Camus," *Yale French Studies,* No. 25 (Spring, 1960).

Albert Camus: Homme de théâtre. Paris: Publications de la Société d'Histoire du Théâtre, No. 4 (Oct.-Dec., 1960).

"Camus l'Algérien," *Simoün,* No. 3. Oran: Bd. Vauchez, 1960.

Configuration critique d'Albert Camus, no. 2. Camus devant la critique allemande, Revue des Langues Modernes, nos. 90-93 [published later by Minard, Paris, 1964].

"Hommage à Camus (1913-1960)," *La Nouvelle Revue Française,* No. 87 (Mar. 1, 1960).

ENGLISH-LANGUAGE BOOKS ON CAMUS,
WHOLLY OR IN PART

Bersani, Leo. *Balzac to Beckett. Center and Circumference in French Fiction.* New York: Oxford University Press, 1970.

Brée, Germaine. *Camus.* New York: Columbia University Press, 1964. (Columbia Essays on Modern Writers, No. 1)

———. Ed. *A Collection of Critical Essays.* Englewood Cliffs, N.J.: Prentice-Hall, 1962.

———, and Guiton, Margaret. *An Age of Fiction.* London: Chatto and Windus, 1958.

Brombert, Victor. *The Intellectual Hero: Studies in the French Novel, 1880-1958.* Philadelphia: Lippincott, 1961.

Clurman, Harold. *Lies Like Truth: Theatre Reviews and Essays.* New York: Grove, 1958.

Collins, James. *The Existentialists: A Critical Study*. Chicago: Regnery, 1952.

Copleston, F. C. *Existentialism and Modern Man. A paper read to the Aquinas Society of London on the 14th of April, 1948*. London: Blackfriars, 1953.

Cruickshank, John. *Albert Camus and the Literature of Revolt*. London: Oxford Univ. Press, 1959; New York: Galaxy, 1960. The latter includes a tribute to Albert Camus.

————. Ed., *The Novelist as Philosopher: Studies in French Fiction 1953-60*. London: Oxford Univ. Press, 1962.

Curtis, Anthony. *New Developments in the French Theatre*. London: Curtain Press, 1948.

Falk, Eugene H. *Types of Thematic Structure: the Nature and Function of Motifs in Gide, Camus and Sartre*. With an introduction by Bernard Weinberg. Chicago: Chicago Univ. Press, 1967.

Fowlie, Wallace. *Dionysus in Paris*. New York: Meridian, 1960.

Gassner, John. *Masters of the Drama*. New York: Dover, 1954.

Hanna, Thomas. *The Lyrical Existentialists*. New York: Atheneum, 1962.

————. *The Thought and Art of Albert Camus*. Chicago: Regnery, 1958; Gateway, 1959.

Jones, R. E. *The Alienated Hero in Modern French Drama*. Athens, Ga.: Univ. of Georgia Press, 1962.

Kaufmann, Walter. *Existentialism from Dostoevsky to Sartre*. New York: Meridian, 1956.

King, Adele. *Camus*. New York: Barnes and Noble, 1965.

Lerner, Max. "Camus and the Outsider," in *Actions and Passions: Notes on the Multiple Revolutions of Our Time*. New York: Simon and Schuster, 1949.

Lewis, Wyndham. *The Writer and the Absolute*. London, Methuen, 1952.

Lumley, Frederick. *Trends in Twentieth Century Drama*. Fairlawn, N.J.: Essential Books, 1960.

Luppé, Robert de. *Albert Camus*. Tr. John Cumming and F. Hargreaves. New York: Minerva Press, 1969.

Mueller, William R. *The Prophetic Voice in Modern Fiction*. New York: Association Press, 1959.

O'Brien, Justin. *The French Literary Horizon*. New Brunswick: Rutgers University Press, 1967.

264 *Bibliography*

Parker, Emmet. *Albert Camus: The Artist in the Arena*. Madison: University of Wisconsin Press, 1965. (Extensive bibliography)

Quilliot, Roger. *The Sea and the Prisons*. Tr. with notes and preface by Emmet Parker. Alabama: University of Alabama Press, 1970.

Rhein, Philip H. *Albert Camus* (Twayne's World Author Series). New York: Twayne, 1969.

Sartre, Jean-Paul. *Literary and Philosophical Essays*. Tr. by Annette Michelson. New York: Criterion, 1955.

Thody, Philip. *Albert Camus: A Study of His Work*. New York: Macmillan, 1957; Evergreen, 1959.

———. *Albert Camus, 1913-1960*. London: Hamish Hamilton, 1961. Revised edition of the previous work.

———. Ed., with notes. *Lyrical and Critical Essays of Camus*. Tr. from the French by Ellen C. Kennedy. New York: Knopf, 1968.

Ullman, Stephen. *The Image in the Modern French Novel*. Cambridge, England: Cambridge Univ. Press, 1960.

Willhoite, Fred H. *Beyond Nihilism: Albert Camus' Contribution to Political Thought*. Baton Rouge: Louisiana State University Press, 1968.

Wilson, Colin. *The Outsider*. London: Gollancz, 1956.

ENGLISH-LANGUAGE ARTICLES ON CAMUS

Abel, Lionel. "Letter from Paris," *Partisan Review*, XVI, No. 4 (Apr., 1949), 395-99.

"Absurdiste," in "The Talk of the Town," *New Yorker*, XXII, No. 10 (Apr. 20, 1946), 22-23.

Ayer, A. J. "Albert Camus," *Horizon*, XIII, No. 75 (Mar., 1946), 155-68.

Bieber, Konrad. "*Engagement* as a Professional Risk," *Yale French Studies*, No. 16 (Winter, 1955-56), 29-39.

———. "The Translator—Friend or Foe?" *French Review*, XXVIII, No. 6 (May, 1955), 493-97.

Biographical sketch, *Saturday Review of Literature*, XXXI, No. 31 (July 31, 1948), 10.

Brée, Germaine. "Albert Camus and the Plague," *Yale French Studies*, No. 8 (1951), 93-100.

———. "Albert Camus: An Essay in Appreciation," *New York Times Book Review*, Jan. 24, 1960, pp. 5, 14.

———. "Camus' *Caligula*: Evolution of a Play," *Symposium*, XII, Nos. 1-2 (Spring-Fall, 1958), 43-51.

———. "Introduction to Albert Camus," *French Studies*, IV, No. 1 (Jan., 1950), 27-37.

Brockmann, Charles B. "Metamorphoses of Hell: The Spiritual Quandary in *La Chute*," *French Review*, XXXV, No. 4 (Feb., 1962), 361-68.

Brombert, Victor. "Camus and the Novel of the 'Absurd,' " *Yale French Studes*, I, No. 1 (Spring-Summer, 1948), 119-23.

Bruckberger, Raymond-Leopold. "The Spiritual Agony of Europe," *Renascence*, VII, No. 2 (Winter, 1954), 70-80.

Burke, Edward L. "Camus and Happiness," *Thought* (Fordham Univ.), XXXVII, No. 146 (Autumn, 1962), 391-409.

Champigny, Robert. "Existentialism and the Modern French Novel," *Thought* (Fordham Univ.), XXXI, No. 122 (Autumn, 1956), 365-84.

Chiaromonte, Nicola. "Albert Camus," *New Republic*, CXIV, No. 17 (Apr. 29, 1946), 630-33.

———. "Albert Camus and Moderation," *Partisan Review*, XV, No. 10 (Oct., 1948), 1142-45.

———. "Sartre versus Camus: A Political Quarrel," *Partisan Review*, XIX, No. 6 (Nov.-Dec., 1952), 680-86.

Chisholm, A. R. "Was Camus a Plagiarist?" *Meanjin*, IX, No. 2 (Winter, 1950), 131-33.

Copleston, Frederick C. "Existentialism and Religion," *Dublin Review*, No. 440 (Spring, 1947), 50-63. Camus, Marcel, Sartre.

Cruickshank, John. "Camus and Language," *Littérature Moderne*, VI, No. 2 (Mar.-Apr., 1956), 197-203.

Duhrssen, Alfred. "Some French Hegelians," *Review of Metaphysics*, VII, No. 2 (Dec., 1953), 323-37.

Durfee, Harold A. "Camus' Challenge to Modern Art," *Journal of Aesthetics and Art Criticism*, XIV, No. 2 (Dec., 1955), 201-05.

"The Eternal Rock Pusher," *Newsweek*, XXVII, No. 15 (Apr. 15, 1946), 97-99.

Fermaud, Jacques. "Humanism in Contemporary French Fiction," *American Society Legion of Honor Magazine*, II, No. 4 (Winter, 1951), 341-53.

Fiedler, L. A. "The Pope and the Prophet," *Commentary*, XXI (Feb., 1956), 190-95.

Fontinell, Eugene. "A Tribute to Albert Camus: Recent Studies of His Work," *Cross Currents*, X, No. 3 (Summer, 1960), 283-89.

Fowlie, Wallace. "The French Literary Mind," *Accent*, VIII, No. 2 (Winter, 1948), 67-81.

———. "The French Literary Scene," *Commonweal*, LVI, No. 8 (May 30, 1952), 202.

Frank, Waldo. "Life in the Face of Absurdity," *New Republic*, CXXXIII, No. 12 (Sept. 19, 1955), 18-20.

Freyer, Grattan. "The Novels of Albert Camus," *Envoy*, III, No. 11 (Oct., 1950), 19-35.

Frohock, W. M. "Camus: Image, Influence, and Sensibility," *Yale French Studies*, II, No. 2 (Fourth Study [Fall-Winter, 1949]), 91-99.

Galand, René. "Four French Attitudes on Life: Montherlant, Malraux, Sartre, Camus," *New England Modern Language Association Bulletin*, XV, No. 1 (Feb., 1953), 9-15.

Galpin, Alfred. "Italian Echoes in Albert Camus: Two Notes on *La Chute*," *Symposium*, XII, Nos. 1-2 (Spring-Fall, 1958), 65-79.

Garvin, Harry R. "Camus and the American Novel," *Comparative Literature*, VIII, No. 3 (Summer, 1956), 194-204.

Gassner, John. "Forms of Modern Drama," *Comparative Literature*, VII, No. 2 (Spring, 1955), 129-42.

Genêt. "Letter from Paris," *New Yorker*, XXIX, No. 15 (May 30, 1953), 82.

Gershman, Herbert S. "On *L'Etranger*," *French Review*, XXIX, No. 4 (Feb., 1956), 299-305.

Glicksberg, Charles I. "The Novel and the Plague," *University of Kansas City Review*, XXI, No. 1 (Autumn, 1954), 55-62.

Grubbs, Henry A. "Albert Camus and Graham Greene," *Modern Language Quarterly*, X, No. 1 (Mar., 1949), 33-42.

Guérard, A. J. "Albert Camus," *Foreground* (Cambridge, Mass.), I, No. 1 (Winter, 1946), 45-59.

Hanna, Thomas. "Albert Camus and the Christian Faith," *Journal of Religion*, XXXVI, No. 6 (Oct., 1956), 224-33.

Harrington, Michael. "The Despair and Hope of Modern Man," *Commonweal*, LXIII, No. 2 (Oct. 14, 1955), 44-45.

———. "Ethics of Rebellion," *Commonweal*, LIX, No. 17 (Jan. 29, 1954), 428-31.

Hart, J. N. "Beyond Existentialism," *Yale Review*, XLV, No. 3 (Mar., 1956), 444-51. On *The Myth of Sisyphus*.

Heppenstall, Rayner. "Albert Camus and the Romantic Protest," *Penguin New Writing*, No. 34 (1948), 104-16.

Hoffman, Frederick. "Camus and America," *Symposium*, XII, Nos. 1-2 (Spring-Fall, 1958), 36-42.

John, S. "Image and Symbol in the work of Albert Camus," *French Studies*, IX, No. 1 (Jan., 1955), 42-53.

Kahler, Erich. "The Transformation of Modern Fiction," *Comparative Literature*, VII, No. 2 (Spring, 1955), 121-28. Zola, Aymé, Rousset, J. Green, Proust, Sartre, Camus, Malraux, Gide.

Kohn, H. "Man the Undoer," *Saturday Review*, XXXVII, No. 7 (Feb. 13, 1954), 14-15.

Korg, Jacob. "The Cult of Absurdity," *Nation*, CLXXXI, No. 24 (Dec. 10, 1955), 517-18.

LeGrand, Albert. "Albert Camus: From Absurdity to Revolt," *Culture* (Quebec), XIV, No. 4 (Dec., 1953), 406-22.

Lesage, Laurence. "Albert Camus and Stendhal," *French Review*, XXIII, No. 6 (May, 1950), 474-77.

McPheeters, D. W. "Camus' Translations of Plays by Lope and Calderón," *Symposium*, XII, Nos. 1-2 (Spring-Fall, 1958), 52-64.

"Man in a Vacuum," *Time*, XLVII, No. 20 (May 20, 1946), 92.

Mason, H. A. "M. Camus and the Tragic Hero," *Scrutiny*, XIV, No. 2 (Dec., 1946), 82-89.

Mohrt, Michel. "Ethic and Poetry in the Work of Camus," *Yale French Studies*, I, No. 1 (Spring-Summer, 1948), 113-18.

O'Brien, Justin, and Roudiez, Leon S. "Camus," *Saturday Review*, XLIII, No. 7 (Feb. 13, 1960), 19-21, 41.

Peyre, Henri. "Friends and Foes of Pascal in France Today," *Yale French Studies*, No. 12 (Fall-Winter, 1953), 8-18.

———. "The Resistance and Literary Revival in France," *Yale Review*, XXXV, No. 1 (Sept., 1945), 84-92.

Politzer, Heinz. "Franz Kafka and Albert Camus: Parables for Our Times," *Chicago Review*, XIV, No. 1 (Spring, 1960), 47-67.

"Portrait," *Saturday Review of Literature*, XXIX, No. 20 (May 18, 1946), 10.

"Portrait," *Saturday Review of Literature*, XXXIV, No. 2 (Jan. 13, 1951), 44.

"Portrait," *Theatre Arts*, XXXI, No. 3 (Mar., 1947), 54.

"Portrait," *United Nations World*, IV, No. 2 (Feb., 1950), 62.

"A Practising Rebel: Albert Camus' *The Rebel*," *Times Literary Supplement* (London), No. 2707 (Dec. 18, 1953), 809-10.

Rolo, Charles. "Albert Camus: A Good Man," *Atlantic*, CCI, No. 5 (May, 1958), 27-33.

Roth, Leon. "A Contemporary Moralist: Albert Camus," *Philosophy* (Oct., 1955), 291-303.

Roudiez, Leon S. "The Literary Climate of *L'Etranger*: Samples of a Twentieth-Century Atmosphere," *Symposium*, XII, Nos. 1-2 (Spring-Fall, 1958), 19-35.

St. Aubyn, F. C. "Albert Camus and the Death of the Other: An Existential Interpretation," *French Studies*, XVI, No. 2 (Apr., 1962), 124-41.

Simpson, Lurline V. "Tensions in the Works of Albert Camus," *Modern Language Journal*, XXXVIII, No. 4 (Apr., 1954), 186-90.

Spiegelberg, Herbert. "French Existentialism: Its Social Philosophies," *Kenyon Review*, XVI, No. 3 (Summer, 1954), 446-62. Camus, Merleau-Ponty, Sartre.

Stern, Alfred. "Considerations of Albert Camus' Doctrine," *Personalist*, XLI, No. 4 (Autumn, Oct., 1960), 448-57.

Stockwell, H. R. C. "Albert Camus," *Cambridge Journal*, VII, No. 11 (Aug., 1954), 690-704.

Stourzh, Gerald. "The Unforgivable Sin: An Interpretation of *The Fall*," *Chicago Review*, XV, No. 1 (Summer, 1961), 45-57.

Strauss, Walter A. "Albert Camus' *Caligula*: Ancient Sources and Modern Parallels," *Comparative Literature*, III, No. 2 (Spring, 1951), 160-73.

Tillich, Paul. "Existential Philosophy," *Journal of the History of Ideas*, V, No. 1 (Jan., 1944), 44-70.

Todd, Olivier. "The French Reviews," *Twentieth Century*, CLIII, No. 911 (Jan., 1953), 36-46.

Vigée, Claude. "Metamorphoses of Modern Poetry," *Comparative Literature*, VII, No. 2 (Spring, 1955), 97-120.

Viggiani, Carl A. "Camus in 1936: The Beginnings of a Career," *Symposium*, XII, Nos. 1-2 (Spring-Fall, 1958), 7-18.

———. "Camus' *L'Etranger*," PMLA, LXXI, No. 5 (Dec., 1956), 865-87.

Wolheim, Richard. "The Political Philosophy of Existentialism," *Cambridge Journal*, VII, No. 1 (Oct., 1953), 3-19.

Index

269